MARINE RADIONAVIGATION
AND
COMMUNICATIONS

MARINE RADIONAVIGATION AND COMMUNICATIONS

JEFFREY W. MONROE, Master Mariner
and
THOMAS L. BUSHY, Master Mariner

CORNELL MARITIME PRESS
CENTREVILLE, MARYLAND

Library of Congress Cataloging-in-Publication Data

Monroe, Jeffrey W.,
    Marine radionavigation and communications / Jeffrey W. Monroe and Thomas L . Bushy
        p. cm.
    Includes index.
    ISBN 0-87033-510-3 (hc)
    1. Radio in navigation. 2. Marine radio stations. I. Bushy, Thomas L. II. Title.
VK397.M66   1998
623.89'32—dc21

98-38876
CIP

Manufactured in the United States of America
First edition, 1998; Second printing, 2008

To our wives, Linda and Peggy, in appreciation for their contributions to our lives, and for their sacrifices during our seagoing years, long semesters of teaching, and endless hours in the preparation of this book

Every once in a while, you have to look out the window.

—Capt. Barney Turlo
Commanding Officer
U.S. Coast Guard Marine Safety Office
Providence, Rhode Island

CONTENTS

FOREWORD

In 1962 when I began my sea career, I remember the master of the vessel telling me, "Don't operate the radar unless you have to because you might wear it out." Just thirty-six years ago, application of electronics, let alone computers and satellites, was fraught with suspicion and unreliability. Today, the application of these tools provides keys to safer navigation, automated engine rooms, cargo operations, and shared management of the vessel. Understanding of electronics, computers, and satellites, and their application, is essential to all the officers and crew of today's merchant vessel. *Marine Radionavigation and Communications* is an outstanding text dealing with these tools. Beginning with basic theory and ending with integrated bridge systems, this book is not only an understandable review of the tools but also an in-depth reference for the user. I believe it is the first book dedicated solely to the electronic systems of the present fleet of merchant ships.

Captains Jeff Monroe and Tom Bushy have completed a most needed compilation and reference for ship's officers and crews. Those who take the time to read *Marine Radionavigation and Communications* will achieve a greater understanding of these tools and should be able to utilize them in the most effective way, providing additional safety and operational efficiency in the operation of their vessel. However, I would be negligent in this foreword if I did not remind those using the tools that they are only tools, and one must be sure to apply reasoning when making decisions using them.

—Jerry A. Aspland
President, California Maritime Academy

ACKNOWLEDGMENTS

No one can prepare a work of this magnitude without the assistance of many individuals who are willing to provide not only valuable advice, but also time and effort. We would like to take this opportunity to gratefully acknowledge the following individuals who helped us in many ways as we prepared this text over the last four years: Our colleagues in the departments of marine transportation at Massachusetts Maritime Academy and the State University of New York Maritime College, including Michael Weaver for relentless editing, Andrew Meleo for technical assistance with radar, James Fitzpatrick for his support in general areas of radio electronics, Malcolm MacGregor for his patience and computer support, Frank Lynch and Ron Labreque for copy assistance, Anne Hammerle of Massachusetts Maritime Academy for her willing administrative support, and Professor Brendan Saburn at SUNY Maritime College, who provided a range of general assistance, including reviewing text; James Isbister, Rufus Lay, Frank Soccoli, and Russ Williamson of Litton/Sperry Marine Systems; Thomas Mackie and Dana Woodward of Trimble Navigation; Marcie Smith of Radio Holland; Rick Wetmore of Raytheon Marine; Dave Williams of Richie Navigation; Tom Pardy of Quincy Electronics; Ed Bizub of COMSAT Mobile Communications; Nick Emord of Bell-Sea Navigation Systems; Donna Manoli and Lt. Stephen Gardiner, USN, who assisted with illustrations; Siobhan Norton of Harbor Express and Michelle Monroe of Mobil Oil Corporation, who helped with the review of text and offered practical suggestions from the operator's point of view; Michelle Worthington for support in preparing the glossary; and the staff at the Maritime

Industry Museum and Stephen B. Luce Library, keepers of the sacred archives.

Special appreciation is due to Jerry Aspland, President of California Maritime Academy, for his eloquent Foreword; to Josh Reiter of the Massachusetts Port Authority, who contributed significantly to the chapter on GMDSS; to Lisa Amaral at Forlivesi Photography for patience in our impatient world; to Tasha and Joe for all the distractions; to Linda Monroe, who slaved over the computer trying to turn poor penmanship and fast dictation into readable text; and to the very talented Van Trong Nguyen, who did an outstanding job preparing many of the computer illustrations for this text.

INTRODUCTION

The last quarter-century has proved an era of growth in marine electronics unparalleled in its rich history. Since Guglielmo Marconi innovated wireless radio transmissions over the ocean at the turn of the twentieth century, radio waves were dedicated primarily to communications. Technological developments during the Second World War demonstrated that radio frequencies were useful in navigation and radar, but limitations remained. With the introduction of computers and solid-state circuits during the 1960s, the possible uses of radio energy were exploited. New equipment has been introduced in nearly every discipline of the marine field, including, but not limited to, navigation, cargo control, communications, collision avoidance, gyrocompass, speed indicating systems, and depth sounding.

Probably the area most improved is electronic navigation systems. Today, worldwide electronic navigation systems capable of 12-meter accuracy have replaced celestial navigation and the traditional methods of position fixing. Where star constellations once were the focus of navigators' eyes, satellite constellations now are listened to by complicated radio receivers that determine a ship's position accurately and reliably. In this book we explore the various areas of this new applied technology and provide some essential user information that has been learned both in the application of theory and through practical experience.

All modern marine electronic equipment can be classified into these major categories: communications, navigation systems, radar, depth sounding, vessel control systems, and computer-aided equipment. Communications include very high frequency (VHF) bridge-to-bridge radiotelephone, single-sideband (SSB) ship-to-shore high-seas radiotelephone, satellite communications (SATCOM), and the traditional radiotelegraph system. The modern vessel operator also has come to rely on the general tools of broadcast reception, including shortwave for time and navigation safety information, equipment developed for the reception of weather facsimile maps, and receivers such as NAVTEX that provide up-to-date notices to mariners. New for the ship's officer is the application of the global marine distress and safety system (GMDSS).

Navigation systems include the familiar radionavigation methods of loran C, Decca, and Omega. These may be technically classified as hyperbolic radionavigation systems. Systems classified as nonhyperbolic include the satellite navigation (SATNAV) systems, such as the U.S.-operated transit satellite navigation system and global positioning system (GPS) and the Russian GLONASS System. Still quite useful is the earliest of radionavigation systems, the worldwide network of marine radiobeacons. Originally designed to operate as directional systems for use with radio direction finders, they are now being used in conjunction with the differential global positioning system (DGPS).

Radar systems have seen dramatic changes in use and design since their introduction in the late 1940s. This category includes the 3-centimeter (3-cm) and 10-centimeter (10-cm) wavelength pulse-modulated marine radars. These systems are now coupled with computer-aided collision-avoidance systems and automatic plotting aids. Equipment used to determine depth or a vessel's speed includes the indicating and recording echo sounder as well as electromagnetic and Doppler speed log systems.

Electromechanical equipment remains the predominant type of vessel control system. This category includes the gyrocompass, associated repeater system, gyropilot, steering control units, and various types of equipment interfaced with these systems.

Finally, there is the computer. With the application of computers to these and many other systems, the operation of the modern commercial vessel has the potential to become almost fully automatic. Computers not only aid us in all of the previously mentioned systems, but add a new dimension to the handling of cargo and supplies, personnel, and many other areas in the marine field that traditionally have been done in slower, less productive ways. They are playing a part in integrated bridge systems and thus have an impact on watchkeepers.

The purpose of this text is to help the modern ship's officer understand not only the complexities of the application of technology to our industry, but the potential problems that may arise with its use. It is hoped this book will serve as a guide for the many professionals who now currently follow, or hope to follow, the way of the sea.

MARINE RADIONAVIGATION
AND
COMMUNICATIONS

.

CHAPTER 1

BASIC ELECTRICAL AND RADIO THEORY

BASIC ELECTRICAL PRINCIPLES

A mariner's first step toward understanding the elements of electronics is to gain a knowledge of electricity and electronics. Electricity is a physical phenomenon, the existence of moving electrons by means of a conducting element such as air, water, or solid material. Electronics pertains to the motion of electrons also, but differs in the control conduction within a component, such as a vacuum tube or a semiconductor. The difference is best clarified by examples. A light bulb is a user of electricity, generating light by increased resistance over a small wire, called the filament. The light bulb's purposeful use of the electricity is just for making light, nothing more. A semiconductor within a computer terminal also uses electricity, but the electrical energy is conducted within the substance at a greater rate than the insulators surrounding it. The semiconductor uses the electricity to enhance its application. Therefore an electronic function takes place within the semiconductor, versus an electrical function within the light bulb. No radio- or electronic navigation device used by mariners could exist without electrical properties, nor could it function without electronic technologies.

The foundation of radionavigation and communications uses the building blocks of electrical theory. The electronic circuits that create radio signals transform basic electrical current into radiant energy. These signals are the reason radios work. The radio signals are composed of electrons that emit from antennas and travel through the atmosphere in the form of radio frequency (RF) energy to be received by another antenna, or in the case of radar by the same antenna.

To produce electricity, electrons are detached from their atoms and are caused to flow through a conductor creating an electric current. Aboard a vessel this electricity production process is accomplished using generators and is generally referred to as power. Generators use a variety of power mediums, such as steam, turbines (turbogenerators), or combustion engines (diesel generators). The cause of electron motion, both initiating and sustaining, is a force, commonly called voltage, or sometimes electromotive force. The moving electrons create direct current or alternating current depending on how the current was initially generated and how the pattern of flow takes place.

Direct current (DC) and alternating current (AC) electrical service are the most common aboard a vessel. As current is produced by generators, it is fed to electrical distribution panels and circuits which service all parts of the vessel. The circuits provide sufficient power to operate all electrical machinery and navigation equipment, as well as hotel services.

Direct current was the primary source of electrical power installed on vessels during the first half of the century. Easy to generate and control, it is called direct because it is continuous as the electrons steadily flow in the same direction. DC is produced by a power source turning a commutator rapidly within a magnetic field, producing a flow of electrons in a single direction. Most steam electric and diesel electric ship propulsion systems use DC for the main engines (electric motors). The same generating systems can be used to provide electrical service throughout the vessel.

Alternating current is produced in a similar manner to DC except that the flow of electrons is interrupted. AC is generated at a controlled frequency that is determined by the equipment in use. The flow of current moving through a conductor creates a surrounding magnetic field. It is critical to understand that all electrical currents, no matter how great the level, are accompanied by a magnetic field. When the source of the electrons is interrupted as it is being generated, the magnetic field collapses and induces a movement of electrons in the opposite direction to the original flow. The source is then restored and the current then moves in the original direction. This on/off process is repeated continually and the electron flow alternates direction on a regular basis as it moves through a conductor. This alternating pattern, called a cycle, creates an energy field with reversing polarities. A specific number of cycles can be established for a period of time, normally a second, which is called the frequency of the electrical current. DC power is only described by voltage, never including frequency because there is none. AC is usually generated at a specified low frequency, such as 60 cycles, to power most lighting and equipment.

Electrons, as well as electrical current through a conductor, move at the speed of light. The force that moves electrons through a conductor is measured in volts. The amount of current moving through a conductor is referred to and measured in amperes or amps. The amount of work that electrical current can accomplish is measured in watts. There is always some opposition to the flow of electrons and there is a direct relationship to the medium to which the energy is transmitted. This opposition is termed resistance. The amount of resistance dictates how a specific electrical circuit can be utilized or how much loss of current or signal strength will be realized. Resistance in electrical components is measured in ohms. It is the resistance of a circuit or conductive element that decreases the strength of electrical current by inhibiting the flow of electrons. The electrical energy dissipates as heat, which is why electrical components get warm.

When electrons build up in an element and do not move because a conductor does not exist, static electricity is created. Static electricity is an excess of electrons in a nonconductive environment, such as in the leading edge of a weather front, or even in the human body after walking across a rug. While not useful in normal electrical service, static electricity has a detrimental effect on both electrical and radio systems.

AC is the most common power found aboard a vessel today, although the current, voltage, and frequency will vary depending on where the vessel was built and the electrical system employed. In North America, general service current is usually 110, 220, or 440 volts at 60 cycles. Alternating current has a number of advantages and is critical in radio circuits. The production of cycles of alternating current is most significant because the basic foundation for the creation of radio waves includes frequency.

Communications and navigation equipment such as radios, radars, and navigation receivers may be powered by AC or DC, depending upon the manufacturer of the equipment. If only DC power is available on board, then a power supply system called an inverter may be used. To generate AC an alternator is coupled with a motor generator or engine to provide AC voltage at high current. Here a DC motor drives an alternating current generator, which in turn feeds critical circuits. In case of a loss of power from the main engineering system, an alternate source of power is produced on larger vessels by an emergency generator. This allows for the use of critical equipment in times of main system casualty. This emergency electrical service is sometimes referred to as vital electrical service, and is designed to supply power to emergency circuits.

BASIC THEORY OF RADIO FREQUENCY (RF) ENERGY

Radio waves are created from alternating current whose cycles are accelerated to a point where their production is measured in thousands or even millions of cycles in a single second. Remember, household electric circuits in North America using 120 volts have only 60 cycles per second. These cycles or oscillations are sped up to a point where the flow of electrons can no longer be accommodated within

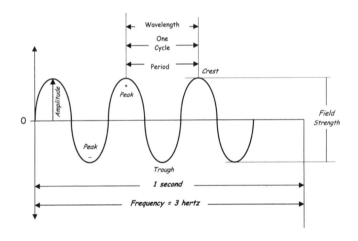

Cycle-One complete revolution equal to 360°

Wavelength-The linear length of one cycle

Period-The amount of time required to complete one cycle

Frequency-The number of cycles per second measured in hertz

Field Strength-Sum of the amplitudes of a cycle of energy

Amplitude-Strength of a cycle of energy above or below the baseline

Peak-Maximum point of energy measured as positive or negative

Formulas to note:

Frequency = 1/period   Wavelength = 3,000,000/frequency

(Wavelength is measured in meters)

3,000,000-Constant: Speed of light in meters/second

Fig. 1-1. Radiowave. Drawing by Van Trong Nguyen.

the generating circuit because of the rapidly changing direction of the electron flow. At this point, radio frequency (RF) energy is being produced. Electrons, in the form of RF energy, begin to disperse from the conductor in the form of radiation. It is important to understand that conductors, such as wires, can no longer provide circuits for RF energy. The subsequent electromagnetic radiation becomes the source of the RF energy needed to produce radio signals. This is the basic principle behind the generation of RF energy as performed in modern complex radio systems.

The RF energy produced in an oscillating circuit due to the creation and collapse of the electromagnetic field within a cycle is emitted in the form of a sine wave.

A cycle of RF energy is measured along an X axis, called the baseline, from crest to crest. The distance in metric units that the cycle occupies in one second is the wavelength. The height of the wave along the Y axis from the baseline of the wave is known as the amplitude, which culminates at positive and negative peaks located at the crest and trough of the wave. The distance between peaks is the field strength of the signal. The leading edge of the propagated signal is known as the wave front. Radio waves have the characteristics of both the electrical and magnetic components of the electromagnetic field.

The number of cycles that a radio wave completes in one second is the frequency. The frequency upon which the radio waves are generated will determine how the signals are classified and used. In modern radio terminology, one cycle per second is called one hertz. To designate large numbers of hertz, metric prefixes are used, such as kilo-, referring to one thousand, mega-, referring to one million, or giga-, referring to one billion.

Cycles per Second	Reference
1	1 hertz (Hz)
1,000	1 kilohertz (kHz)
1,0000,000	1 megahertz (MHz)
1,000,000,000	1 gigahertz (GHz)

Fig. 1-2. Frequency chart

Radio signals are grouped according to their frequencies, a classification called the electromagnetic (EM) spectrum. The EM spectrum takes the various frequencies and categorizes them into bands that have descriptive names. Their initials serve as abbreviations, for example, very high frequency-VHF. Alphabetical labels have also been assigned to the categories, with A having the lowest cycles and Z the highest, for example, X band radar. Normal hearing range is referred to as acoustic energy and is measured in audiohertz as a reference point. Acoustic energy is entirely different from RF energy but it can be referenced to provide a method of comparison.

Normal human hearing detects sounds within a low range of cycles called the audio frequency (AF: 15 and 15,000 Hz). AF has a wavelength of between 15,000,000 and 15,000 meters. The electromagnetic spectrum, comprising radiated EM waves (RF energy), begins within the higher range of AF. In the very low frequency (VLF: 10 to 30 kHz) range, distinct RF frequency is found. The first marine use of that energy was for a radionavigation system called Omega. (The names of navigation and radio systems are mentioned here for clarity. Detailed discussion follows within this volume.) Higher along the spectrum is the low frequency (LF: 30 to 300 kHz) range, where the loran system and low-frequency radiotelegraph are used. The next band is medium frequency (MF: 300 kHz to 3 MHz), where the marine radio beacon system is found. The old radiotelegraph international calling and distress frequency (500 kHz) was located here as well as the familiar AM broadcast band. Shortwave broadcast and single-sideband ship-to-shore communications occupy the next area of the spectrum, high frequency (HF: 3 to 30 MHz). Many nations broadcast radio time signals, or time ticks, in the high-frequency bands, as well as shortwave programming.

Bridge-to-bridge radiotelephone is found in the very high frequency band (VHF: 30 to 300 MHz). Television channels 2 to 13 lie within the VHF band. Ultra high frequency (UHF: 300 to 3,000 MHz) contains the majority of shipboard walkie-talkie communications and the global positioning L-band system, as well as television channels 14 through 83. In the super high frequency area (SHF: 3,000 to 30,000 MHz or 3–30 GHz) the familiar 10-cm wavelength and 3-cm wavelength radars are found, the S and X band radars, respectively.

Marine equipment uses no bands beyond those mentioned above. The EM spectrum continues, however. The next range is the extremely high frequency band (EHF, beginning at 30 GHz) including the heat and infrared ranges, invisible light, ultraviolet light, X rays, gamma rays, and finally cosmic rays.

It is important to understand the relationship that frequency has with the propagation of RF energy. Depending on the frequency of the RF energy, radio waves will have different characteristics, which will affect a signal's clarity and the range it will travel. For example, the higher the frequency of a signal, the clearer the signal will be when received, provided certain physical interference does not occur. While this is important in communications, it is even more critical in radionavigation, where the accurate measurement of a radio signal is the key to the determination of position. The clarity arises from the signal being less subject to interference due to the large number of cycles contained within a small wavelength.

Since higher-frequency transmissions are usually clearer, a general assumption can be made that as the frequency of a signal gets lower, the less clear or less accurate the associated system will be.

There is also a relationship between frequency and usable distance. While higher-frequency systems may be clearer and more accurate, they have a tendency to lose their strength faster and thus

Band	Abbrev.	Range of frequency	Range of Wavelength
Audio frequency	AF	20 to 20,000 Hz	15,000,000 to 15,000 m
Radio frequency	RF	10 kHz to 300,000 MHz	30,000 m to 0.1 cm
Very low frequency	VLF	10 to 30 kHz	30,000 to 10,000 m
Low frequency	LF	30 to 300 kHz	10,000 to 1,000 m
Medium frequency	MF	300 to 3,000 kHz	1,000 to 100 m
High frequency	HF	3 to 30 MHz	100 to 10 m
Very high frequency	VHF	30 to 300 MHz	10 to 1 m
Ultra high frequency	UHF	300 to 3,000 MHz	100 to 10 cm
Super high frequency	SHF	3,000 to 30,000 MHz	10 to 1 cm
Extremely high frequency	EHF	30,000 to 300,000 MHz	1 to 0.1 cm
Heat and infrared*		10^6 to 3.9×10^8 MHz	0.03 to 7.6×10^{-5} cm
Visible spectrum*		3.9×10^8 to 7.9×10^8 MHz	7.6×10^{-5} to 3.8×10^{-5} cm
Ultraviolet*		7.9×10^8 to 2.3×10^{10} MHz	3.8×10^{-5} to 1.3×10^{-6} cm
X rays*		2.0×10^9 to 3.0×10^{13} MHz	1.5×10^{-5} to 1.0×10^{-9} cm
Gamma rays*		2.3×10^{12} to 3.0×10^{14} MHz	1.3×10^{-8} to 1.0×10^{-10} cm
Cosmic rays*		$> 4.8 \times 10^{15}$ MHz	$< 6.2 \times 10^{-12}$ cm

Fig. 1-3. The electromagnetic spectrum

cannot be used over great distances. Lower-frequency systems have greater range but may sacrifice clarity and accuracy.

Frequency	Wavelength	Abbrev.	Marine Use	Other Uses
30 GHz	1.0 cm	EHF	satellite communications	
3 GHz	10.0 cm	SHF	GPS, marine radar	
300 MHz	1.0 m	UHF	inter-ship communications	TV (ch. 14–78), portable transceivers
30 MHz	10.0 m	VHF	bridge-to-bridge radiotelephone	TV (ch. 2–13)
3 MHz	100.0 m	HF	SSB/SITOR	shortwave radio
300 kHz	1,000.0 m	MF	radiobeacons, DGPS	
30 kHz	10,000.0 m	LF	loran C, Decca	
3 kHz	$1 \cdot 10^5$ m	VLF	Omega	

Fig. 1-4. Marine systems in the EM spectrum

Marine radionavigation and communication systems are designed to take advantage of the natural characteristics of propagation at the frequency that the radio signal is generated. The more dependent the mariner becomes upon a system using RF energy, the more he or she must understand its properties and its limitations.

PROPAGATION OF RF ENERGY

Radio waves travel as electrons at the speed of light: approximately 164,000 nautical miles per second, or 186,000 statute miles per second, or 300,000,000 meters per second. The radio waves are generated and amplified in a transmitter. The transmitter will convert high-frequency electrical current into radio waves through its transmitting antenna or aerial. These radio waves are generally transmitted omnidirectionally, picked up by antennas or receivers, then reconverted into radio frequency current. The receiver amplifies and recreates the original signal for the operator to use.

As mentioned, radio waves are generally transmitted from an antenna omnidirectionally. This can be modified, however, depending upon the transmitting antenna array, called directional transmitting. Omnidirectional radio waves travel outward in the same manner as ripples in a pool of water from a dropped stone. The RF energy contained within the radio waves possesses an electrical component and a magnetic field.

The direction of the electrical component, the polarization of the field, can be horizontal or vertical. Radio waves traveling in outer space can be polarized in any direction. Radio waves traveling along the surface of the earth, however, are vertically polarized. The magnetic and electrical fields of a radio wave are perpendicular to each other, and the wave moves in a direction perpendicular to these fields. To clarify, imagine sitting on the beach and watching waves rolling in. The vertical height of the wave is the electrical field and the length of the wave along the beach is the magnetic field. The direction of travel is determined by the expanding volume of water, which forces the ocean wave to move toward the beach. In a radio wave, it is the electrical and magnetic components of the field that expand and force the radio wave's movement outward from the antenna and perpendicular to its components.

Upon leaving the antenna, radio waves travel through the atmosphere along differing paths. The radio signals travel directly (direct waves) from their source to a receiver or they can travel indirectly (indirect waves) due to conditions along the path of travel. How the signal is received will determine whether they travel as ground waves or sky waves. Ground waves travel parallel to the earth's surface due to the refractory tendency of RF energy in the atmosphere. Sky waves move upward and away from the emitting antenna into the atmosphere. Some sky waves pass completely through the atmosphere into space while others are reflected back toward the earth's surface. Sky waves that bounce back skip or hop, and they are so nicknamed. Ground waves have a tendency to be steadier and will produce a clearer signal. This usually results in clearer communications and more accurate positions from radionavigation systems. Sky waves, on the other hand, being generally reflected, have a tendency to bounce around frequently, creating a variation in signal strength and clarity, and often resulting in poor radionavigation fixes.

A combination of the characteristics of the atmosphere, the earth's natural forces, and topographic features of the earth determines the path that the radio waves travel. According to the path of travel, each of the signals will have certain characteristics that impact clarity, strength, and range.

As a radio wave passes through the atmosphere, it encounters changes in atmospheric density due to humidity, particle content, and the general composition of the air. A signal passing through the atmosphere or over the surface of the earth begins to lose strength. The decrease of signal strength due to the medium through which it passes is called attenuation.

Attenuation of signals within the atmosphere are caused by the signals being absorbed, scattered, or reflected. Ultimately, the absorption of the radio energy, the scattering of the electrons, and the reflection of the radio wave will cause the signal to disappear entirely. These changes affect its direction of travel as well as its strength. These three primary attenuating factors impact the propagation of radio waves, as they affect all radio signals, no matter what path they travel. They also have a direct effect on clarity, signal strength, and usable range. The path of travel of a radio wave is predominantly determined by the effects of refraction, diffraction, reflection, and trapping.

Refraction is the tendency of a radio wave to follow the curvature of the earth due to the characteristics of the atmosphere. Refraction occurs when radio waves pass through the atmosphere, bending according to the varying densities of air. The air mass's density depends primarily on temperature and pressure, as well as humidity, particle content, and other factors. Gravity also contributes to refraction since the atmosphere's layers are influenced by this effect. The general empirical formula used to determine the range of RF energy is 1.22 times the square root of the antenna height.

Diffraction occurs when radio waves reach the geometric horizon or strike a solid object. They will pass over the horizon or around the object. The resulting effect causes the radio waves to be picked up in the area over the horizon or around the other side of the object. This is similar to being able to pick up light in the shadow area of an object. Radio waves, like light waves, will bend around the object and fill in behind it. While this is acceptable for radio communications, it can have a detrimental effect on systems used for direction finding, such as radar or marine radio beacons. Diffraction can cause an error in determination of the true direction of a signal's transmission.

Reflection occurs when a radio wave's direction of travel is diverted upon encountering a dense atmospheric level or a topographic feature. Reflection is the primary reason why sky waves can be picked up at long distances, particularly at night. It is also the reason that the usable range of certain signals decreases. The higher the frequency of a radio wave, the more it will be reflected. This proves to be very useful in super high frequency systems such as radar, which are entirely dependent upon reflected signals for their operation.

Trapping, or ducting, is an extreme condition of reflection resulting in radio waves, particularly SHF, rebounding between the earth's surface and an atmospheric layer, or within atmospheric layers, causing a tunnel effect. This dramatically increases the transmitted range of a signal. In radar navigation, trapping has been responsible for the reception of radio waves well beyond their detectable and useful range.

Refraction affects all frequencies and is responsible for bending radio waves, which allows reception of a signal beyond the visible horizon. This circumstance can be exaggerated if certain atmospheric conditions prevail that allow the atmosphere to become layered, forming radio ducts. A temperature inversion layer of dry air sitting on top of a layer of warm, moist air causes extreme conditions of refraction resulting in superrefraction, which increases signal distances. Subrefraction occurs when reverse conditions exist. In that case, radio waves that would normally bend toward the surface of the earth due to refraction will instead bend upward toward the sky, thus reducing range of reception by surface stations.

Passage of signals over land or near coastlines can also cause refraction of radio waves. This is caused by the difference in the characteristics of the land and water. Change in a signal's direction can occur significantly where prominent land masses meet the sea. This coastal refraction can have a serious impact on some ground-based radionavigation systems such as radio beacons, loran, and Decca. Refraction due to radio signals passing over or near large land masses is called land effect. Although these effects are termed refraction, symptoms of diffraction are basically what is occurring.

In summary, radio waves will travel as ground waves or sky waves no matter how they are emitted. However, due to atmospheric conditions and weather patterns, transmission efficiency can change substantially before reception.

IONOSPHERIC PROPAGATION

Located above the surface of the earth, beginning at around 30 miles and extending out to about 250 miles, is an area of the earth's atmosphere called the ionosphere. The structure and reflective properties of the ionosphere have a very definite effect upon the way we send and receive radio signals.

During the day the ionosphere is not very dense and generally consists of four layers. The D layer is closest to the surface of the earth, about 30 miles out. Next there is an E layer, an F-1 layer, and an F-2 layer. Maximum layering of the atmosphere occurs shortly after the sun's maximum elevation.

As the sun sets, the ionosphere begins to undergo a tremendous physical and electrical change. At night the ionosphere collapses and the D and E layers disappear, raising the bottom level of the ionosphere up to about 100 miles above the earth's surface. Also at this time, the F-1 and F-2 layers combine to form a dense single layer.

This newly formed dense layer reflects sky waves back to the earth more frequently than during the day. These reflected sky waves have a dramatic effect on radio reception, clarity, and usable range. In the morning, the opposite occurs: the ionosphere once again becomes less dense as it extends in the atmosphere. Mariners relying on HF radio transmission must be keenly aware of these atmospheric changes.

The critical time when tremendous changes occur during the transition from day to night or night to day is known as twilight. As the sun rises or sets, there is a tremendous amount of sun-induced RF energy, which enters and sometimes leaves the atmosphere. This occurrence creates the changes in the ionosphere by varying the polarization of the electrical components within the atmosphere itself.

During twilight, the operator of communications or radionavigation equipment will pick up substantial interference which can become so extreme that radio signals may not be heard. This interference to radio signals at twilight is called polarization error. Extreme polarization error can cause the blackout of a signal, called night effect.

As mentioned, the ionosphere can also affect signal range. For example, the strength of a transmitted signal traveling as a ground wave will attenuate until it can no longer be received. During the day, when ground waves are the only signals received, the reception of that transmitted signal is limited to the range of the ground wave.

At night a transmitted signal traveling as a sky wave will be reflected back to the earth's surface and will substantially increase in reception range. Radio waves travel in the form of ground waves and

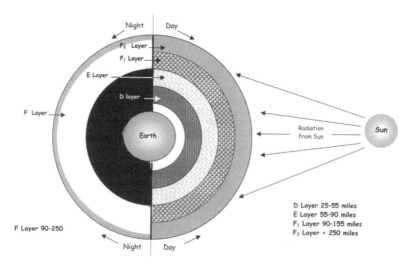

Fig. 1-5. Ionosphere. Drawing by Van Trong Nguyen.

sky waves simultaneously after they are emitted from the antenna. Ground wave signals are generally strong and steady during day or night, but sky wave signals generally fluctuate and are stronger at night. This phenomenon can hinder radionavigation systems such as Decca and marine radio beacons, because their accuracy is based solely on ground-wave reception. When sky waves mix with ground waves, interference affects the accuracy of the navigational information provided.

Long-range reception due to ionospheric propagation depends upon the number of times the signal will be reflected before it is fully attenuated. The range of a signal's reception after it is reflected is its skip distance. Occasionally, a vessel may be located in an area where it is beyond the range of the ground wave but is not far enough from a station where it can begin receiving the reflected sky waves. The receiver will be in an area of no reception called the skip zone. In this situation, the transmitter will not be heard until the receiver moves close enough to pick up the ground wave or further away so it can receive the sky wave.

Sky waves will also affect the steadiness of radio wave reception, causing the signal to vary in strength at the receiver. This is the result of the simultaneous reception of two sky waves or the simultaneous reception of a sky wave and a ground wave. Since the ionosphere does not have a consistent reflective surface, the radio waves will rebound

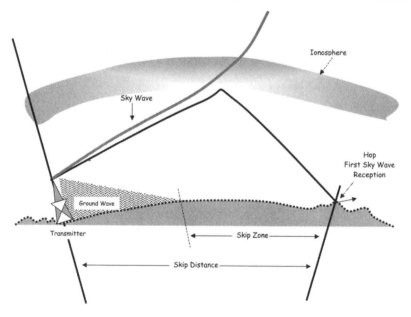

Fig. 1-6. Radio signal propagation. Drawing by Van Trong Nguyen.

in random patterns. When the receiver picks up the waves together, the signal will be stronger. As the sky waves shift direction, they will no longer be received at the same time and the signal strength will fluctuate. This will also occur when ground waves and sky waves are received simultaneously. The clarity will be affected because a phase shift occurs due to the longer distance the sky wave travels. The variation in strength of the received signals is called fading.

Multiple sky-wave reception differs from sky-wave/ground-wave reception. Multiple sky-wave signals will generally fade out completely, while sky-wave/ground-wave reception will not because the loss of the sky wave will diminish the signal; the ground-wave signal will continue to be received.

When radio waves enter the ionosphere, there will be a slight change in wavelength due to the signal's interaction between free electrons and free ions. The wavelength tends to elongate, causing a slight distortion in the signal. This effect will be enhanced during daylight hours, when solar radiation levels are higher, and during the 11-year sunspot cycle, when solar radiation creates upheaval in the ionosphere.

It is critical that the operator understand the effects of sky waves on the particular communication or radionavigation system in use. Also critical is the understanding that, due to the tremendous changes that occur during twilight, the accurate use of most radionavigation systems is severely limited.

NOISE

Unwanted signal reception in any form is technically called interference. The normally encountered, unintentional interference is called noise. When noise occurs from reception of extraneous RF energy being specifically targeted by a transmitter, jamming occurs. Jamming is used as a military tactic, and it may be experienced as the impact of powerful transmissions that impregnate several frequencies. Jamming is rarely encountered during peacetime.

Sometimes noise results from faulty equipment, such as receivers with faulty circuits, connections, antennas, or cables. One common type of noise created by equipment is hum, caused by antenna lines picking up the magnetic fields of power lines when they are located too close to each other. Another is microphonic noise, commonly caused by moving elements within a unit. It results from connections becoming loose from vibrations aboard the vessel, or sometimes because components within the unit were improperly assembled or soldered.

Crackling or sizzling may arise from faulty parts in a receiver, poor contacts, or improper grounding. Static electricity from power systems aboard or electric charges in the atmosphere can build up in electrical components of the equipment, creating sizzling. Grounding is critical to the installation process, protecting units from noise and eventual damage.

Most often, however, noise results from atmospheric conditions beyond the control of the mariner. Atmospheric noise is usually caused by the buildup of static electrical charges in the atmosphere. This commonly is caused by thunderstorms associated with a passage of a cold front. Noise can also occur in the case of unique atmospheric phenomena such as Saint Elmo's fire, the result of an excessive static buildup of electrified particles in still air. Saint Elmo's fire causes rigging and other components of a vessel to glow with a dim green light. It is easily attracted to antennas and the connected components. Large variations in signal readings or loud static noise on radios is the result. The operator should not discount severe weather conditions involving lightning, which not only fills the atmosphere with electric particles but also may strike antennas.

Other atmospheric noise occurs when the ionosphere undergoes its twice-daily change at twilight. At these times the polarity fields change, creating polarization error or night effect. This change also produces unwanted interference by noise in the signal reception. This condition can become extreme, creating a radio blackout as mentioned. More often it only creates enough interference to render communications difficult and radionavigation systems inaccurate.

Note that atmospheric noise is not confined to specific frequencies, but will generally be experienced across the entire radio spectrum. The higher the frequency the less it will be affected by atmospheric noise. Higher-frequency systems such as VHF radio, SATNAV, or radar will be less affected, but do not conclude that atmospherics will have no impact on these systems. Low- and medium-frequency signals suffer especially from atmospheric interference.

PHYSICAL OBJECT INTERFERENCE

A solid obstacle can interfere with the transmitted signal, as discussed earlier. RF energy striking these objects can be scattered or absorbed, decreasing signal strength. Generally, when a signal encounters a solid object, a shadow or area of no signal occurs just beyond that object. Eventually, like water passing around a rock in a stream, the radio waves close back in and continue at reduced strength. This is noticeable when radar antennas are located ahead of masts due to construction constraints, causing shadow areas. The shadow area will appear on the radar screen, and targets at close range in that area may be lost.

When many obstacles are located ashore, between the vessel and the transmitter, interference problems arise. Signals passing over land are deflected, changing their direction. This is particularly important in the case of radio direction finding, where the direct path of a signal from the transmitter to the receiver is vital. This interference is called land effect and occurs most often when, due to topographic features, the signal path becomes affected.

Physical object interference of radio signals is noticed when driving in an automobile. A broadcast station's signal fades out when passing through a short tunnel or past tall buildings in densely populated areas. This example demonstrates how objects can cause interference, and how differing frequencies are affected by them. The lower the frequency, the greater the chance of interference, the higher the frequency, the smaller the chance.

SIGNAL RANGE

The range over which a usable signal can be received depends on several factors. These include the transmitted power of the signal, the signal's route of travel, and atmospheric conditions. Higher-frequency signals will be attenuated faster than lower-frequency signals because they are scattered and reflected more significantly. This leads to the rule that the higher the frequency of the signal, the shorter the range of reception.

Variations in signal strength or fading will also affect signal range. Fading can be caused by interference between a sky wave's single- and double-hop reception, the reception of multiple sky waves, the fluctuation of a sky wave with a steady ground wave, the variations in the path of the wave through the ionosphere, or the fact that the receiver is located at the edge of a skip zone.

Other critical factors include the type and size of antenna used, the condition of the equipment, and the installation. The presence of extraterrestrial phenomena, such as fluctuations in the Van Allen radiation belt, which surrounds the earth, and variations in solar radiation, will have a dramatic effect on radio signals. Particularly noteworthy is excessive sunspot activity. Sunspots generate large amounts of RF energy, which have a dramatic impact on radio signals in the earth's atmosphere. This effect can go from one extreme to another. In some cases, signals become totally blacked out due to excessive interference, and in other cases, excessive signal range has been experienced. Most communication and radionavigation systems have calculated ranges which are generally accurate. Remember that numerous factors can change the calculated range to a significantly different range.

The operator must assume that the equipment used is of good quality and in proper working order. If the operator understands the characteristics of radio-wave propagation and the forces that affect it, he or she can work communications systems effectively and avoid potentially dangerous situations when using radionavigation systems.

BASIC TYPES OF RADIO TRANSMISSIONS

Transmission, reception, and antenna systems are closely related in design and construction to provide optimum use. A transmitter produces radio frequency current and supplies it to an antenna, which converts it to electromagnetic radio waves (RF energy) and sends it through the atmosphere. The receiving antenna picks up these electromagnetic waves, inducing a current in the aerial, which in turn is amplified and converted into a usable form.

There are four general transmitting systems associated with marine use. These are continuous wave (CW), modulated continuous wave (MCW), voice-transmission systems, commonly known as radiotelephony, and the pulse-modulated systems found in radar.

The most basic form of RF energy is continuous wave. This is literally energy that is dispersed into the atmosphere at a specific frequency. The only way to communicate intelligence with continuous wave is through the use of Morse code. Morse code has been used effectively in telegraphy, and for this reason continuous wave is also known as radiotelegraphy. The transmitted base signal of continuous wave, as well as all other transmitting systems, is the carrier wave.

In the second type of transmission system, modulated continuous wave, RF energy emitted by a transmission system carries no information. Information must be superimposed on the carrier wave so that it can be used to send intelligence. In the case of a continuous-wave system, the carrier wave remains unaltered. Only after it is received is an audio signal attached in the form of a simple audio tone. With modulated continuous wave, the audio information is superimposed on the carrier wave prior to transmission. This altered or modulated signal is then broadcast and received by any simple receiver. Most modern radiotelegraph systems use modulated continuous wave for Morse code radio transmissions.

Keep in mind that in discussion of the frequency of a radio signal, general reference is to the frequency of the carrier wave, which occupies a very narrow area. This does not take into account the frequency spread that encompasses the modulated signal and may occupy a wide band of hertz on either side of the carrier. The carrier wave is so called because it literally carries the intelligence in the form of a modulated signal. The signals attached to the carrier wave are called sidebands, in the form of single sideband or double sideband.

The next type of system is the voice-transmission system, or radiotelephony. Voice-transmission systems modulate or change a signal by varying either amplitude or frequency to produce voice communications. Radiotelephony systems require an additional input component, such as a microphone, which changes acoustic energy to electric energy. Amplitude modulation (AM), often used in marine communication systems, is very common and utilizes frequencies in the medium- to high-frequency bands. AM radio is also a common commercial broadcast system. The prime advantage of the AM systems is that they can broadcast over greater distances with lower power because they utilize lower frequencies.

An AM signal consists of a carrier wave and an upper and lower sideband, which contains the modulated signal. In standard AM broadcasts, such as commercial radio, the signal consists of both sidebands. In marine communications, this system has been modified by using only one of the sidebands and channeling the energy of the other sideband and a portion of the carrier wave into the other transmitted sideband signal. This allows very long-range broadcasts with lower power, but dramatically compromises the clarity of the signal.

The need for clearer communications, particularly in commercial broadcast systems, even at the expense of range, led to the development of the second type of voice-transmission system, which is known as frequency modulation (FM). FM broadcasts are very clear but have short usable ranges. Marine communication systems of this type are generally "line-of-sight," such as marine VHF radio. Line of sight means the transmission and reception ranges are determined by antenna height. FM commercial broadcasts occupy a lower frequency and are more powerful with greater range. FM transmission is denoted in bridge-to-bridge radiotelephone, such as VHF-FM (very high frequency, frequency modulated).

FM systems are based on a principle similar to AM, where a modulated signal varied by a microphone or other device will change the frequency of the transmission while maintaining the signal's amplitude. Note that for both AM and FM, it is the amplitude of the modulated signal and the frequency of the modulated signal that are changed, not the frequency or amplitude of the carrier wave. Since FM broadcasts use a higher frequency, they are less subject to interference and are more useful for clear, short-range communications such as bridge-to-bridge radiotelephone.

Pulse-modulated systems are created through the modulation of the amplitude and frequency of the signal attached to the carrier wave, which are in turn molded into short bursts of RF energy. Since these pulses can be accurately measured to determine frequency variation and distance, they are very effective in the application of RF energy to radionavigation systems and radar.

COMPONENTS OF RADIO SYSTEMS

The effective use of radio waves for transmitters and receivers are complementary, opposite parts of this system. They have similar components and methods for conversion of power into radiation and radiation back into communications. Radionavigation depends on producing specific RF energy at a precise frequency and sufficient power to ensure that the signals can be utilized for their intended purpose. Radio signals are generated and shaped in the circuitry of radio transmitters, converted into and out of radiated waves of energy, and converted back into a useful form in a receiving system. To accomplish this simple task, four basic component parts exist: the power supply, the transmitter, the receiver, and the antenna system.

Power Supply

All transmitting and receiving units begin with one fundamental component, the power supply. The power supply receives electricity from the ship's generators and distributes filtered voltages as required for the production of RF energy and for the components of the operational controls. The power supply performs the key function of providing regulated and constant operating current throughout the entire unit, providing protection from the variations of current often found in a vessel's electrical system. To control these current fluctuations, power supplies require stringent filtering systems.

Transformers are one of many components in a power supply. Typically they step up or down the input voltage as required, and may serve as an isolation device between the ship's power and the electrical components. Power supplies also clean the electrical power through the use of filters. In general, there are three common types of filters employed in power, amplifier, and receiving systems: high-pass, low-pass, and band-pass filters.

High-pass filters allow all frequencies above a certain cutoff frequency to pass into the system. Low-pass filters pass all frequencies below a certain cutoff frequency into the system. Band-pass filters pass all frequencies between a high- and low-cutoff frequency into the system.

Transmitters

Modern transmitters and receivers employ microprocessors that handle nearly all functions in a system, including accurate frequency selection, levels of amplification, filtering, and, in radionavigation systems, accurate measurement of radio signals to determine position. Transmitters and receivers have amplifiers and tuning devices for selecting frequencies. Occasionally in marine radio and radar systems, transmitting and receiving units are installed within one apparent unit, a transceiver. This section will present these two components separately.

The unit that generates the radio frequency signals is called the transmitter. Transmitters consist of two main sections, the oscillator circuit and the power amplifier circuit. Each of these segments is divided into multiple components that have specific functions in the production and amplification of a radio signal.

The oscillator converts direct electrical current into RF signal of the carrier frequency. A controller, such as a variable-frequency oscillator (VFO), is attached to this element and is used to determine the frequency of the signal to be transmitted. The amplifier circuit increases the oscillator's output. In communications systems, devices added to convert acoustic energy to electrical energy, or vice versa, are known as microphones and speakers. The microphone ac-

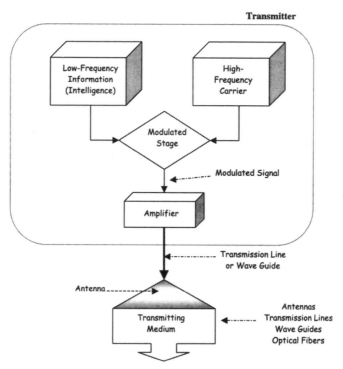

Fig. 1-7. Transmission system. Drawing by Van Trong Nguyen.

tivates a modulator which changes the carrier wave sufficiently to create the voice transmission.

As mentioned previously, there are many different types of transmitted radio waves in use. The Federal Communications Commission (FCC), the U.S. government agency charged with control of all forms of communications, classifies these emissions according to their characteristics.

Theoretically, a signal could be transmitted directly, but in reality it is much too weak. Once the RF current (carrier) is created, it is sent to an amplifier stage, where the signal level is increased. At this point the carrier is modulated with the intelligence generated from the microphone. A series of amplifiers and filter networks is employed to deliver the correct frequency and power level to the antenna. It is at the antenna where the RF current is converted into RF radio energy.

It is important to understand that in some systems, mostly in lower frequency, the transmitter will use both the antenna and the

---

Amplitude Modulation

A1A:	Continuous-wave telegraphy
A2A:	Telegraphy by on/off keying of tone-modulated carrier
A3E:	Telephony
A3C:	Facsimile
A9W:	Composite emission of telegraphy and telephony
G1D:	Data transmission
G3E	Telephony
H2A	Telegraphy by on/off keying of tone-modulated carrier
H2B	Selective calling using sequential single frequency code
H3E	Telephony
J3E	Telephony
N0N	Unmodulated continuous-wave emission
R3E	Telephony

Frequency (or Phase) Modulation

F1B:	Narrow band direct printing (NBDP); Telex
F2A:	Telegraphy by on/off keying of tone-modulated carrier
F3C:	Facsimile
F3E:	Telephony

Pulse Modulation

kHz:	kilohertz
MHz:	megahertz
GHz:	gigahertz

Fig. 1-8. Transmission classifications

earth as part of the transmitting system. As the RF wave is emitted, the positive half of the wave is emitted through the antenna element and the negative half is emitted through the ground. It is for this reason that lower-frequency systems not grounded properly at the antenna element will not function. This is also true of transmitters used on vessels, which must have a good ground to the sea. In the case of a lifeboat radio or emergency position-indicating radio beacon (EPIRB), if the grounding wire or unit is not put into the water, the transmitter will not work properly.

Marine radio operators only control the use of a transmitter by the keying of a microphone. Otherwise the electrical functions of the transmitter are not influenced by the operator. Certain legal responsibilities arise when using a transmitter. Only certified technicians may perform repair work on transmitters, and only certified operators may actuate a transmitter by keying the mike.

Receivers

At this moment thousands of radio signals travel through the air, surrounding the reader. The unit that enables us to utilize these radio signals is called the receiver. The first task of a receiver is to pick up and sort the numerous RF signals to find the specific frequency required. Initially the signals are received by the antenna and a current is induced, which is conducted to the first-stage amplifier, an RF amplifier. Through a tuning control the frequencies of the desired signals are located and passed on to the next stage, which in most receivers is the detector.

The detector separates the intelligence from the carrier and passes it on to the next stage of the receiver. This is the process if the radio signal has been modulated at the transmitter. In continuous-wave transmissions, the signal is unmodulated and must be mixed with a lower frequency developed by a local oscillator in the receiver. The local oscillator mixes its signal with the carrier and produces an intermediate frequency. The intermediate frequency is then passed to the last stage of the receiver.

In the last stage of the receiver, filters are used to eliminate unwanted frequencies, and finally the desired signal, either from the intelligence detected on modulated signals or signals produced from an intermediate frequency, is sent to the final-stage amplifier. For communications equipment, this is usually an audio amplifier, which generates input to a speaker, finally converting electrical energy into acoustic energy, or sound. For other types of radio equipment, such as radionavigation receivers, the signal is provided to a microprocessor, which measures the signal according to the type of system being utilized, then forwards it to an appropriate information display.

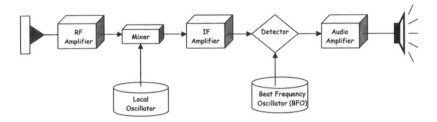

Fig. 1-9. Receiver system. Drawing by Van Trong Nguyen.

The receiver must be installed correctly and be in excellent working condition, including having a proper ground to the vessel to eliminate excess static electron buildup. The quality of reception will depend upon the quality of each of the unit's characteristics in the areas of frequency range, selectivity, sensitivity, stability, and fidelity.

The frequency range of a receiver determines what specific signals can be tuned and reproduced. A unit may cover a broad group of frequencies, such as in a multiband communications receiver, or a single frequency, as in a radionavigation receiver like loran C.

Selectivity is the ability of a receiver to limit reception to signals of a specific frequency and filter out interfering signals near that specific frequency. Very selective receivers can break a signal down to a few microhertz.

The sensitivity of a receiver is its capability to amplify weak signals received to a useful level so that they can be detected above the existing background noise. Many receivers have special filters that can block out the background noise without blocking the desired signal, or are capable of varying the amplification at the initial RF amplifier stage to increase signal strength.

A receiver's stability is its capability to lock onto a desired signal without drifting off frequency. Frequency drift can occur when a unit is unable to remain tuned into a signal and adjusts itself within its internal circuitry to changes caused by current flow, inductance, or dissipation of heat.

Finally, fidelity is the capability of a receiver to reproduce the original characteristics of a received signal as clearly and completely as possible. The higher the fidelity, the better the received signal will be heard, in the case of audio receivers, or the clearer the picture, in the case of video receivers. Clarity resulting from high fidelity is desirable in all of the commonly used marine systems, particularly radionavigation systems.

All of these receiver characteristics are interrelated; when a unit is deficient in one, overall reception can be severely limited. Numerous factors can affect and compromise these characteristics, even in the best of receivers. Improperly connected or mismatched antennas are a common problem.

Receiver controls vary according to their use and their manufacturer. A general communications receiver will have various types of controls that are commonly designed to assist with the reception of signals over a broad range. These include the RF gain, which boosts the signal at its primary stage of amplification, and the volume or gain control, which boosts the signal at its final stage of amplification. Every unit will have a form of frequency control, normally a tuner, which can be variable, crystal controlled, or synthesized, and is capable of receiving one or more frequencies. The frequency control may have an additional selectivity control that allows the operator to search a broad or narrow selection in the desired band.

Some receivers are equipped with a beat frequency oscillator (BFO) control. This device provides a locally generated signal which can be mixed with a CW transmission when received, allowing the user to hear the carrier wave. The device "beats" the two signals together to put them into a form capable of being heard. Operators use the BFO to hear continuous-wave Morse code signals.

The unit may also have a noise limiter, or squelch control, to block out unnecessary background noise or signals. Noise limiters block out signals above or below a certain frequency. The squelch control can be used to block out all signals below a certain level of strength. Since squelch is useful in reducing noise, mariners must also be careful not to eliminate useful transmissions. Squelch should be adjusted to "quiet" the static noise.

While there are many other controls associated with radio receivers, these are among the most common. As with any piece of electronic equipment, the operator should study the operational manual for each piece of equipment to understand his or her unit thoroughly.

Antennas

An antenna system component is usually common to both transmitters and receivers. The antenna system can be considered to consist of the antenna as commonly understood, the feedline to the transmitter and receiver, and any coupling devices for transferring power from the transmitter to the feedline.

For every specific frequency there is an optimum length and style of antenna that allows the system to work on that frequency at peak efficiency. The proper type and installation of the antennas is critical to each of the various types of equipment used on vessels. The antenna must also be of a suitable design and construction to tolerate the harsh marine environment.

Basically, all marine antennas fall into the following categories: whip antennas, parabolic antennas, slotted wave-guide antennas, loop antennas, and bar antennas. Each of these types of antennas is designed for specific systems, with some acting as both transmitting and receiving elements and others used specifically for receiving.

Whip antennas are a single wire, either stretched horizontally between two supports, such as ship's masts, or supported vertically by a nonconductive shell, such as fiberglass. Common use of the term whip supposes vertical installation, but technically this may not be the case. Whip antennas are the most common type found aboard vessels today. Vertical fiberglass whips are used with almost every type of radio receiver or transmitter, including VHF bridge-to-bridge radios, single-sideband ship-to-shore radios, and most radionavigation receivers.

Horizontal whip antennas are most commonly used by radiotelegraphs aboard ship. Due to smaller-vessel construction constraints, a wire whip may be supported at two points, creating almost any angle. The general rule concerning these types of antennas is that vertical receiving antennas work best on systems using vertical transmitting antennas, and horizontal receiving antennas work best with horizontal transmitting antennas. The lower the frequency of a system the longer the antenna required, because of the longer wavelength. It is necessary to understand that a specific proportionality exists between wavelength and antenna length or height. With receivers, the longer the antenna and the higher it is placed, the more efficient it will be.

The most fundamental antenna is the half-wave type, where the total length of the antenna is equal to half of the wavelength of the transmitted frequency. The length of a transmitting antenna is critical, but receiving antennas need not be as accurately cut. This antenna is so basic that it is the unit from which many more complex types of antennas are built. For practical purposes, the length in feet of an antenna can be computed using the formula:

Length in feet = 468/frequency (MHz)

When power is fed to an antenna, the current and voltage vary along its length. When transmitting, the current is at maximum at the center and nearly zero at the ends, while the voltage level on the antenna is just the opposite. The resistance and capacitance along the antenna length will vary as well. Since antenna lengths cannot be cut for every frequency used, an antenna tuner matches the antenna to the transmitted frequency by varying the capacitance and resistance that the signal will encounter as it moves to the antenna.

Fig. 1-10. Antenna types: (A) vertical and horizontal whips,
(B) SATCOM, (C) slotted wave-guide radar antenna.
Photographs by Forlivesi Photography.

The radiation from a transmitting antenna is not uniform in all directions. It is strongest in directions perpendicular to the wire and is nearly zero along the direction of the wire ends. For this reason, vertical antennas are more commonly used in marine systems, except where high power and longer antennas are required for efficient range.

A common variation of the whip antenna is the half-wave dipole. The half-wave dipole antenna mounted over earth is a bidirectional antenna, meaning that it radiates equally well in both horizontal directions perpendicular to it. For a half-wave dipole to take on unidirectional characteristics, it needs additional elements. It has excellent directive capabilities and is very efficient when placed at least a half wavelength above the ground. Antennas with these extra elements are usually called beams. Beams make the antenna more directive by changing the shape of the emission pattern.

In most beams, the additional elements receive power by either induction or radiation from the driven element. They then reradiate it in the proper phase relationship to achieve directivity or gain over a simple half-wave dipole in free space. These elements are called parasitic elements. They draw power from the driven element. The driven element receives its power directly from the transmitter via the transmission line.

There are two types of parasitic elements. A director is shorter than the driven element and is located at the front of the antenna. A reflector is longer than the driven element and is located at the rear of the antenna. Maximum radiation from a beam therefore travels from the reflector element through the driven and director elements. The strength of the emission will vary according to the pattern the antenna creates. This variation in the pattern of an antenna is expressed as a front-to-back ratio, which is the ratio between the power radiated in the direction of maximum radiation to the power radiated in the reverse direction. The structure of the antenna also affects the strength or gain of the output signal. In a beam antenna, the gain of an antenna with parasitic elements varies with the spacing between the elements and the element length. Antenna gain is defined as the ratio of output voltage (or signal strength) to input voltage (or signal strength).

The signal leaving a transmitting antenna must be powerful enough to induce a current in a receiving antenna. This is called effective power gain. It is expressed as the ratio of the power required to produce a certain signal strength at a receiving comparison antenna to the power needed to have as strong a signal with another specific antenna. The comparison antenna is usually a half-wave dipole in free space.

As versatile as the dipole antenna is, the vertical whip antenna remains the most popular aboard vessels today, due to compactness and ease of installation. Vertical whips are usually used for VHF, SSB, loran C, Decca, Omega, and SATNAV. They are efficient for long-distance transmitting and receiving because of the low radiation angle. By standing vertically, the antenna transmits in a more uniform omnidirectional pattern. When installing a whip, it is important to try to locate it away from objects such as masts, king posts, superstructure, fishing towers, or other antennas. Proper grounding, as in every antenna system, must be ensured.

Another type of common marine antenna is the parabolic reflector antenna. The emitter/receiver element is usually a feed horn. Parabolic antennas use a curved section behind the element to focus transmitted or received signals. Generally, marine types are reflector antennas with signals emitted back into a curved dish, where they are focused and then sent outward. In reception, the opposite occurs. Because this type of antenna is very directive, unlike a whip antenna, it cannot pick up or distribute signals in all directions at the same time. It does have better output range and detection ability from a single direction. A parabolic antenna is most commonly used with standard A SATCOM or older radar systems.

The slotted wave-guide antenna is the more common type of radar antenna today. Like the earlier parabolic reflector, it is highly directive. The radar scanner is actually a hollow tube with slots in its side allowing short bursts of high energy to radiate out and be subsequently received. A long-angled reflector behind the slotted wave guide shapes and concentrates the signals during transmission and reception. Its primary advantage over the older parabolic type is that it reduces the output of interfering side lobes from the antenna in the radiated pattern. It is also easier to maintain and install on masts.

Directional-loop antennas and crossed-loop antennas are the next common type of marine antenna, designed for radio direction

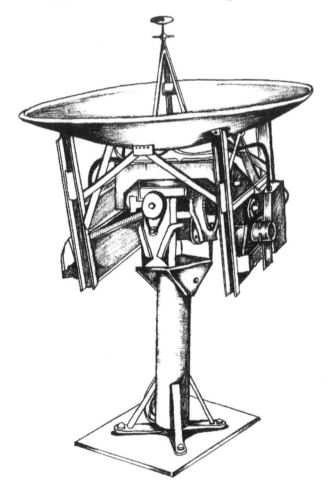

Fig. 1-11. Satellite communication (SATCOM) antenna.
Courtesy of Litton/Sperry Marine Systems.

Fig. 1-12. Radar antenna. Courtesy of Furuno Corporation.

finding. In a crossed-loop system, also known as a Bellini-Tossi antenna system, the signals are picked up at varying levels at different points on the antenna. These levels are analyzed by the receiver to determine transmitter direction. This type of antenna is easier to position on a vessel than the older directional loop, which was mounted directly above the receiver unit and turned by hand.

Some direction finders use the bar antenna, which is usually a piece of soft iron with a section of wire wrapped tightly around it. It is most commonly found as a directional antenna on small portable radio direction finders (RDFs). Bar antennas are commonly used in transistor radios for AM reception. The wrapping of wire around soft iron eliminates the need for external antennas because of their efficient pickup and induction of weak RF currents. They are still limited in use and are not effective in most marine systems except smaller RDF units.

Fig. 1-13. An ADF, cross-looped antenna.
Photograph by Forlivesi Photography.

Several critical factors must be kept in mind when considering the efficient functioning of an antenna. The lower the frequency, the longer the antenna must be. Also important with lower frequency systems is a proper ground. The proper functioning of the lower-frequency system involves not only the antenna itself but its ground to earth for the transmission and reception of radio waves. This is why communications systems below 30 MHz must be specifically grounded to the ship for efficient operation, even though all antenna systems need to be grounded to diffuse static electricity. Portable lifeboat radios must be grounded by having a ground wire in the sea to transmit a signal. In addition, EPIRBs are designed to float in seawater, an important grounding source.

Another critical element for the antenna is its height above the level of the earth. In lower-frequency systems, the more vertical the separation between the antenna and the level of the earth, the more efficient the system. Height achieves clearance above structural members such as the ship's mast, stack, or even other antenna. It is vital that an antenna be placed aboard a vessel with a clear line of sight in all directions so that signals may be transmitted or received unhindered. Such is the case when setting up a lifeboat search and rescue transponder (SART), where more height increases the chance of rescue.

Finally, the installation and the length of the lead, or feedline, from antenna to receiver/transmitter is critical. If antenna leads are very long, much of the signal is lost between the antenna and the actual receiving unit. If antenna wires are inadvertently strapped to power cables, magnetic fields surrounding these cables can interfere with signal reception even if both the power cables and antenna cables are shielded. An efficient antenna line must be used to minimize signal loss.

The most popular type of antenna lead is coaxial cable, called coax for short. It consists of one conductor placed in the center of a nonconductive tube. This is the center conductor. A second conductor is placed around the nonconductive tube, called the shield, which in turn is surrounded by thick insulation. The most popular types of cable have either a solid or stranded-wire center conductor surrounded by polyethylene to form a nonconductor, a web wire or braided wire shield covering the insulated case, and waterproof vinyl covering the shield. With coax cable, the fields are entirely inside the tube, which prevents RF energy from appearing outside the cable and keeps other fields from mixing with the signal in the line. The shield is grounded to protect the internal fields of the cable and to dissipate any external RF energy.

To determine the strength of any signal emitted from a given antenna, the RF output must be measured. The most common meas-

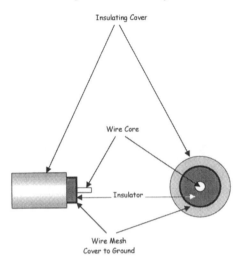

Fig. 1-14. Coax cable. Drawing by Van Trong Nguyen.

urement of an antenna system is the standing-wave ratio (SWR). Standing waves are variations of current and voltage along a transmission line. These occur when the impedance of the line is different from that of the antenna at the operation frequency, creating a mismatch.

SWR is the ratio of maximum current to minimum current (or maximum voltage to minimum voltage) along the transmission line. The instrument used to measure SWR is called a reflectometer. SWR is important because it is a direct indicator of how well the system will work. The ratio should be as close as possible to 1:1 to obtain the best performance from the equipment.

Since it is unusual for the antenna and feedline to be perfectly balanced (where SWR is 1:1), the operator will usually use an antenna tuner to get the SWR as close to 1:1 as possible. The device is installed between the transmitter and the antenna. It is used in conjunction with the reflectometer to make up for impedance differences between the antenna and the feedline. An SWR meter is commonly installed on VHF and SSB transceivers to indicate the best tuning of the antenna system. SWR meters are required aboard vessels with FCC station licenses.

Keep in mind that antenna systems are not indestructible. High winds, extreme weather conditions, vessel vibration, and inadvertent damage can all affect the antenna and thus the entire system. Regular inspections, cleaning of contacts, instructions to crew, and other maintenance will ensure the system will work when needed.

COMMON SYSTEM PROBLEMS

Modern technology is such that the common problems associated with transmitting and receiving systems are not due to the way the equipment is manufactured, but to the method of installation. Poorly placed antennas or antenna cables or ungrounded components may render systems less effective.

Since all electrical current is accompanied by a magnetic field, its presence can induce electron flow in any conductor, including antenna cables. Many installations on vessels have antenna lines that are attached to power cables, because this is the easiest way to install the cables throughout the vessel. The adjacent power lines induce a current in the antenna cables, creating an interfering hum that will mask the radio signal.

Another common mistake is the failure to ground a system, which will cause static electricity buildup and system noise. In addition, blocked antennas, installed without regard to a vessel's structure or other antennas, will compromise both transmission and reception efficiency.

One task vessel personnel commonly neglect is the frequent inspection of system components, particularly those on weather decks. Connections can become loose or can short out due to moisture. This moisture, along with excessive static electricity or dissimilar metals can fuel corrosion, which is a common cause for malfunction. Fiberglass antennas can crack and break after long periods of direct UV rays, exposing wires to the elements. People tend to notice a problem only when something stops working, which is generally during abnormal or emergency situations. In the worst case scenario, undetected problems in a radionavigation system can result in errors leading to grounding or other serious casualty.

CHAPTER 2

RADIO DIRECTION FINDING

BASIC THEORY

The mariner is required to determine his or her position skillfully and accurately. This being the case, it has become a basic tenet of seamanship that the navigator possess the necessary skill and equipment to accomplish the task. The practice is such that although land-based systems have been developed to assist in positioning, the mariner must accept that information and determine where his or her ship is located. In other words, given universal assistance from shore, mariners gather such information deemed necessary to fix their ship's position single-handedly. With this in mind, the discussion of marine radionavigation can begin with the most basic and fundamental of systems.

The use of radio signals to determine a line of position was one of the earliest radionavigation systems developed. Although many more sophisticated systems have been developed in recent years, basic radio direction finding remains a useful system because of its simplicity and usefulness during emergency situations requiring search and rescue. Offshore navigators will find the need to apply error corrections for proper use and accuracy. An automated approach to the use of radio beacon signals using this system is popular among recreational boat operators, and in many emerging nations by their maritime community, as an inexpensive method of determining position.

Students of navigation should be familiar with the basic principles of navigation, which are also used with radio direction finders (RDF). A radio wave is received and recognized as being broadcast from a known location. This procedure is no different from the mariner sighting a lighted aid to navigation along a coastline at night. Upon sighting the light, the navigator carefully assesses the light's characteristics as being from a particular light on the chart in use. Once confirmation is made, a bearing is taken on the light using a gyrorepeater, pelorus, or hand-held compass. The data is then plotted on the chart as a line of position. More than one line of position is required to be used to determine the vessel position. In radio direction finding, the procedure is nearly the same: a charted radio station is tuned in on a specific RDF receiver, recognition of the station is made, then a line of position to the station is obtained using a directional antenna. See figure 2-1 as a demonstration of this principle of position fixing.

The navigator must understand the weakness of obtaining merely one line of position at any one time. Knowledge of being on a line may be useful, but cannot be construed as fixing a vessel's position. Of course, use of a previous line of position with a present line, the principle of running fixes, can always be used. The concept of being limited to only one line of position from one discipline of navigation may offer an argument against the usefulness of radio direction finding. The following scenario and argument may help clarify this: a ship at sea has lost advanced radionavigation aids from some circumstance and must face the task of landfall. A single radio direction finder station is available. Assume the sun was available for a celestial observation for a line of position; certainly only one obtainable line of position is insufficient to make a safe landfall. However, were the

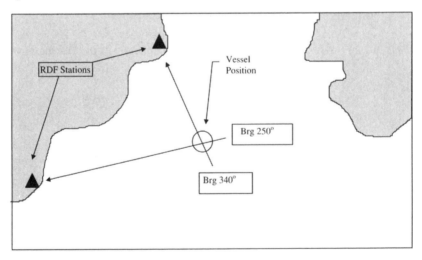

Fig. 2-1. Principle of lines of position and position fixing.
Drawing by Thomas Bushy.

navigator able to obtain both the sun line and the radio direction line, a position fix might be more than possible.

Radio direction finders (RDFs) are radio receivers installed aboard vessels and at shore stations with direction-sensitive antennas receiving identification code signals from shore transmitters. While these systems are generally designed to provide a single bearing or line of position to the operator, they are more commonly used as a backup to visual or other radionavigation systems. Direction-finding equipment is also used to determine radio bearings to vessels in distress when transmitting on emergency frequencies. Depending upon the range of the radio receiver's bandwidth, operators may use commercial radio stations and aeronautical radio beacons for directional information as long as the antenna position can be accurately determined on a chart.

The most accurate positions are determined by multiple lines of position which are derived from different sources. This includes not only radionavigation systems but visual bearings, celestial observations, hyperbolic lines, or even a chain of soundings. There is a tendency to forget that a line of position from any discipline of navigation is a mere pencil mark on a chart and that any additional information, if deemed accurate, can be used with any other information to confidently access your location.

While direction systems can provide lines of position, a popular method of using these aids has been for a navigator to tune a signal and allow the bearing to be used as the vessel's course. Fishing vessels, recreational boats, and other craft record directional information when leaving port and then return on the reciprocal signal. This may be why many radio directional stations are still being maintained throughout the world. Homing should be used carefully since it could lead to grounding or collision with a transmitting station.

There are several radio direction systems available for use by the mariner. Best known is the marine radio beacon system, found worldwide in coastal areas, which will be the most thoroughly discussed in this text. While the marine radio beacon system is used by operators aboard a vessel to ascertain position, there is a duplicate shoreside system of radio direction-finding stations which can receive a vessel's radio signal, at which point a radio bearing from shore to the ship may be given. In addition, coastal port radar and radio stations operate direction finding services for vessels operating in heavily traveled areas. Finally, a navigation system called Consol was designed to provide long-range navigation from shore stations and was considered a radio directional system. Consol has been shut down virtually all over the world.

This chapter will discuss the various types of directional systems remaining in use today. The modern navigator should not discount these systems because of the apparent low level of technology or the arduous corrections they may require. They still provide a viable backup to newer systems and in some cases may become the primary navigation system aboard the vessel, for both routine position fixing and locating vessels in distress.

THEORY OF OPERATION

Shore-based radio stations that transmit coded signals intended to be received by ships for positioning purposes are called marine radio beacons. Radio receivers equipped with direction-sensitive antennas are called radio direction finders. This worldwide system of marine radio beacons is one of the oldest and most frequently used radionavigation systems in the world. In the United States, radio direction-finding equipment remains a minimum requirement for navigation aboard oceangoing ships. A ship so equipped can obtain useful radio bearings from any known radio beacon within reception of the transmitting antenna, provided the station's position is indicated or can be indicated on a chart, allowing a fix to be determined with reasonable accuracy. With more than nine hundred radio beacons worldwide broadcasting a simple signal continuously, uncluttered by infinitesimal timing problems or orbiting satellites, a navigator can use a radio direction finder for navigation on just about any coastline.

Mariners can expect marine radio beacons to operate in the most severe circumstances because of their simplicity, much the way shoreside radio listeners rely solely upon their clock radio to wake them for work each morning. And as an added benefit to all mariners, the same receiving equipment doubles as a useful tool in searching for vessels transmitting distress messages.

All specifically designed radio beacons broadcast continuously in the medium-frequency band (285–395-kHz). Modern radio direction finders are also capable of receiving 500 kHz, the international call and distress frequency for radiotelegraph, and 2,182 kHz, the international call and distress frequency for single-sideband radiotelephony. Special low-power transmitters are available throughout the world for calibrating shipboard RDF units.

The station broadcasts a carrier frequency continuously, which allows the operator to have a steady signal for tuning. On the carrier frequency, a specific identifying signal is superimposed, involving long dashes and Morse code designator letters. For example, a radio beacon broadcasting from Chatham Light may use 292 kHz, signaling itself by the letters *CL* (dash-dot-dash-dot/dot-dash-dot-dot) followed by a 10-second dash. This method of station identification is being eliminated in the U.S. system. The mariner must be cautioned that identification of a transmitting beacon may be more challenging: reliance on specific frequency selection combined with an accurate dead-reckoning position is required. Radio beacons do provide an excellent backup when using other radionavigation systems.

In many areas of the world marine radio beacons are sequenced. Sequencing involves several different stations broadcasting on the same frequency, one at a time, in a specific order. This allows the user to get more than one bearing for a fix without changing frequencies, often involving time-consuming tuning and station recognition. A reconfiguration of the marine radio beacon system is currently under way in the United States that will eliminate sequenced radio beacons. Some radio beacons are being relocated to provide better application when used for homing. In addition, a number of marine radio beacons are being modified to carry signals for the differential global positioning system, discussed in chapter 4. This policy shift by the United States is mandated by fiscal constraints within the Federal Radionavigation Plan and the apparent decreased use of radio beacons by mariners. However, there remains a strong commitment to continue a skeletal RDF system because of its strengths in time of emergency, and as a backup system for navigation.

A marine radio beacon system is very cost effective for the government and serves a large civilian user community. The U.S. Federal Radionavigation Plan predicts that marine radio beacons will be part of the radionavigation mix well beyond the year 2000. This stance may not be globally accepted, especially by Third World nations committed to providing a basic radionavigation system to protect their coastlines.

Marine radio beacons are designed to provide bearing accuracy relative to a vessel's heading in the range of plus or minus 2 degrees to plus or minus 10 degrees. In most cases, however, marine radio beacons have been found to have a useable accuracy around plus or minus 2 degrees within 150 miles from the radio beacon, when utilized by skilled operators. Usually used offshore, RDF can be carefully used in bays and sounds of coastal waters but should not be considered sufficiently accurate within restricted channels or harbors. RDF is generally looked upon as a medium-accuracy system by mariners, sufficient to fix a vessel's position where high degrees of accuracy are not required.

As an example, figure 2-2 demonstrates the levels of accuracy a navigator can expect. Assume a ship's dead-reckoning position is 50 miles from shore, and two radio beacons are equidistant from that position.

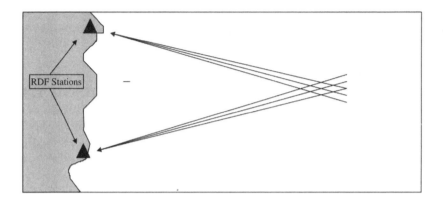

Fig. 2-2. Principle of RDF accuracy. Drawing by Thomas Bushy.

Aeronautical radio beacons located along the coast can also be used for marine navigation. Aeronautical radio beacons operate in the same frequency ranges as marine radio beacons.

EQUIPMENT

There are various types of radio beacon receivers in use today aboard vessels. Recreational radio beacon receivers or RDFs are generally portable with built-in bar antennas that can be moved to determine a line of position. Aboard commercial vessels, there are generally two types of receivers in use.

The original style of RDF was known as an aural null indicator. This type of receiver, similar to the portable recreational boat receiver, depends on the ability of the user to listen for the "null," or weakest point, of a transmitted signal to determine direction, sometimes with visual assistance. The null of the signal is used to determine a station's direction because one can locate the null more precisely than one can locate the strongest signal. Often the RDF will have a visual indicator, such as a meter or split beam tube, to assist the user in more accurately determining the null.

The second type of marine radio beacon receiver is the automatic direction finder (ADF). The ADF searches for the direction of the carrier wave and then locks onto the broadcaster signal. This simplifies the process for the user, as the older style RDF unit required a more complicated process for determining position. The ADF can also be used in a similar method as the older RDF.

Earlier style RDF systems employed a single movable-loop antenna that was moved by a hand wheel above the receiver. The wheel was turned to pick up the strongest signal so it could be easily identified. Then the antenna was rotated until it was perpendicular to the original position where the signal was strongest. At this point the signal would almost disappear, which is referred to as the null point. By carefully moving the antenna back and forth slightly, this null area could be defined within a couple of degrees. This was how the direction of the transmitter could be determined.

When the movable RDF antenna was placed end-on to a signal it would pick up a large portion of a radio wave and cause a current to be induced and flow in a single direction, similar to water pouring over a water wheel. When the antenna was turned perpendicular to find the null, the RF energy would strike the antenna face and flow in two different directions at the same time. The antenna was designed to have a positive and negative pole, so that when the two currents reached the receiver, they had different polarities. The current literally canceled itself out and at this point a null was experienced. A direction indicator on the antenna stem was aligned with this point on the receiver, which could be used to determine the direction of the null.

Movable-loop antennas have been replaced with fixed crossed-loop antennas on newer RDF/ADF receivers. These antennas are placed higher up for better reception since they do not need to be located just above the receiver. This crossed-loop antenna uses the same principle as the movable-loop antenna but determines the direction of a radio signal using a device in the receiver. Most antennas of this type use two loops perpendicular to each other. There are variations of this antenna type using multiple loops but the system is still based on the same principle.

The antenna as a whole will pick up the signal at varying strengths in different areas of the antenna. The signals then pass to the receiver where a device called a goniometer separates the incoming signals by their varying strengths. To determine direction, the operator turns the goniometer to determine the strength of the signal in various directions. Like the movable loop, once the loudest signal is heard and the station identified, the goniometer is rotated 90 degrees to determine the radio null and to find direction. A direction indicator is connected to the goniometer and when it is turned, it can be used to determine direction over a compass.

A loop antenna will pick up a signal when either edge of the loop is aligned with the transmitter, thus the user can have a potential 180-degree error in his radio bearing. This is called radio bearing ambiguity, and is eliminated by the simple addition to the unit of a sense antenna system. The sense antenna system consists of a second antenna, usually a simple wire whip, which is connected to the

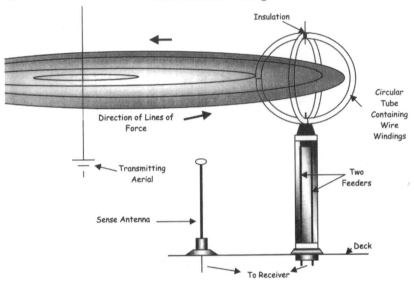

Insulation

Direction of Lines of Force

Circular Tube Containing Wire Windings

Transmitting Aerial

Two Feeders

Sense Antenna

Deck

To Receiver

Fig. 2-3. Radio direction finder reception.
Drawing by Van Trong Nguyen.

receiving circuit. A switch allows the current flow from the second antenna to mix with the flow from the loop antenna. If the polarities are the same, the signal direction will be indicated by the stronger mixed signal. If the polarities are different, the input from the sense antenna will cancel the input from the loop antenna and a weaker or no signal will be heard, thus indicating the loop is facing the wrong direction. All loop antennas have a definite positive and negative side which allows this system to function. The user should carefully consult the instructions for a particular unit and become familiar with the specific manner in which the sense system works.

Automatic direction finders operate in a similar manner except that the goniometer has a motor attached to it. As with the traditional RDF, the operator must identify the station before switching to the automatic mode. When it is put into automatic mode, the goniometer focuses in on the null point of the received signals and the motor moves the direction indicator, allowing the user to determine a bearing to the station. The signal strength is measured off the carrier wave, not the modulated signal of the transmission. Use of an ADF eliminates the need to employ a difficult "sense" process because the sense system is automatically incorporated in the process. ADF bearings can be backed up with aural null bearings.

Another type of radio direction finder which is no longer manufactured but still found on some vessels is the rotating antenna

Fig. 2-4. ADF receiver. Photograph by Forlivesi Photography.

system. Rotating antenna systems operate differently than the earlier movable-loop or crossed-loop systems. The antenna, which looks like a movable loop unit, is turned in a continual rotation by a motor located at the base of the antenna. The rotating loop picks up the transmitter signals as it passes through the RF field. The receiver utilizes a cathode ray tube indicator to show the RF pattern as perceived by the rotating antenna. The pattern can be narrowed to a single line on the screen and can actually determine the bearing of the transmitter with more accuracy than the aural null system. Higher acquisition and maintenance costs eventually limited the marketability of rotating antenna systems.

RDF receivers can receive designated frequencies in the medium-frequency bands, including signals above 200 kHz up to and including 500 kHz, and in some cases the lower end of the commercial broadcast (AM) band. Direction finders on oceangoing vessels must meet the requirements set forth by the International Convention for the Safety of Life at Sea (SOLAS). These units must be capable of determining the direction of distress calls on several frequencies. These include the traditional international calling and distress frequencies for

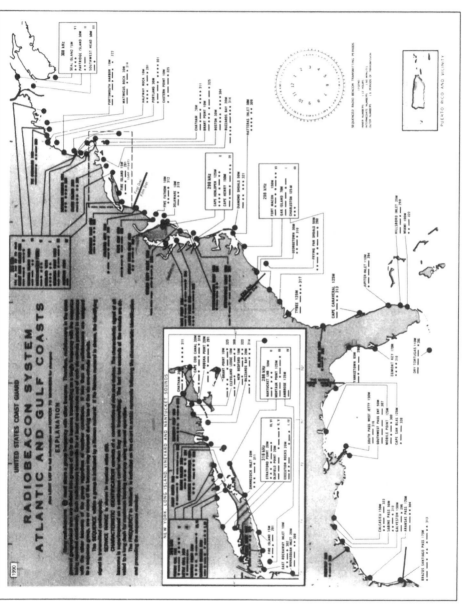

Fig. 2-5. Radiobeacon system. Courtesy of National Ocean Service/U.S. Government.

radiotelegraph, on 500 kHz, and medium-frequency single-sideband radiotelephony, on 2,182 kHz.

RADIO DIRECTION-FINDER NAVIGATION

The accuracy of a radio bearing depends on several important factors. As with any radionavigation system, variables which introduce error are minimized. Errors involving radio waves include quadrantal error, which is deviation introduced by the vessel itself; land effect or coastal refraction; polarization error or night effect; and operator error, particularly ambiguity. Another impact on the accuracy of radio bearings is the distance to the station from which bearings are taken.

Quadrantal error is introduced by the vessel and must be accounted for when using the RDF. This error is caused by the ship's metal, masts, and stays, deck cargo such as containers, and the electrical/magnetic character of the ship. Placing the antenna as high up as possible and clear of any interfering structures can generally reduce this error but will not eliminate it. To compensate, correction factors are applied to the user's radio bearings. These factors are determined by carefully comparing visual bearings of a transmitting antenna with a radio bearing taken at the same time. Called "swinging the ship," this determination of correction factors is required to be done annually and checked periodically. Before this process is begun, however, the ship's rigging, including masts and concentrations of anticipated deck cargo, should be in the same position as if stowed for sea. Once the factors are calculated, the unit may be corrected if a trained technician cuts a correction cam for the unit and it is installed.

Every unit must have a copy of the calibration curve posted adjacent to it. The calibration table will be clearly marked, if the unit has been corrected. After installation of the correction cam, the RDF accuracy must be compared again against visual bearings. Minor correction factors are then posted adjacent to the RDF unit for use by the operators in a similar fashion as with compass deviation tables.

Land effect or coastal refraction is another significant error that can be introduced into RDF readings. When a radio signal passes over land or near a land mass, particularly where topographic features are prominent, the radio signals will bend. The altered direction of these signals will create a substantial difference in the readings and affect the accuracy. There is little that can be done to compensate for land effect or coastal refraction, and the operator should be aware that when using a radio beacon, where there is substantial amount of land between the receiver and the transmitter, directional errors can occur. In addition, bearings that cut near a

DO NOT APPLY TO BEARINGS
THE R. D. F. HAS BEEN COMPENSATED

ITT Mackay Marine

MV/SS EMPIRE STATE ...... D.F CORRECTION CURVE, TYPE 4003A ..... NR 56 M003 ......

SCALE READING	CORRECTED READING	SCALE READING	CORRECTED READING
0	0	180	−1
5		185	
10	+5	190	+3
15		195	
20	+8	200	+5
25		205	
30	+10	210	+6
35		215	
40	+10	220	+8
45		225	
50	+8	230	+7
55		235	
60	+7	240	+6
65		245	
70	+6	250	+3
75		255	
80	+3	260	+3
85		265	
90	+1	270	−2
95		275	
100	−1	280	−3
105		285	
110	−4	290	−7
115		295	
120	−5	300	−8
125		305	
130	−7	310	(−)
135		315	
140	−8	320	−7
145		325	
150	−7	330	−5
155		335	
160	−6	340	−5
165		345	−4
170	−4	350	−8
175		355	
180	−1	360	0

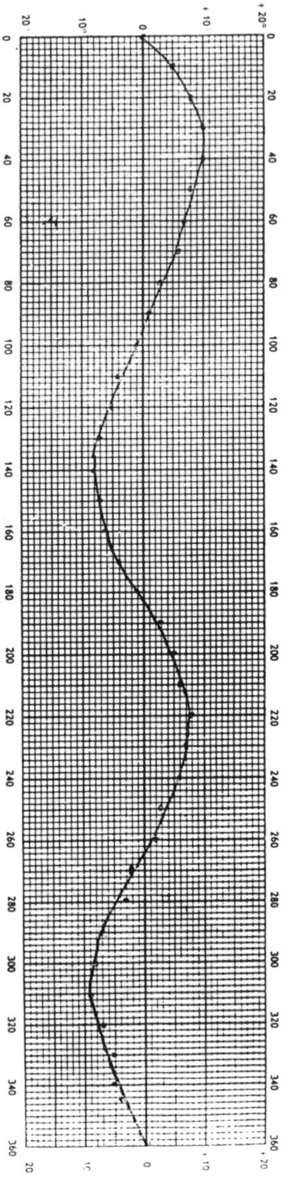

CALIBRATION DETAILS

DATE: 5-26-80

AT: SAYBROOK CN

FREQUENCY: 320 KC

CHOKE SETTINGS NIL

SHIP'S RIG CONDITIONS

MAIN AERIAL: OPEN

EMERGENCY AERIAL:

OPEN

DERRICKS: NONE

BOATS IN/OUT OUT

SIGNATURES

RADIO OBS: W. Winter

VISUAL OBS: MANY GOOD MEN

REMARKS

ALL OK

NEW CAM INSTALLED

Fig. 2-6. RDF correction curve.
Courtesy of State University of New York Maritime College.

coastline at an oblique angle may also produce significant errors. Coastal refraction or land effect is most prominent when bearings are taken within 15 to 20 degrees of being parallel to a shoreline. It is noteworthy that the use of dead-reckoning navigation is very important to the accurate use of RDF navigation.

Polarization or night effect also can create major inaccuracies in RDF bearings. When bearings are taken within a half hour before

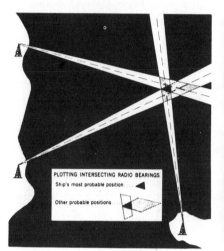
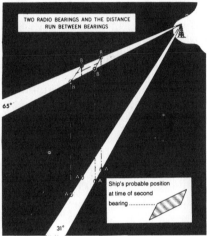

Class	Bearing Error (Degrees)	Observational Characteristics					
		Signal Strength	Bearing Indication	Fading	Interference	Bearing Swing (Degrees)	Duration of Observation
A	±2°	very good or good	definite (sharp null)	negligible	negligible	less than 3°	adequate
B	±5°	fairly good	blurred	slight	slight	more than 3° less than 5°	short
C	±10°	weak	severely blurred	severe	strong	more than 5° less than 10°	very short
D	more than ±10°	scarcely perceptible	ill-defined	very severe	very strong	more than 10°	inadequate

Fig. 2-7. Classification of bearings.
National Ocean Service/U.S. Government.

sunset to about a half hour before sunrise, introduction of sky waves as well as the radio errors that occur during twilight can be very problematic. It is important to note that radio bearings are dependent upon ground waves and that sky waves will cause inaccurate readings because of the fluctuation in the direction in which they are received.

Ambiguity is the most significant error the operator can experience. As discussed previously, when signals are received from a single radio station, the operator cannot tell whether the signal reading is the true bearing or the reciprocal bearing. Modern radio directional finders have sense systems that employ a second antenna and can be utilized to determine the true direction of a single station as stated. In lieu of a sense system an operator must rely upon a basic tenet of navigation: maintain an accurate dead-reckoning (DR) position. Because ambiguity errors are reciprocal, or 180 degrees, knowing the approximate bearing to the receiver from the DR position can avoid problems. Additionally, ambiguity can be reduced by cross-checking RDF fixes to other navigational systems if available.

Another key error involves the vessel's distance from the receiver. All radio signals travel in a great circle but are usually plotted on Mercator charts for navigation. When bearings are taken when the station is within 50 miles, they can be plotted as a straight line on a Mercator chart with no correction. Over 50 miles, the radio bearings must be corrected prior to being plotted. This is done by the application of a correction factor from a conversion angle table, commonly found in publications that list or contain information about marine radio beacons. Instructions for the application of the correction are given in the table explanation. Navigators may also calculate a conversion angle correction by using the following formula when navigating in midlatitudes between the equator and 85 degrees, and when there is a difference of longitude of less than 4½ degrees between the receiver and the transmitter:

$$\tan \text{ conversion angle} = \sin Lm \tan \tfrac{1}{2} DLo$$

where

Lm = mid-latitude
DLo = difference of longitude

If the receiver is in north latitude, the correction is added if the transmitter is eastward, and subtracted if the transmitter is westward. If the receiver is in south latitude, the correction is subtracted if the transmitter is eastward, and added if the transmitter is westward.

As with visual bearings, the navigator should try to make sure that the angle of intersection of several bearing lines is as close as possible to 90 degrees. Keep in mind that bearing lines from radio beacons can be utilized with visual bearing lines or lines of position from other radionavigation systems.

The quality and proper installation of the equipment is also important. As previously mentioned, it is important that the antenna for your receiver be located in such a manner that no obstructions will interfere with its line of sight to a transmitter. The sense antenna should also be mounted in an unobstructed location. Antenna cables should be run clear of high-voltage power lines and radar wave guides. The unit should be properly grounded and voltage-protected.

Finally, as with any piece of equipment, it is the operator's degree of experience that is most significant. The navigator should make every effort to use RDF/ADF whenever possible and to become well versed in its operation in preparation for the time when he or she may be forced to use the equipment as the primary means of navigation. As often stated by the U.S. Coast Guard, the prudent navigator using the dictates of good seamanship will never rely on any single means to determine a position.

RADIO DIRECTION-FINDER STATION INFORMATION

In the United States, comprehensive information about the marine radio beacon system is found in National Imaging and Mapping Agency (NIMA) Hydrographic Office Publication No. 117, *Radio Navigational Aids*. Information on the range, frequency, characteristics, and position of radio beacon transmitters, however, must be found in the U.S. Coast Guard *Light Lists* or NIMA's *List of Lights*. There are also numerous other publications produced by other nations that list radio beacons, most notably *The Admiralty List of Radio Signals,* published by the hydrographer of the Royal Navy of the United Kingdom.

Just as an operator should be well-versed in his or her vessel's aids to navigation when navigating, he or she should also be familiar with radio aids that may be encountered during the watch. Many watchstanders regard the marine radio beacon system as being old-fashioned and choose not to use it. However, under the general agreements of SOLAS, direction finders are required aboard vessels making voyages outside of coastal areas for the purposes of determining the direction of vessels in distress. The operator can easily master the use of the direction finder as part of his or her normal

RADIO DIRECTION FINDER AND RADAR STATIONS

(1) No.	(2) Name	(3) Type	(4) Position Rx	(4) Position Tx	(5) Frequency	(6) Range	(7) Procedure	(8) Remarks
NORWAY								
1005	**Ragaland (LGQ).** 2-0727	RDF	58°48′48″N 005°40′10″E	58°56′48″N 005°42′16″E	A. 500 kHz, A1A, A2A; 2182 kHz, A3E. B. 255–535 kHz band, A1A, A2A. 1600–3200 kHz band, A3E. C. 516 kHz, A1A, A2A. 1.0 kW; 1729 kHz, A3E, 0.5 kW			CALIBRATED SECTORS: 100–009°
1006	**Lista Lt. (LGZ).** 2-0722	RDF	58°07′03″N 006°34′14″E				Call Farsund Radio (LGZ)	
1007	**Hillersoy (LGL).** 2-0752	RDF	61°16′45″N 004°37′26″E				Call Floro Radio (LGL)	
SWEDEN								
1015	**Goteborg (SAG).** 2-0665	RDF	57°24′55″N 011°56′15″E	57°27′55″N 011°56′05″E	A. 500 kHz, A2A; 2037, 2182 kHz, A3E. B. 410, 500 kHz, A2A; 1605–3800 kHz band, A3E. Pref. freq.: 2182 kHz. C. 450, 500 kHz, A2A, 2.0 kW; 1785, 2182 kHz, A3E; 2.0 kW.		Ship's call sign is transmitted for 50 sec., followed by 10 sec. dash.	CALIBRATED SECTOR: 159–345° CHARGES: 3.5 gold francs
DENMARK								
1020	**Blavand (OXB).** 2-0311	RDF	55°33′36″N 008°05′55″E	55°33′14″N 008°06′58″E	A. 500 kHz, A2A; 2076, 2182 kHz, J3E, H3E. B. 410, 500* kHz, A2A; 2076, 2182* kHz, H3E. C. 429, 500* kHz, A1A, A2A, 0.9 kW; 1813, 2182* kHz, J3E, H3E, 0.5 kW.			CHARGES: 1 Special Drawing Right (SDR) per bearing

*NOTE: In case of distress only.

Fig. 2-8. Excerpt from Pub 117 listing of radio direction finder and radar stations

watchkeeping responsibilities in case the time ever comes when the system may have to be used in a life-or-death situation. Even with the transition of radio beacons to DGPS, the system is still broad-casting a carrier frequency for the DGPS. It may not have a clear ID signal, but it is useful for a radio bearing nonetheless.

OPERATION

The operator should identify the stations to be encountered in an area where the vessel is navigating. Always cross-check charted information against the information published in the *Light List* and list the stations to be utilized as part of a voyage plan. The stations may have a specific Morse identification code; if not, other identification factors should be determined. The station's position, type of transmission, range, and other key data are listed in the previously mentioned publications.

Signal range varies with the power of each transmitting station, and a station's range will be indicated in the station identification list. Generally, however, the maximum range does not exceed 200 miles during the day; due to sky-wave reception, it decreases to approximately 100 miles at night.

As previously mentioned, corrections for conversion angles for bearings received from stations more than 50 miles distant must be applied when using other than gnomonic projection charts. If your unit has not been calibrated with a correction cam, be sure to use the RDF correction curve or scale. The FCC requires that you check your RDF unit by taking a series of bearings on either side of the vessel and comparing them to visual bearings on a regular basis between inspections, which are required annually.

Radio bearings are usually not in error more than 2 degrees for distances less than 150 nautical miles. For every degree in error encountered when taking a bearing, you have a 0.17-nautical-mile position error per every 10 miles of range from the station.

To increase plotting accuracy and because accuracy is not greater than 2 degrees at the null, you should plot bearing lines indicating the limits of the null, especially at longer distances from the transmitter. This will produce a narrow zone of probability where the vessel is most likely located.

To reduce error, avoid taking bearings at sunrise or sunset. Be sure to take land effect or coastal refraction into account. This type of error can be somewhat avoided by not using bearings that are within 15 to 20 degrees of being parallel to the shoreline. Finally, check to ensure your gyrorepeater or course heading indicator is aligned with the ship's heading.

If you decide to home in on a radio beacon, be sure to keep continuous track of how close you are getting to the beacon. Also, with floating radio beacons, be sure to avoid constant bearings at a closing range, as you may wind up running over the radio beacon.

Many of the same principles that apply to navigating with visual bearings are applicable to radio bearings. Special case bearings such as doubling the angle on the bow can be very useful in determining

RADIO NAVIGATIONAL AIDS
RADIO DIRECTION FINDER AND RADAR STATIONS

Correction to be applied to radio bearing to convert Mercator bearing

Mid. Lat	0.5°	1°	1.5°	2°	2.5°	3°	3.5°	4°	4.5°	5°	5.5°	6°	6.5°	7°	7.5°	Mid Lat
4				0.1	0.1	0.1	0.1	0.2	0.2	0.2	0.2	0.2	0.2	0.2	0.3	4
5		0.1	0.1	.1	.1	.2	.2	.2	.2	.3	.3	.3	.4	.4	.4	5
6		.1	.1	.1	.2	.2	.2	.3	.3	.3	.3	.4	.4	.5	.5	6
7		.1	.1	.2	.2	.2	.3	.3	.3	.4	.4	.4	.5	.5	.5	7
8		.1	.1	.2	.2	.2	.3	.3	.4	.4	.5	.5	.5	.6	.6	8
9		.1	.1	.2	.2	.3	.3	.4	.4	.4	.5	.5	.6	.6	.6	9
10		.1	.1	.2	.2	.3	.3	.4	.4	.5	.5	.6	.6	.6	.6	10
11		.1	.1	.2	.2	.3	.3	.4	.4	.5	.5	.6	.6	.7	.7	11
12	0.1	.1	.1	.2	.3	.3	.4	.4	.5	.5	.6	.6	.7	.7	.8	12
13	.1	.1	.2	.2	.3	.3	.4	.5	.5	.6	.6	.7	.8	.8	.8	13
14	.1	.1	.2	.2	.3	.4	.4	.5	.6	.6	.6	.7	.8	.8	.9	14
15	.1	.1	.2	.3	.3	.4	.4	.5	.6	.6	.7	.8	.8	1.0	1.0	15
16	.1	.1	.2	.3	.4	.4	.5	.6	.6	.7	.8	.9	1.0	1.0	1.1	16
17	.1	.2	.2	.3	.4	.5	.5	.6	.7	.8	.9	.9	1.0	1.1	1.2	17
18	.1	.2	.2	.3	.4	.5	.6	.6	.7	.8	.9	1.0	1.0	1.1	1.2	18
19	.1	.2	.3	.3	.4	.5	.6	.7	.7	.8	.9	1.0	1.1	1.2	1.2	19
20	.1	.2	.2	.3	.4	.5	.6	.7	.8	.8	.9	1.0	1.1	1.2	1.3	20
21	.1	.2	.3	.4	.5	.5	.6	.7	.8	.9	1.0	1.1	1.2	1.2	1.4	21
22	.1	.2	.3	.4	.5	.6	.7	.8	.9	.9	1.0	1.1	1.3	1.4	1.5	22
23	.1	.2	.3	.4	.5	.6	.7	.8	.9	1.0	1.1	1.2	1.3	1.4	1.5	23
24	.1	.2	.3	.4	.5	.6	.7	.8	1.0	1.0	1.1	1.2	1.4	1.5	1.6	24
25	.1	.2	.3	.4	.6	.6	.7	.8	1.0	1.1	1.2	1.3	1.4	1.5	1.6	25
26	.1	.2	.3	.4	.6	.7	.8	.9	1.0	1.1	1.2	1.4	1.5	1.6	1.7	26
27	.1	.2	.3	.4	.6	.7	.8	.9	1.0	1.1	1.2	1.4	1.5	1.6	1.7	27
28	.1	.2	.4	.5	.6	.7	.8	.9	1.1	1.2	1.3	1.4	1.5	1.6	1.8	28
29	.1	.2	.4	.5	.6	.7	.8	1.0	1.1	1.2	1.3	1.4	1.6	1.7	1.8	29
30	.1	.2	.4	.5	.6	.8	.9	1.0	1.1	1.2	1.4	1.5	1.6	1.8	1.9	30
31	.1	.2	.4	.5	.6	.8	.9	1.0	1.2	1.3	1.4	1.6	1.7	1.8	1.9	31
32	.1	.3	.4	.5	.7	.8	.9	1.1	1.2	1.3	1.4	1.6	1.7	1.8	2.0	32
33	.1	.3	.4	.6	.7	.8	1.0	1.1	1.2	1.4	1.5	1.6	1.8	1.9	2.0	33
34	.1	.3	.4	.6	.7	.8	1.0	1.1	1.2	1.4	1.5	1.7	1.8	2.0	2.1	34
35	.1	.3	.4	.6	.7	.9	1.0	1.2	1.3	1.4	1.6	1.7	1.9	2.0	2.2	35
36	.1	.3	.4	.6	.7	.9	1.0	1.2	1.3	1.5	1.6	1.8	1.9	2.1	2.2	36
37	.2	.3	.4	.6	.8	.9	1.1	1.2	1.4	1.5	1.6	1.8	2.0	2.1	2.2	37
38	.2	.3	.5	.6	.8	.9	1.1	1.2	1.4	1.5	1.7	1.8	2.0	2.2	2.3	38
39	.2	.3	.5	.6	.8	1.0	1.1	1.2	1.4	1.6	1.7	1.9	2.1	2.2	2.4	39
40	.2	.3	.5	.6	.8	1.0	1.1	1.3	1.4	1.6	1.8	1.9	2.1	2.2	2.4	40
41	.2	.3	.5	.6	.8	1.0	1.2	1.3	1.5	1.6	1.8	2.0	2.2	2.3	2.5	41
42	.2	.3	.5	.7	.8	1.0	1.2	1.3	1.5	1.7	1.8	2.1	2.2	2.4	2.6	42
43	.2	.3	.5	.7	.9	1.0	1.2	1.4	1.5	1.7	1.9	2.1	2.2	2.4	2.6	43
44	.2	.4	.5	.7	.9	1.1	1.2	1.4	1.6	1.8	1.9	2.1	2.3	2.5	2.6	44
45	.2	.4	.5	.7	.9	1.1	1.3	1.4	1.6	1.8	2.0	2.2	2.3	2.5	2.7	45
46	.2	.4	.5	.7	.9	1.1	1.3	1.5	1.7	1.8	2.0	2.2	2.4	2.6	2.8	46
47	.2	.4	.6	.7	.9	1.1	1.3	1.5	1.7	1.9	2.1	2.2	2.4	2.6	2.8	47
48	.2	.4	.6	.8	1.0	1.1	1.3	1.5	1.7	1.9	2.1	2.3	2.4	2.6	2.8	48
49	.2	.4	.6	.8	1.0	1.1	1.3	1.5	1.7	1.9	2.1	2.3	2.5	2.7	2.9	49
50	.2	.4	.6	.8	1.0	1.1	1.3	1.5	1.7	1.9	2.1	2.3	2.5	2.7	2.9	50
51	.2	.4	.6	.8	1.0	1.2	1.4	1.6	1.8	2.0	2.2	2.4	2.6	2.7	2.9	51
52	.2	.4	.6	.8	1.0	1.2	1.4	1.6	1.8	2.0	2.2	2.4	2.6	2.8	3.0	52
53	.2	.4	.6	.8	1.0	1.2	1.4	1.6	1.8	2.0	2.2	2.4	2.6	2.8	3.0	53
54	.2	.4	.6	.8	1.0	1.2	1.4	1.6	1.8	2.1	2.2	2.4	2.7	2.9	3.1	54
55	.2	.4	.6	.8	1.0	1.2	1.4	1.7	1.9	2.1	2.3	2.5	2.7	2.9	3.1	55
56	.2	.4	.6	.8	1.0	1.2	1.4	1.7	1.9	2.1	2.3	2.5	2.7	2.9	3.2	56
57	.2	.4	.6	.9	1.1	1.3	1.5	1.7	1.9	2.1	2.3	2.6	2.8	2.9	3.2	57
58	.2	.4	.6	.9	1.1	1.3	1.5	1.7	1.9	2.1	2.3	2.6	2.8	3.0	3.2	58
59	.2	.4	.6	.9	1.1	1.3	1.5	1.7	2.0	2.2	2.4	2.6	2.8	3.0	3.2	59
60	.2	.4	.6	.9	1.1	1.3	1.5	1.7	2.0	2.2	2.4	2.6	2.8	3.0	3.2	60

Receiver (latitude)	Transmitter (direction from receiver)	Correction Sign	Receiver (latitude)	Transmitter (direction from receiver)	Correction Sign
North	Eastward	+	South	Eastward	−
North	Westward	−	South	Westward	+

Fig. 2-9. Radio bearing conversion table.
Courtesy of National Ocean Service/U.S. Government.

approximate distance off. Be sure, however, to account for the 2-degree probability of error.

RADIO DIRECTION-FINDING STATIONS

Under international agreement as part of the maritime navigation service, a number of shore stations have been designated to provide radio direction-finding capabilities. This service is offered on specific radio frequencies. Any vessel should be able to use this service, which can be requested by the deck watch officer through a shore station. In addition, the same shore stations are able to take bearings on distress frequencies to help locate vessels that send distress signals.

Radio direction-finding services are generally provided in the medium-frequency bands, between 1,605 kHz and 2,850 kHz, and include the international calling and distress frequency for single sideband, 2,182 kHz. To obtain a radio bearing from a shore station, the vessel should call the radio direction-finding station on the listening frequency indicated in the List of Radio Determination and Special Service Stations (these lists are reprinted in the United States by NIMA in Publication 117, *Radio Navigational Aids* and in the United Kingdom by the Hydrographer of the Navy in *The Admiralty List of Radio Signals*).

Depending upon the type of information required, the vessel calling should transmit the appropriate service or abbreviation as indicated in the station list. The vessel should also indicate the desired frequency that the vessel wants to use to transmit so that a radio bearing can be taken. The shore station will then give the vessel instructions on how the bearing will be taken. Once the instructions are received and understood and the frequency agreed upon and tested, the vessel is asked to transmit a long signal. The shore station may ask the vessel to repeat this to ensure it has an accurate reading. Once the shore station is satisfied that it has an accurate bearing on the vessel, it will then transmit back to the vessel the information indicating *the true bearing in degrees from the radio direction-finding station to the vessel,* the class of bearing, the time of observation, and the position of the radio direction-finding station. The vessel should acknowledge and confirm that it has received the information from the shore station. The vessel can then plot the bearing on a Mercator chart. Keep in mind that the same rules that apply to the correction of RDF bearings must be applied to these bearings. In addition, the operator must take into account that the bearing received is from the shore station to the vessel and that the reciprocal bearing will need to be plotted.

Class A— positions the operator may reasonably expect to be accurate
to within 5 nautical miles
Class B— positions the operator may reasonably expect to be accurate
to within 20 nautical miles
Class C— positions the operator may reasonably expect to be accurate
to within 50 nautical miles
Class D— positions the operator may not expect to be accurate to
within 50 nautical miles

Fig. 2-10. Bearing classifications.
Courtesy of National Ocean Service/U.S. Government.

The class of bearing refers to the expected accuracy of the radio
signal. These classifications are acceptable for frequencies utilized
under 3,000 kHz.

Bearings from several stations may be requested simultaneously,
which would allow the vessel to fix with reasonable accuracy its position. For all the modern wonders of satellite navigation as well as numerous other systems, and keeping in mind that the communications
system is generally tied to an emergency battery power source, this
system could prove very useful if you are dead in the water and drifting, or even worse, in a lifeboat or a life raft awaiting rescue.

COASTAL AND PORT RADAR AND RADIO STATIONS

There are a number of shore-based stations that provide navigational assistance to vessels on request. They primarily provide radar
information and can be determined on a chart because they are indicated by the description "Ra." These stations are not worldwide, but
are located in some of the prominent areas around the globe including Canada, Northern Europe, South America, Asia, and New Zealand.

Coastal radio stations provide information based on shore-based
radar systems that can be supplied to vessels upon request, including
traffic in harbors and harbor approaches and information regarding
the vessel's position. These shore-based stations provide navigational
assistance but do not necessarily exercise control over traffic as in a
vessel traffic system. It should be noted that the type of information
supplied by a shore-based station does not relieve the master of the
vessel of his or her responsibility for safe navigation. Port radio stations operate in a similar fashion except that they are located in a port
area. These stations broadcast traffic, navigational, weather, and
other important information concerning only their particular port

limits and approaches. Both coastal and port stations require operators. They may not necessarily be available at all times because of
shutdown due to equipment malfunction or maintenance.

RADAR BEACONS

Radar beacons (RACON) are radar transponder devices designed to
produce a distinctive image on the screen of ship's radar sets, thus
enabling the mariner to determine his position with greater certainty
than would be possible using a normal radar display alone. Although
this topic could be presented in the radar chapter, it does provide a
specific direction-finding function, and so will be discussed here.

RACON are short-range radio devices used to provide fixed radar reference points in areas where it is important to identify a special location. They are viewed on a radar screen and have a distinctive presentation. Specifically designed for the marine environment,
RACON are used for landfall identification, identification and ranging of inconspicuous coastlines, identification of particular aids to
navigation, directional information to a specific point, and identification of dangerous hazards to navigation.

RACON transponders are triggered ("interrogated") by a vessel's
radar, usually on the 3 cm marine radar frequency. They provide
range and bearing information and differ from the older RAMARK
system, which broadcast continually and only provided bearing information. When a RACON transponder is triggered by the radar
signal from an approaching vessel, it will produce a directional line
on a radar screen that will show the specific characteristic of the station identity code. This line can be measured to determine range and
bearing to the transmitter.

Most RACONs are operated by the U.S. Coast Guard, which
plans to eventually maintain approximately 110 units throughout
the United States. The Coast Guard also approves privately operated and maintained RACONs.

The U.S. Coast Guard presently operates approximately 50
RACONs as maritime aids on the Atlantic, Pacific, and Gulf coasts
and in the Great Lakes. Aids that the Coast Guard mandates should
be clearly distinguishable and include stations on shore, large navigation buoys (LNB), harbor entrance buoys (Mo A), channel en-
trances under bridges, and uncharted hazards to navigation. The
RACON is activated by the vessel's radar, transponding a Morse
code echo from the navigation aid, which is then displayed on the radar unit radially away from the target in lengths of approximately
one to two miles. The Morse code signal always begins with a long
dash, followed by the Morse code letter distinguishing the station.

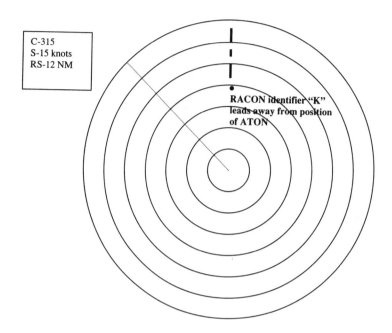

C-315
S-15 knots
RS-12 NM

RACON identifier "K"
leads away from position
of ATON

Fig. 2-11. RACON. Drawing by Thomas Bushy.

Uncharted hazards are always displayed using the Morse Code letter D (dash-dot-dot). RACON locations and information may be obtained in abbreviated form on a navigational chart or in detailed form in the *Light List*.

RACON should be visible to most commercial shipboard radar systems on vessels 6 to 20 miles from the RACON installation, regardless of radar size. No additional receiving equipment is required. Some precautions are necessary if use of the RACON is desired. Radars that operate in the 10-cm band (2,900–3,100 MHz) are usually installed as a second radar on larger vessels, and may not respond to RACON. The Coast Guard now installs dual-band (3-cm and 10-cm), called frequency-agile, RACON in most locations. In addition, rain clutter control switches on radars must be switched off or, if necessary, remain on low to ensure that the RACON is visible. Pulse correlation circuitry (interference or clutter rejection on some radars) installed on most newer radars, if on, may prevent the radar from displaying some RACON. Therefore this circuitry should be switched off for maximum RACON potential. Only by referencing detailed RACON information in the *Light List* will the mariner be prepared to utilize transponder functions and RACON capabilities.

CHAPTER 3

HYPERBOLIC RADIONAVIGATION SYSTEMS

BASIC THEORY

Hyperbolic radionavigation systems are among the most accurate and still frequently used systems employed in marine navigation today. The key advantage of these systems is that they can provide instantaneous multiple lines of position, which are then utilized to establish a navigational fix. Mariners should remain aware of hyperbolic systems despite reliance upon satellite systems since land-based transmitters can be both protected and maintained with greater ease than orbiting satellites.

Most hyperbolic systems are considered to be long-range radio navigation aids. They were originally broken down into two categories, which included coastal confluence systems and global coverage systems. Coastal confluence systems are designed to provide highly accurate position-fixing information in potentially hazardous navigation areas. Their accuracy decreases with the greater distance traveled from shore. Global coverage systems were designed to provide position-fixing information in all areas with the same average accuracy throughout the system. There was only one global hyperbolic system, Omega, and it was terminated in September 1997. The navigator's reliance on hyperbolic systems will most likely continue to remain viable in coastal coverage areas.

There are two types of hyperbolic radionavigation systems employed today. These are the coastal confluence systems loran C and

Decca. Loran C appears to be the only system that will remain a useful navigation aid for the foreseeable future.

Hyperbolic radionavigation systems are created by establishing a specific hyperbolic radio pattern over a geographical area. An understanding of hyperbola is necessary in order to understand how the pattern is created. A hyperbola is a locus of all points in a flat plane that have a constant difference of distance from two fixed points. A hyperbolic navigation pattern is created by establishing two points at a specific distance from each other at which transmitting stations are placed. Although the pattern is calculated through a series of mathematical equations, this discussion will concentrate on the pattern formation rather than the mathematics behind it.

Assume for a moment that two points have been established, at approximately one hundred miles apart, labeled A and B in figure 3-1. We can establish the first part of the pattern, called the *baseline*, which is a straight line drawn between the two points, A-B. Where the line goes beyond the fixed points, this is referred to as the *baseline extension*, A-A' and B-B'. At the approximate midpoint of the

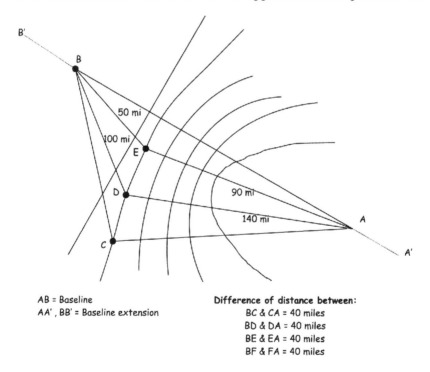

AB = Baseline
AA' , BB' = Baseline extension

Difference of distance between:
BC & CA = 40 miles
BD & DA = 40 miles
BE & EA = 40 miles
BF & FA = 40 miles

Fig. 3-1. Hyperbolic pattern concept.
Drawing by Van Trong Nguyen.

baseline, another segment of the pattern can be established which is called the *centerline*. The centerline is approximately halfway between the two fixed points and is drawn perpendicular to the baseline. If a measurement to any part of the hyperbolic pattern is made from both of the original points, it will be discovered that while the distance from the points may increase or decrease, the difference of distance between the two legs that are measured from the fixed points, AB, will remain the same.

If we take these measurements on either side of the centerline, then a similar situation will occur. Using the premise that the difference in distance must remain the same, in figure 3-1, we have established two points, AB, with B one hundred miles northwest of A. We have selected some points (C, D, E) which will fall within the hyperbolic pattern.The difference of distance between A-E and B-E is forty miles. Although the distance is greater between A-D and B-D, the difference of distance remains the same. At location D, the distance between B and D is one hundred miles. The difference between A and D is one hundred and forty miles, and the difference of distance remains forty miles.

Continuing to use the same technique, a locus of points will be created with the same difference of distance. When the points are connected, a curved line is created. This process is repeated to establish a series of lines between each fixed point and the centerline. The end result will be a group of curved lines that bend toward the fixed points on either side of the centerline. This navigation pattern is established, as previously mentioned, through a series of mathematical calculations which define the exact coordinates of each point, leading to a tool that can be used by a navigator. It is important to remember that although the patterns are precisely calculated, radio signals are used to make the pattern a practical tool. Atmospheric disturbances and other forces can impact the signal's path of travel which in turn can affect the accuracy of the pattern.

To utilize this as a navigation system, transmitting antennas are placed at each of the points that broadcast signals in a specific sequence on a specific time base. The receiver can measure the difference in time in microseconds (one millionth of a second), or the variance in the phase of the two received signals. This information is used to determine where the vessel is within the hyperbolic pattern. The hyperbolic pattern, when placed over a geographical area, creates an infinite number of lines of positions, some of which can then be superimposed on a chart in the form of overprinted lattice lines. The measurement of the various radio signals by the receiver produces a series of coordinates that when interpolated by the navigator renders vessel position. The key advantage of a hyperbolic radionavigation system is that multiple transmitters can be used to establish a series of overlaying patterns that the navigator can utilize to develop several lines of position simultaneously, thus developing a fix.

The hyperbolic patterns are very broad and when printed on large-scale Mercator charts, appear nearly parallel to each other. The difference between each hyperbolic line represents a specific distance in nautical miles known as the gradient. The gradient is very important to the mariner in attempting to establish the useable signals from transmitting stations. The steeper the gradient, the closer

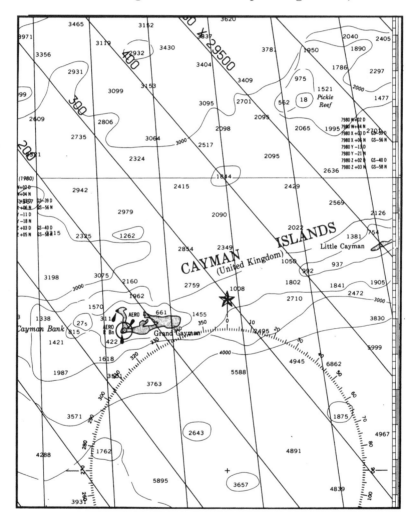

Fig. 3-2. Loran C chart.
Courtesy National Ocean Service/U.S. Government.

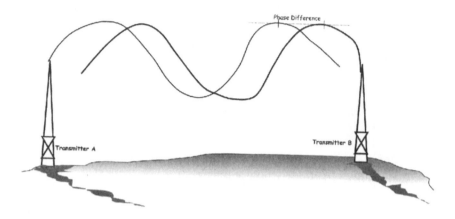

Fig. 3-3. Phase comparison. Drawing by Van Trong Nguyen.

the receiver is to the baseline, and therefore the more reliable the line of position (LOP). The shallower the gradient, the closer the receiver is to the baseline extension, and the less reliable the LOP.

Although the systems produce basic information in several different forms, when applied to the hyperbolic pattern they will ultimately produce a fix based on two or more lines of position derived from the pattern. This is what gives these types of systems a major advantage over the directional systems discussed previously.

Modern hyperbolic radionavigation receivers are equipped with microprocessors that can very easily convert time-delay or phase-comparison information into coordinates of latitude and longitude. There is discussion currently going on among various governments in regard to eliminating the hyperbolic overprints on nautical charts because the microprocessor technology is so reliable. Ultimately however, this argument continues to be balanced by the reality that the raw measurements from each of the systems are more finite and thus more accurate than latitude and longitude coordinates.

System	Coverage	Band	Frequency	Measurement Method
Loran C	coastal	LF	100 kHz	time delays/phase comparison
Decca	coastal	LF	70–130 kHz	phase comparison

Fig. 3-4. Hyperbolic radionavigation system

Each radionavigational system establishes its hyperbolic pattern in a separate manner and in turn uses a slightly different method for allowing the user to determine where they are in the pattern. In the case of loran C, the time difference between received signals, as well as a comparison of the phases of these signals, is used to determine position. In the case of Omega and Decca, phase comparison is the only method used in which the differences in received cycles of radio waves are measured at their reception point.

As stated earlier, hyperbolic radionavigation systems are established with a series of transmitters placed at specific points with a navigation pattern established between them. They can be based on individual stations which interact with each other, such as in the Omega system, or on groups of specific stations that interact with each other in what is referred to as chains, as in loran C or Decca. Once the hyperbolic pattern is established, a series of transmitters can create additional patterns criss-crossing an area. The use of two or more patterns and the subsequent lines of position determined from them provides a fix. It should be kept in mind that radionavigational receivers are like all other radio receivers, with system signals subject to the forces and errors that affect all radio transmissions.

LORAN C NAVIGATION SYSTEM

Loran is an acronym derived from the term long-range navigation system. Designed for accurate coastal and harbor navigation, the system provides rapid position determination by continuously measuring the time delay between signals received from a master and secondary station. The loran reading corresponds to a line of position on a calculated pattern established through a mathematical scale of probable propagation based on ground-wave radio transmissions. The loran A system was originally developed during World War II by the scientists at the radiation laboratory of the Massachusetts Institute of Technology. After testing, it was deployed by the U.S. Coast Guard and in its initial form was used to assist allied bombers in missions over Europe. Referred to as standard loran, it was in use until 1980 in the United States and was only recently shut down in the developing nations of Asia.

Loran A's successor, loran C, was developed in the 1950s and was fully deployed in the 1970s. Loran C provides a better level of accuracy and a more expanded area of coverage than the original system. Loran C is considered to be reasonably free of the effect of most atmospheric disturbances except when weather conditions are severe.

The United States, which developed and operated loran C in areas throughout the world, plans to eliminate its support of the system in favor of the newer GPS in the United States. In coverage areas outside of the United States, maintenance and operation of the system is being turned over to local authorities. In some cases, those authorities have elected to expand the system as a replacement for Decca and as an alternate to the U.S.- or Russian-controlled satellite systems.

It is key that the mariner understands that loran C is a land-based, cost-efficient system that is unlikely to be affected by strategic actions of nations in conflict. Its current widespread use and its accessibility as a backup navigation system in coastal coverage areas should support its continued operation for the foreseeable future. The U.S. federal radionavigation plan indicates continued operation through 2015 in the United States, but other government authorities may support loran C even longer.

Theory

Loran C is a low-frequency hyperbolic system broadcasting on a frequency of about 100 kHz. The navigator's position is established through the combined measurement of time delays (TD) and phase comparisons, which gives the system more accuracy than its predecessor. Transmitters broadcast pulsed signals of about 250 microseconds in duration. Originally designed to cover the U.S. coastal confluence zone, it is now in use throughout many key coastal areas throughout the northern hemisphere.

Loran C coverage is divided into chains comprised of three to five land-based transmitting stations consisting of a master station and two, three, or four secondary stations (also known as slaves). The master station is designated as M (master) and the secondary stations are designated as W (whiskey), X (xray), Y (yankee), and Z (zulu). Each of the secondary station transmitters is synchronized with the master transmitter so that there is a precise time interval between the master transmission and the transmission from each of the secondary stations. This is accomplished through a precise timing control mechanism located at each of the transmitters.

The stations transmit in a particular sequence at a specific rate called the group repetition interval (GRI). The group repetition interval is the amount of time it takes for a chain to broadcast all of its signals in sequence from the beginning of the first pulse of the master station transmission to the beginning of the first pulse of the master in the next cycle. Group repetition intervals are established between 40,000 and 99,000 microseconds. The particular chain is designated by dividing the GRI by 10. For example, if the GRI was 99,600 microseconds, the chain designation would be 9960.

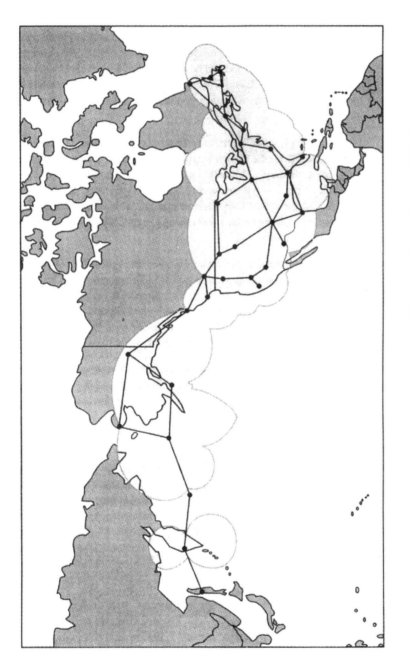

Fig. 3-5. Loran C coverage diagram. Courtesy of National Ocean Service/U.S. Government.

Pulse: The Master (M) station sends a signal consisting of nine pulses, the ninth being the identification pulse. The secondary stations send a signal consisting of eight pulses.

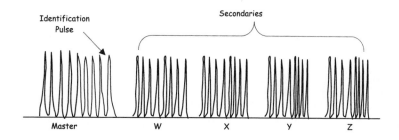

Group repetition interval (GRI):

Each station transmits these groups of pulses at specified interval called the GRI. This interval keeps the loran receiver from tracking signals from other stations not within the chain being used.

Example: A GRI of 9960 means that there are 99,600 microseconds between each group of pulses. This is how the receiver identifies the correct chain being used.

Fig. 3-6. Loran chain designation. Drawing by Van Trong Nguyen.

The stations broadcast in the order master-whiskey-xray-yankee-zulu. This is how the receiver determines the differences between chains, as all loran C stations transmit on the same frequency.

The master station and each of the secondary stations broadcast eight pulses of approximately 250 microseconds in duration. The signal envelope of a loran C pulse contains a variation in both frequency and amplitude. This allows the receiver to do a precise measurement of the transmission through phase comparison of the pulse cycles within the envelope. This combined technique of timing measurement and phase comparison gives loran C greater accuracy than its predecessor.

The master station also broadcasts a ninth pulse called the performance pulse. The performance pulse allows the receiver to determine which of the transmissions is coming from the master, which will give it an indication of where the cycle of transmissions begin. The performance pulse is also utilized to tell the receiver whether the system is functioning correctly.

Broadcasting at a specific GRI, signals are received at the specific rate designated for that chain. The hyperbolic pattern is established between the master and each of the secondary stations with

North Pacific	9990
Chenka (Russia/USA)	5980
Russian Chain	7950
Northwest Pacific	8930
Korea Chain	9930
North China	7430
East China	8390
South China	6780
Gulf of Alaska	7960
West Coast, Canada	5990
West Coast, USA	9940
East Coast, Canada	5930
Newfoundland, East Coast	7270
Great Lakes, USA	8970
Northeast, USA	9960
Southeast, USA	7980
Ejde Chain	9007
Bo Chain	7001
North Saudi Arabia	8830
Southern Saudi Arabia	7030
India Bombay Chain	6042

Fig. 3-7. Loran-C GRI rate table (1997)

the baseline lying directly between the master and each secondary station, with an average separation of about 650 nautical miles. The difference between each hyperbolic line is expressed in microseconds and labeled according to the measured TD.

Operation

The navigator using loran C must consider the coverage area over which navigation is required. Of course the coastal areas provide the greater probability of danger to the ship when inadequate navigation is conducted. The concepts of loran C accuracy are very important in this phase of operation. There are three types of accuracy. Absolute accuracy is the accuracy of a position as compared to the actual geographic coordinates of the earth. Repeatable accuracy is the ability of the receiver to determine a similar position in comparison to the same position measured at a previous time. Relative accuracy is the comparison of two operators using the same system at the same time. As a clarification, a user can actually determine the absolute accuracy when stationary in a known location such as a harbor mooring. A reasonable measurement of absolute accuracy can be obtained when comparing loran C to more sophisticated satellite navigation systems if terrestrial positioning is not available. Repeatable accuracy can be measured when returning to a known location when the previous receiver readings are known. Relative accuracy is least measurable since few vessels have more than one loran C receiver aboard. Of the three, the comparison between absolute and repeatable accuracy is the most critical. The navigator is warned that absolute accuracy should be +/– 0.25 nautical miles (NM) under most circumstances, but can expect repeatable accuracy of as close as +/– 0.1 NM. Most navigators will therefore hold the position of the vessel as relatively accurate, but will enjoy greater confidence that they are where they want to be if returning to a known position.

Although the loran C system has been designed for overall accuracy of about 0.25 NM, in most cases the navigator can rely on +/– 0.1 NM in near coastal areas. This accuracy decreases the farther the receiver gets from the geographic center of the chain, and can decrease significantly at night due to sky-wave propagation. In addition, the accuracy of the system is compromised twice daily during twilight, and during periods of extreme weather.

The navigator must also consider nonuniform propagation rates. Keeping in mind that the loran C radionavigation pattern is based on a theoretical concept that assumes a constant speed of radio signals within the system, the actual speed of radio waves can vary due to atmospheric conditions, weather, or when the signals pass over land masses. There are three factors that need to be incorporated when navigating with loran C. The first is the primary phase factor (PF), which is generally accounted for in the lattices overprinted on a chart and in a receiver's microprocessor. This factor is based on an average variation of signal propagation in the geographic area due to atmospheric conditions. The secondary phase factor (SF) is developed by taking into account the effect that traveling over water has on a signal. Like the PF, the SF is accounted for on charts and in the receiver's microprocessor. The operator does not need to consider this in practical navigational usage.

The last factor concerning accuracy is called the additional secondary phase factor (ASPF). This factor is based on the variation that is introduced when signals travel over or near land masses, since the loran C navigational patterns are based upon signal propagation over water, not over land. Therefore, a correction must be utilized by the navigator seeking a high degree of accuracy. The ASPF corrections are mathematically determined using Millington's method, and are presented either on chart lattices or in correction tables. It should be noted that some charts have the lattice lines corrected for ASPF, others do not, and the navigator must inspect the chart's notes in order to determine whether ASPF must be applied. In particular, if a chart has been corrected for ASPF and the loran C receiver is operating in latitude and longitude readout function, it will not render the same level of accuracy as when using TD lattice plotting.

Loran operation must begin with the user providing sufficient time for the receiver to pick up and measure the appropriate signals that have been selected. Modern receivers use two methods to select geographical chains. The first is manual selection, where the user enters the desired chain into the receiver. The second is where the user enters an approximate geographical position in latitude and longitude, and the receiver selects the appropriate chain. Once the receiver has identified the chain's transmission and the cycle of the transmission, it will automatically track all stations in the chain. One of the biggest advantages of loran C over other hyperbolic radionavigation systems is that once the proper GRI is selected, the unit will eventually provide viable navigational information. This will continue until the receiver leaves the coverage area or the user selects another chain. Although the receiver is tracking all the secondaries in a chain, most receivers only accommodate the display of two secondaries at one time.

Every loran C receiver indicates the strength of the signal being picked up by providing a numeric reading of the ratio between the strength of the received signal in comparison to the existing background noise. This indication is called the signal-to-noise ratio (SNR) and is generally rated on a scale from 0 to 999. The higher the number, the stronger the signal. For a reading to be considered reasonably measurable and thus reasonably accurate, at least 60 percent of what is being received should be a loran C signal. The SNR in this case would be 600 (or 60 on receivers that provide only a two-digit indication). Between 600 and 999 is considered the usable strength of a signal. Below 600, the receiver has difficulty taking an accurate measurement, thus signals below that level should be suspect. In addition, there should be a steady indication that reasonably assures the user that the unit is receiving only ground waves, the type of signal upon which the established hyperbolic pattern is based.

A receiver has several alarms associated with it that indicate a problem with reception. These alarms include (1) the blink alarm, which is triggered by the performance pulse of the master station indicating a system-wide transmitter malfunction, (2) the lost signal, which indicates that the received transmissions are unusable or unheard above background noise, and (3) the cycle alarm, which will appear when initializing the receiver or when the signal is lost. This indicates the receiver is not reading the transmission pattern correctly because it has not picked up the performance pulse.

Some receivers are equipped with notch filters, which are used to eliminate unnecessary background noise on the broadcast frequency. This allows the receiver to process a clearer signal. Many units have automatic filtering capability, but some of the more sophisticated units allow the user to adjust the filters. This can prove particularly useful when the receiver is at greater distances from the transmitters.

Most receivers have integrated microprocessors, which can provide the user with information based on the reception of loran C signals. It is important to understand that these capabilities are separate from what the system was designed to provide and that the ability and accuracy of these types of measurements depend on the quality and type of receiver. Most receivers can provide the user with the ability to establish and navigate using waypoints, determine course and speed made good, provide bearings and distances to navigation marks, and determine cross-track error.

Most of the determinations that the modern loran C receiver can render are common to navigators. Interestingly however, an evolution in navigation terminology has been caused by the modern microprocessor-based loran C receiver. What once was considered a navigation point to navigators, where course and/or speed changes were required and labeled on a chart, has now become known as a waypoint. Waypoints are merely a navigation point which has been programmed into the loran C receiver. Additionally, cross-track error (XTE) is the new term for a vessel's ability to navigate on a straight rhumb line from point A to point B. Navigators will recall that this was once referred to as set and drift, or leeway.

Navigation

From the perspective of the U.S. Coast Guard or the professional seafarer the prudent navigator should never rely solely upon one method of navigation to determine a position. This same perspective needs to be applied to the use of loran C, or for that matter, any other type of radionavigation system. The larger a vessel, the higher the probability of a significant marine casualty such as a grounding, which could have disastrous impacts on the environment, not to mention the career of the navigator.

Vessel size and the type of operation will dictate how this type of system is utilized. For example, a ship leaving port may or may not note its position by loran C as a waypoint for return. This means that once coming back to that port, relying upon the constraints of absolute accuracy of +/– 0.25 NM is adequate, since by that time loran C position fixing may be secondary to radar navigation. But the coastal fishing vessel may want to retain a loran C position after a successful catch. Although the exact location of the catch isn't important, relying upon loran C repeatability is, since the fisherman definitely wants to come back to that spot.

Using loran C in daily navigation is relatively easy, depending upon the type of receiver. Virtually all modern receivers allow for the selection of time delay readout, or latitude and longitude (lat/long) readout provided by the microprocessor. Reading the lat/long merely requires the navigator to observe the electronic position of the vessel at a particular time, then plot this position on the chart. Using TD can be a little more confusing. The navigator must read the microsecond TD off the receiver at a particular time, then find the closest overprinted TD on either side of the receiver reading, then measure the gradient between the two TDs and interpolate where their microsecond reading falls. A line is drawn parallel to the hyperbolic pattern closest to the interpolated point, thus establishing a single line of position. The navigator then goes to a second station and follows the same procedure, establishing a second line of position. The navigator may choose to select yet another secondary station, utilizing the basic navigation principles of LOP selection. The intersecting LOPs thus create a fix.

The loran C overprint found on coverage charts is based upon probable propagation under normal conditions for the specific area. As mentioned previously, the user has to keep in mind that while the patterns calculated may be relatively precise, signal reception and position determination will differ from the calculated pattern according to variations in the path the signals will travel and any atmospheric conditions that interfere with the signals.

The operator should keep the following basic concepts in mind when using the system. The maximum daytime range of a loran C chain is between 700 and 1,200 miles, which is the normal range of a ground-wave signal. At night, sky-wave reception can extend the range of loran C to between 2,300 and 3,400 miles; however, sky-wave readings become increasingly inaccurate at range because of their random reflection pattern. There are sky-wave correction tables available for loran C, but even with applied corrections, signals received in the form of sky waves should be limited to general offshore navigation only. The question now becomes, How does the operator recognize sky-wave reception on a loran receiver?

Remember that reception based on sky waves will fade in and out depending on how they are picked up by the receiver. A sky wave that is received simultaneously with a ground wave or with another sky wave will cause the signal strength to vary depending on whether or not the signals are received simultaneously. This is heard very clearly on a radio receiver. On a loran C receiver, the operator should look at two indications to see if this is happening. First are the readings themselves. If they change rapidly back and forth, this is an indication that you are picking up sky waves. However, a better indication is the SNR. If it changes rapidly between a strong indication or a weak indication, sky waves are being received.

Many operators include SNR indications as a normal part of the process of taking loran C lines of position. Microprocessing units with latitude and longitude readout are often misused when the operator fails to check the strength of the selected signals the receiver is using to determine a position. This can lead to a substantial decrease in the accuracy of a loran C fix. For this reason, as well as the fact that microsecond measurements are more finite than latitude and longitude, better fixes are obtained through the measurements of time delays, providing proper plotting interpolation is accomplished by the navigator.

Remember also that component signals mean all of the transmissions. If good signals from the secondary stations are received, but the reception from the master station is poor, then the accuracy of the entire system is compromised. On the other hand, if good signals are received only from the master and one or two secondary stations, do not discount the information. The LOPs can be crossed on the chart with LOPs from other radionavigation systems or even visual bearing lines.

Loran C patterns are overprinted on some navigational charts, but usually only in areas where loran C is normally considered to be reliable. Overprinting places a finite number of LOPs on a navigational chart, relying upon the navigator to interpolate for the infinite number of possible LOPs. A color coding of the different secondary stations is universally used on U.S. National Oceanic and Atmospheric Administration (NOAA) charts. W slave is light blue, X is magenta, Y is gray, and Z is green. Notes are included on charts to assist the navigator in determining which slaves are available on a particular chart. Since the United States intends to phase out loran C over the next decade or so, it too has indicated that overprinting loran C lattice lines is no longer required. At this time, NIMA (the former Defense Mapping Agency) has ceased overprinting charts with loran C lattice lines. Some charts produced by the British admiralty and other non-U.S. government agencies still produce charts which have detailed loran C information.

Lattice tables are available to navigators that usually exceed the coverage areas overprinted on charts. Mariners involved in offshore navigation may have to rely upon these tables more frequently than coastwise sailors. Lattice tables are numeric tables that assist the mariner in developing lines of position based upon dead-reckoning positions. Once provided aboard most vessels equipped with loran C receivers, these bulky loose-leaf binders are of questionable necessity because of the reliability of latitude and longitude microprocessors, comprehensive overprinting on U.S. charts, and global navigation systems. If navigating in an area where lattice tables are required due to non-overprinted charts, signals received in these areas should be used for general navigation purposes only. Loran C reliability diagrams are available from various government agencies for all coverage areas.

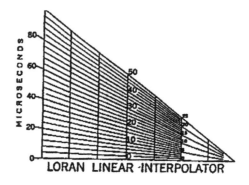

LORAN LINEAR INTERPOLATOR

1. Locate your position as closely as possible using the loran grids on the chart.

2. Pick a reference chain and choose the two closest to your estimated position. Spread dividers perpendicularly between this pair, taking note of the difference in microseconds (10, 20, 50, etc.). Mark one of this pair as your reference time delay (TD).

3. Using the interpolator on the chart, place one pin of the dividers on the reference line (0, horizontal axis) while placing the other pin on the vertical axis. Move the dividers to the right until the top pin rests on the line which indicates the microsecond difference between the pair of TDs (this was found in step 2).

4. Now squeeze the dividers to the microseconds desired. (This is the difference between the reference TD you chose on the chart and the TD read on the loran.)

EXAMPLE: 43820   Chart reference
             43815.5   Loran receiver reading

                 4.5   Desired spread of dividers

5. Without changing divider spread, place the dividers perpendicular to the TD reference and make a mark on this point.

Fig. 3-8. Loran linear interpolator. Drawing by Van Trong Nguyen.

Finally, keep in mind that loran C has certain limitations that the navigator needs to incorporate within normal usage. Loran C should not be used within 30 nautical miles of a transmitting station, or counted on for accurate navigational fixes more than 1,200 nautical miles from the center of a chain's pattern. Caution should be utilized in selecting gradients, keeping in mind that the larger the gradient, the poorer the LOP. When intersecting two LOPs, the closer to perpendicular they are the better. Avoid using loran C information near the baseline extension. Take several readings and average the figures.

The loran C system remains one of the most accurate radionavigation systems available for use in the world today. However, as in all situations, the navigator should rely on additional systems to double-check position finding.

Ranging Mode

Sophisticated loran C receivers are available with ranging modes for vessels that require a higher degree of accuracy than that which the system was designed to provide.

The ranging mode permits the receiver to determine its range from the transmitting stations, both master and secondaries, by using a time measurement coordinated through the signal pattern. Through calculating its exact range to the transmitter, the receiver can determine a more exact fix by crossing several range lines. This is used in conjunction with normal time-delay and phase-comparison measurements to calculate a more precise position by accounting for variations in signal travel due to external influences on the signal's path of travel.

Loran C ranging capabilities are found only on the more sophisticated receivers commonly aboard research vessels, cable ships, or other similar vessels. There are also some loran C chains established with specific ranging capabilities where the full configuration of master and secondary stations is not in place.

Outlook

Loran C was initially developed to provide the military with a radionavigation system with a better coverage and accuracy than the older loran A system. Eventually it was selected as the U.S. government's federally provided radionavigation system for civilian maritime use in the U.S. coastal areas. In addition, it was designated by the Federal Aviation Administration (FAA) as a supplemental system in the national air-space system. Since 1974 the system has been a mainstay for maritime users; however, with the global positioning system becoming operational, loran C's future is in question in the United States. Several studies have been completed to look into expansion of coverage into the Caribbean and parts of the Pacific. The conclusions were that the expansions were not cost-beneficial for marine use. However, the FAA has expanded loran C coverage across the continental United States and Alaska. The federal government is terminating the operation of overseas loran C stations or has been turning the stations over to local authorities outside of the United States. Working together with Canada, the U.S. Coast Guard is replacing some of the loran C transmitters with newer and more technically advanced equipment.

Because loran C has been in widespread use for several decades and is used by the maritime community, aviation interests, and the recreational and fishing communities, loran C has developed an extensive constituency. In addition to the users in the United States, there are loran C chains in operation overseas for the purpose of serving U.S. Department of Defense requirements. These chains are located in Japan, the North Atlantic, and in the Mediterranean Sea. Canada also operates several loran C chains and several other nations have now specified loran C as their national radionavigational system. The International Association of Lighthouse Authorities (IALA) is helping to facilitate the planned expansion of loran C for maritime use in northern Europe as a replacement for the Decca navigation system. There is also a planned expansion of loran C into South America by the nations on that continent. Because of the cost associated with maintaining numerous navigation systems, there are currently plans to develop a method of cost-sharing or full takeover of loran C operations outside of the continental United States. In addition, there is now a jointly operated U.S./Russian loran C chain that was placed in operation as of January 1, 1995.

DECCA NAVIGATION SYSTEM

Decca is a phase-comparison hyperbolic system first developed in Europe by the British. It is considered to be a relatively accurate, short- to medium-range radionavigation system that, like loran C, is designed for use in coastal confluence areas. Decca operates in the low-frequency band, 70 to 130 kHz. The application of the information derived by the receiver is very similar to loran C, although the hyperbolic navigation pattern is developed through phase comparison while disregarding time delays.

Continuous broadcasting signals provide coverage in limited areas between 250 and 500 NM from the transmitting stations. Worldwide Decca chains are available in very specific areas including Northern and Western Europe, South Africa, the Arabian/Persian Gulf, the northern Indian Ocean, and Japan.

The system is entirely dependent upon ground waves. Continuous-wave transmissions are carefully synchronized among all the transmitters. The receiver does an accurate phase comparison to determine where the user is within the hyperbolic pattern.

The Decca system consists of eleven groups of basic frequencies that are numbered from 0 to 10. Within those eleven base groups, there are six master frequencies lettered A to F. The user selects the appropriate chain by numeric selection of the base frequency and alphabetical selection of the master frequency.

Each Decca chain consists of a master and three slaves, separated from each other by between 60 and 120 miles, forming the baseline of the system between the master and each slave transmitter. There is a master station (A) and two or three slave stations designated as red (B), green (C), and purple (D). Like other hyperbolic systems, the pattern is the same and is imposed on a geographical area for navigational purposes. The baseline between the master and each slave is broken down into ten zones labeled A through J. Within each zone, there is a designated number of lanes, depending on which of the slaves is being received.

Between the master and the red slave, each zone will have 24 lanes per zone, numbered 0 to 23; between the master and the green slave there are 18 lanes per zone, numbered 30 to 47; and between the master and the purple slave there are 30 lanes per zone, numbered 50 to 79. Each of these lanes is in turn divided into 100 equal segments called centilanes or percent of lane. The receiver determines its location within the Decca pattern through phase comparison. The receiver will provide a reading consisting of a zone, lane, and centilane numbers. The readings will always be given in the order of master, then red, green, and purple slaves.

On the baseline, the width of each zone is approximately 6 to 12 nautical miles, depending on the distance between the master and each slave. Within the zones are the lanes, which vary in width depending on which slave they are attached to. The red lanes are approximately 450 meters in width, the green lanes 590 meters, and the purple lanes 350 meters.

Operation

Decca receivers, originally equipped with analog phase meters, now have digital readouts called decometers that simultaneously indicate the phase comparisons between the master and each of the slave stations. The hyperbolic lattice lines which separate Decca lanes are based upon the point where there is a zero phase difference between the reception from the master and the respective slave signal. The distance or interval between each successive zero phase point is called a Decca lane.

The system assumes that at least two of the three master-slave groups will be readable at any time, thus providing a fix based on at least two lines of position. While Decca can accurately indicate to the user what percent of a lane the receiver is located in, it cannot indicate through direct radio reception the lane in which the receiver is located. The receiver must keep track of the lanes it passes after it is synchronized when it is initially turned on. If it loses count, it will give a bad lane identification, although the centilane reading will remain accurate. This is one of the disadvantages of phase-comparison systems.

For the Decca receiver to give you an accurate and complete reading, it has to be initialized within the chain. The system will then determine where it is in the hyperbolic pattern. At this point, the receiver will literally count each lane it passes every time it

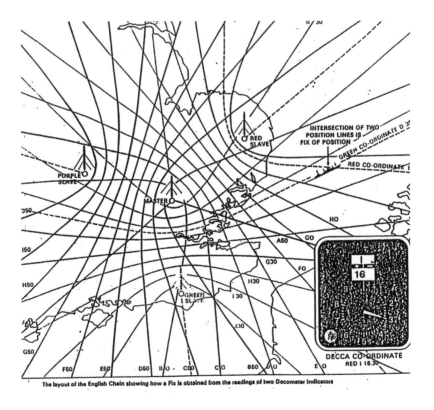

The layout of the English Chain showing how a Fix is obtained from the readings of two Decometer Indicators

Fig. 3-9. Decca coverage pattern. Courtesy of Decca Ltd.

crosses a zero phase point. The initial correct lane value is determined by a lane identification transmission by utilizing a comparison frequency with the base frequency. This comparison is done when the receiver is initialized within the Decca coverage area, and through a synchronization process will indicate to the receiver which lane number it is in within a zone. The correct zone is determined by the receiver's internal count and by the navigator utilizing navigational techniques such as maintaining an accurate DR position plotted on an overprinted Decca chart. This makes the system potentially less user friendly compared to loran C, which, after initialization, will eventually provide an accurate fix without synchronizing the receiver to the chain.

During the day, the usable range of Decca is about 450-500 miles, but at night the usable range decreases to about 250 miles due to sky-wave reception. The system is also subject to errors from land effect and is very sensitive to weather conditions, as are other medium-frequency systems.

When correctly initialized and tracking, Decca will generally give a continuous record of position. The major error encountered with Decca is lane slip, which results when the receiver fails to keep a continuous count of the lanes it passes through. This lane slip or incorrect lane identification usually results from an interruption or disturbance in transmissions, incorrect initializing or referencing of the receiver, or interference. Interference is generally caused by excessive Decca sky-wave signals, flooding of the Decca frequencies by shipboard radio transmissions, weather conditions such as electric storms, or other similar atmospheric disturbances.

Navigation

As mentioned previously, Decca is considered a highly accurate system, and in some cases is considered to be more accurate than loran C. If used properly and under favorable conditions, the user can expect the highest level of accuracy to be plus or minus 0.05 NM if within 50 miles of a transmitting station. This accuracy will decrease the farther the receiver is from the transmitting stations. On the average, Decca signals are accurate to around a tenth of a mile.

The two types of common errors associated with Decca are fixed errors and variable errors. Fixed errors are those errors in the Decca system that are relatively constant and are caused by the path that the ground waves travel, particularly over or near land. This type of travel introduces diversions in the signal path because of the terrain and can cause the speed of the signal to vary from its point of transmission until the time it is received. This can introduce an error in the positional information which can be as substantial as plus or minus half a lane (0.5 lane). These errors are most noticeable around 3 miles offshore, unfortunately in approaches to important port areas. This can be compensated for by applying pattern corrections, available in various publications.

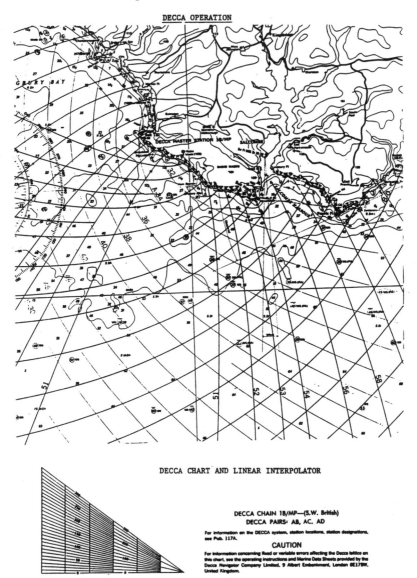

Fig. 3-10. Decca chart /interpolator.
Courtesy of National Ocean Service/U.S. Government.

Chain	Chain	General Location
English	5B	Europe
South West British	1B	Europe
North British	3B	Europe
North Scottish	6C	Europe
Irish	7D	Europe
Vestlandet	0E	Europe
Lofoten	3E	Europe
Trondelag	4E	Europe
Danish	7B	Europe
German	3F	Europe
North Baltic	4B	Europe
South Bothnian	8C	Europe
North Bothnian	5F	Europe
Helgeland	9E	Europe
Frisian Islands	9B	Europe
South Baltic	0A	Europe
Gulf of Finland	6E	Europe
Finnmark	7E	Europe
Skagerrak	10B	Europe
Holland	2E	Europe
Northumbrian	2A	Europe
Hebridean	8E	Europe
Cape	6A	Africa
Natal	10C	Africa
Eastern Province	8A	Africa
Namaqua	4A	Africa
Southwest Africa	9C	Africa
Salaya	2F	India
South Persian Gulf	1C	Persian Gulf
Hokuriko	9C	Japan

Fig. 3-11. Decca chains (1997)

Fixed errors are determined at the time of acceptance trials and correction factors are supplied by the manufacturer of the system, Racal-Decca Ltd. The Swedish chain, however, has been monitored regularly by the Swedish hydrographer and pattern corrections have been applied regularly to the overprinted lattice lines. The navigator should keep in mind that coastal refraction and land effect can have a serious impact on Decca accuracy, and so should use signals received with caution when approaching land.

Variable errors are generally caused by sky-wave interference, which becomes more considerable the farther you travel from the transmitters. Sky-wave interference is greatest at night and is more significant in winter than in summer. Changes in the ionosphere that cause polarization error or night effect also have a significant impact on Decca accuracy.

A rule of thumb is to assume that the useful nighttime range of Decca is about half of that predicted for the chain during the day. Generally, however, when you are more than 150 miles from a transmitting station, attenuated signal strength or interference will decrease the accuracy of Decca readings. Both variable and fixed errors may cause the receiver to encounter lane slip, and as in other forms of navigation, it is extremely important to maintain an accurate DR position. In addition, the navigator should back up Decca fixes with other types of position fixing data determined from radionavigation or terrestrial sources.

As with loran C, the angle of intersection of Decca lattice lines should be as near to 90 degrees as possible. Do not depend on Decca positions during times of bad weather or at twilight. Lane slip due to variable errors can occur very easily. Always maintain an accurate DR position when using Decca and cross-check with other methods of navigation when possible. Interruptions or disturbances in Decca transmissions are broadcast as "Decca warnings" by selected coast stations in those areas where coverage is present. Stations broadcasting these warnings are listed in government publications published by the United Kingdom, United States (NIMA Publication 117), and other cooperating nations.

Outlook

Although very accurate, Decca is tedious to use, is considered too short-range, and is prone to errors of interpretation. It has been reported that Decca chains have been unreliable in non-European areas. The IALA is working to facilitate a planned expansion of the loran C system in Northern Europe for the maritime community. It is currently anticipated that loran C will eventually replace Decca in this area as the primary coastal navigation system due to loran C's greater range and ease of use. Expanding coverage of loran C into other areas may facilitate this same procedure in other Decca coverage areas not currently served by loran C.

OMEGA NAVIGATION SYSTEM

Omega was developed by the U.S. Navy in 1957 to be used as a long-range, worldwide, continuous radionavigation system. The system was originally designed for use by submarines that could receive signals on special antennas trailed astern while submerged. Like Decca and loran, Omega was considered a hyperbolic radionavigation system. Its coverage extended beyond the coastal zone areas to include the open ocean, making it the first global coverage system. The system operated in the very low frequency (VLF) band in the internationally agreed upon frequencies between 10.2 and 13.6 kHz.

With the introduction of high-accuracy global satellite systems, the relative low accuracy of the Omega system made its continuation questionable. The U.S. Coast Guard, which operated the system, determined that better global coverage and improved accuracy could be obtained with the U.S.-operated global positioning system and its supplemental system, DGPS. On September 30, 1997, the U.S. Coast Guard terminated all Omega operation worldwide.

CHAPTER 4

SATELLITE NAVIGATION SYSTEMS

INTRODUCTION

Satellite navigation systems are the most technologically advanced and most accurate radionavigation systems deployed globally today. They provide a number of significant advantages over ground-based radionavigation systems because the propagated signals are not subject to the same types of interference that the ground-based systems must overcome.

These systems are also the most expensive to operate because the sophisticated equipment is deployed in orbital locations above the surface of the earth. Originally designed as military navigational systems, they have been made available for civilian use for the safety of the civilian maritime community.

The satellite systems discussed include Doppler-based, two-dimensional systems, such as the transit system, formerly operated by the United States, and Russian low-earth-orbit (LEO) systems, which include the Parus and Tsikada systems. Discussion will also include ranging-based systems, such as the global positioning system (GPS) operated by the United States and the GLONASS system operated by Russia.

All satellite navigation systems have three basic components. The first component is the space segment, which provides transmitted radionavigation information. The space segment includes all of the deployed satellites, placed in precise orbits via unmanned booster rockets or the space shuttle. The second component is the control segment, which involves earth-based tracking stations that monitor the satellite's orbit and provide corrective information to the system. The third component is the receiver segment, consisting of government provided- or commercially-available receiving units.

One of the key components of each of the satellite navigation systems is the fact that it is carefully synchronized to a single time standard, and is dependent upon it for operation. This permits a vast user community to always have access to precision coordinated universal time (UTC) information for scientific work, surveys, or navigation.

DOPPLER SATELLITE NAVIGATION SYSTEMS

In 1967 the U.S. Navy released signals from its Transit Navsat or Navy Navigation Satellite System for commercial use. Commonly referred to as the transit SATNAV system, it was initially designed for military use. The system became very popular because of the difficulties users had been facing with ground-based systems, particularly the low-frequency, hyperbolic Omega global system. The transit system was found to be very accurate, but was slightly inconvenient to use since the radio signals were useful only while a satellite was in a visible orbit from the receiving unit. This off-demand system was therefore used in conjunction with land-based systems. The system was turned off by the U.S. government in 1996.

The former Soviet Union, also in 1967, launched its very first navigation satellite into a low-earth orbit for the purposes of testing the feasibility of satellite navigation development. The operation of the system was based upon the Doppler technology demonstrated by the U.S. Navy's transit system. Due to the low-earth orbit of the satellites, the systems became known as LEO SATNAV systems.

Russia maintains two Doppler-based LEO systems, each utilized in different communities. These include the military Parus or Tsikada-M system, which utilizes six satellites, and the Tsikada system, designed for civilian use and consisting of four satellites. The same operational theory that was utilized in the U.S. system also applied to the Russian systems.

Although the U.S. system is now inoperative, the continued operation of the LEO system requires the inclusion of transit systems in this text.

Theory of Operation

This Doppler-based system's space segment includes numerous satellites in relatively shallow polar orbits between 400 and 700 miles above the earth's surface. Polar orbits describe satellites moving at a constant speed, passing over both the poles approximately 12 to 15 times per day. The average time between orbital passes is normally around 2 to 3 hours. The closer you get to the poles, the more frequent the passes due to the polar orbit. Satellites broadcast information concerning their orbital path simultaneously on multiple frequencies. This broadcast technique helps to defeat the effects of ionosphere interference. The orbital paths are determined and monitored through the control segment on the earth's surface.

Each of the satellites is tracked by earth stations positioned at various locations. The earth stations send their information to a coordinating and processing facility, where variances in the orbital path and gravitational effects are monitored. The information is then used as a basis for predicting the orbital path of each satellite over a subsequent period of time. This information is transmitted to the satellite, which in turn broadcasts to the receivers as it moves in its orbit.

The broadcast is synchronized to within one second with UTC and consists of orbital data and satellite identification information. The signal, which is broadcast in a period of 2 minutes, contains information on deviation from elliptical orbit, time of perigee, mean motion, argument of perigee, rate of change of argument of perigee,

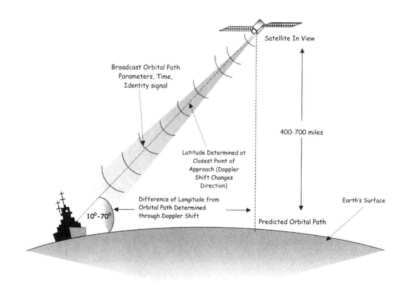

Fig. 4-1. Doppler transit satellite navigation.
Drawing by Van Trong Nguyen.

eccentricity, semimajor axis, right ascension of ascending node, rate of change of right ascension of ascending node, cosine of inclination, right ascension of prime meridian, and sine of inclination.

The receiver on the surface of the earth picks up the satellite's broadcast when it rises above the horizon, and continues receiving for an average of about 15 to 20 minutes. The satellite must be above the horizon at an elevation of more than 10 degrees but less than 70 degrees in relation to the receiver for optimum fixing. The path of the satellite approximates a meridian of longitude. The receiver needs only to determine where it is in relation to the orbital path of the satellite to determine its own longitude. It does this by measuring the frequency Doppler shift of the approaching signal because of its velocity/distance relationship. This is called the Doppler effect.

The Doppler effect describes the frequency changes at a certain rate. As subsequent signals, called counts, are received, the receiver calculates how far it is from the satellite's path. This allows the receiver to determine the first coordinate, the longitude of the receiver. When the satellite reaches the zenith in relation to the receiver, the frequency shift begins to change in the opposite direction. It is at this point the receiver determines the second coordinate, latitude. Latitude is computed based on the orbital parameters broadcast by the satellite. Broadcast signals are synchronized on a precise time-based pattern, allowing the receiver to display accurate UTC as well as position in latitude and longitude.

Operation of Doppler-based SATNAV

Doppler-based systems provide position information derived from the orbiting satellites on an as-received basis, therefore creating a limitation for the mariner, since fixes can become rather infrequent. Once initialized, the microprocessor receiver calculates DR position information based on manual or automatic course and speed inputs. Dead-reckoning information is updated when satellite position information is successfully received. This function has caused significant navigational errors by users mistakenly using DR data as position-fixing data. As with any DR track, it is an educated approximation of where the ship is positioned, not an actual position determination.

There are, however, numerous advantages for the user that may outweigh limitations. The foremost advantage is that, in comparison with ground-based systems, Doppler-based SATNAV can be used in almost all types of weather in all oceans, and is not subject to ground-wave or sky-wave propagation interference because of space-wave propagation along a line of sight. A vessel's two-dimensional position may be determined from a single satellite. The system is considered to be very precise, with accuracy to within one-quarter of a nautical mile.

The accuracy of the receiver is vitally dependent upon input information. The receiver must be initialized with proper antenna height, a DR position, speed, heading, and time and date within a reasonable variation. After initialization is input, data must be adjusted frequently when using manual input, or checked frequently when using automatic inputs. Small errors in receiver speed can introduce large errors in position determination calculation. For example, an incorrect input of one knot into the receiver, either by manual or speed log input, can cause a position error of two-tenths of a nautical mile.

If several satellites are in view, the receiving unit may not be able to distinguish the difference between signals coming from several satellites and will result in an inaccurate or totally useless fix. Most receivers have visual or audible indicators telling when a satellite is in view and when it is tracking. Some units maintain a satellite prediction page, which allows the user to plan on when the next fix will become available. A quality receiver can be programmed to block out signals coming from satellites that are too high or too low, usually indicative of a poor pass. All units will store last-pass information in memory, and some will print the information when the pass occurs. The last-pass information contains time, your position at the last fix, and whether it was considered useable.

The user should also allow the receiver to take a full set of measurements before and after the satellite passes its zenith. This will ensure that the receiver has had sufficient information to calculate the Doppler shift as it approaches and check its calculations as the satellite moves away.

As with other radionavigation systems, signals should not be trusted in unusual weather conditions, during periods of extensive atmospherics, or during twilight.

Doppler SATNAV Errors

There are errors associated with transit SATNAV that must be taken into account by the user. These errors are found in all segments of the system.

Some of the error estimates were based upon data collected from stationary receivers. Generally, it can be assumed that system errors will not introduce more than 50 meters of position error in user readings. Incorrect initialization and input information can, however, introduce substantial errors in receivers above the predicted accuracy. It is critical the user take the time to properly set up the receiver, as baseline accuracy of the system can be severely compromised if this is done incorrectly.

Doppler-based satellite navigation systems provide two-dimensional data with approximately a 500-meter predictable and probable accuracy in each of the coordinates (latitude and longitude), 95 percent of the time. This is based on a single frequency observation from a single satellite pass. When multiple satellites are in view, the receiver often switches back and forth between observations, failing to provide a calculated set of coordinates. It has also been determined that certain areas on the earth's surface, such as off the African coast and in the polar regions, have a higher incidence of poor readings. It should also be noted that errors due to refraction will be higher when a satellite is viewed at lower elevations.

GLOBAL MULTIDIMENSIONAL SYSTEMS

Both the United States and Russia have designed and deployed global multidimensional systems based on constellations of orbiting satellites providing continuous navigation information. The receiver can determine its position in latitude and longitude in relation to several satellites using extremely accurate ranging information. The receiver can also determine position in multiple dimensions, namely in geographic coordinates and altitude in relationship to the surface of the earth. These newer systems will replace all previous Doppler-based/transit systems in the near future.

There are two global multidimensional systems currently deployed. The U.S. global positioning system (GPS), or Navstar system, and the Russian global navigation satellite system or GLONASS.

Global Positioning System (GPS), or Navstar

The U.S. Navstar global positioning system (GPS) is a satellite-based radionavigation system designed to provide continuous worldwide coverage of navigation, position, and timing information to marine-, air-, and land-based users. GPS is operated and controlled by the Department of Defense (DOD) and is under U.S. Air Force management.

The system was originally intended for military use only, but federal radionavigation policy was changed to allow the civilian community to use the GPS standard positioning service to increase safety in transportation. Today, GPS systems can be found almost anywhere position information is needed. Obviously marine and aeronautical use has benefited, but highway trucking, land surveying, and even mountaineers routinely utilize GPS. The system's initial operational capability was established in 1993 and it met its full operational capability, based on military standards, in 1995. The system, like Doppler-based systems, is divided into the space, control, and user segments.

THEORY OF OPERATION

The space segment consists of twenty-four satellites in six separate circular, semisynchronous orbital planes around the earth. The layout and spacing is referred to as the GPS constellation. There are twenty-one operational units with three orbiting spares in each plane. Satellites orbit at 10,900 nautical miles (20,200 kilometers) above the earth in 12-hour periods at an inclination angle to the equator of 55 degrees. They are placed in orbit in such a manner so that at any given time, at least five satellites will be in view to a user anywhere in the world.

The satellites broadcast continual position and time data. Each GPS satellite transmits a modulated spread spectrum signal on two L-band frequencies, 1,575.42 MHz (L1) and 1,227.6 MHz (L2), which, like in older satellite systems, allows the signals to be picked up with minimal interference caused by the ionosphere.

The transmissions are pseudo-random noise (PRN), sequence-modulated radio signals containing a coarse acquisition code (C/A code) and precision code (P code). There is a navigation message superimposed on the codes which contains satellite ephemeris data, atmospheric propagation information, and satellite clock bias.

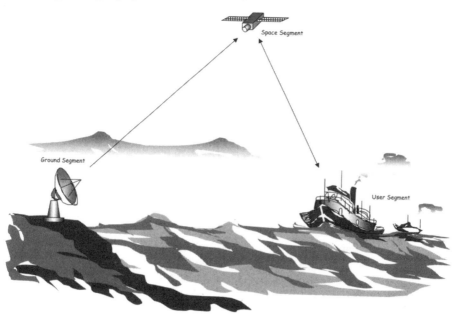

Fig. 4-2. GPS segments. Drawing by Van Trong Nguyen.

The second segment of the system is known as the control segment and consists of a master control station located in the United States in Colorado Springs, Colorado. In addition, there are five additional monitoring stations in Hawaii, Colorado, Kwajalein (Philippines), Diego Garcia, and Ascension Island, and three ground antennas at Ascension Island, Kwajalein, and Diego Garcia. The monitoring stations track all GPS satellites within view and collect ranging information from the satellite broadcasts. The monitor stations send the collected information to the master control station. This information is used to compute very precise orbital information for the satellites. This information is updated, formatted, and sent back to the satellites through the ground antennas, which also transmit and receive satellite monitoring and control signals.

In the third segment of the system, called the user segment, the GPS receiver calculates its position and determines exact UTC through a series of calculations it performs when in operation. Depending on whether it is receiving or utilizing signals from three or four satellites, the system will provide two-dimensional position information, requiring three satellites, in the form of latitude and longitude, or three-dimensional position information, requiring four satellites, which will include altitude in addition to latitude and longitude. From this information it can derive the accurate course and speed of the receiver. The signals are measured on a single-channel or multiple-channel receiver depending on its type, manufacturer, and built-in capabilities.

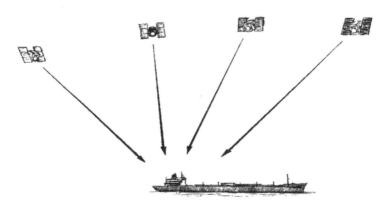

GPS receivers are capable of viewing four to six satellites. Position is determined by electronically calculating the range from each satellite to the receiver.

Fig. 4-3. GPS user segment. Drawing by Stephen Gardiner.

The first piece of information that is determined is the position of three or four satellites at an exact time. Satellite position information, as well as the satellite's identity signal, are broadcast as part of the transmission. The second determination is radio propagation time between the satellites. The receiver uses the propagation sequence to determine a measuring point, done by measuring the phase of the spread spectrum signal that is being received.

Finally, the receiver determines its exact position by calculating the distance between itself and each satellite based upon the speed of radio energy. This is done by calculating its range to each satellite, called ranging, and using the information to establish a coordinate position that consists of latitude, longitude, and altitude.

For the receiver to do accurate ranging, it must first adjust its internal clock so it matches the time maintained by the satellite. Each satellite has an atomic clock installed in it for precise timekeeping. The satellite broadcasts a coded signal, which the receiver measures to determine how much adjustment of its internal clock is necessary. Phase comparison for the determination of the precise time is accomplished through the production and comparison of pseudo-random codes. Both the satellite and the receiver generate the same code at exactly the same time. The receiver synchronizes itself to the satellite time frame by comparing the two codes and correcting for the discrepancy. The pseudo-random code information also permits the receiver to do a preliminary calculation of propagation variance. Once the receiver and satellite clock are on the same time frame, the receiver then measures the delay in receiving the transmitter's signal to determine how far it is from the satellite. All of this is accomplished within about 40 microseconds.

For identification, each satellite has a pseudo-noise generator (PN), which produces a specific code corresponding to each satellite. It also produces a second signal that is used in the ranging circuit. All of these pieces of information are utilized by a microprocessor contained in the GPS receiver. The microprocessor handles all of the calculations and provides the information in a digital, menu-driven format to the user.

As the receiver begins to determine range from each of the satellites, it begins to adjust itself to determine the most precise position. A pseudo-range is developed that contains some error, primarily in timing. The microprocessor in the GPS receiver continues to adjust the pseudo-ranges until the signals from at least three satellites intersect as closely as possible. The computer accomplishes this adjustment by subtracting or adding time to the pseudo-range. Once the ranges coincide at a single point, the receiver can determine a position point based on the position information it received from the satellites. The high level of accuracy in this system is very dependent upon receiving at least three satellite broadcasts. The precision of a GPS fix is determined by the receiver as it continually adjusts the pseudo-ranges. The receiver actually takes a series of pinpoint adjustments and then calculates the most probable intersection of the satellite ranges.

Nonmilitary users of the GPS system can expect horizontal position accuracy of 100 meters or better and vertical accuracy of 150 meters or better, 95 percent of the time. Practical use of the system has demonstrated that in most cases, there is a reasonable expectation of accuracy of around 25 meters for most areas in the world. Since the reason for system development was defense-based, the military operators build additional inaccuracies into the system. This intentional downgrading of the accuracy for nonmilitary systems is called selective availability (SA). Military receivers are rated as having a spherical accuracy of 16 meters or better. However, they have been reported to be accurate within 1 meter, and in some configurations near half a meter, horizontally and vertically. GPS time is measurable in military and certain survey receivers to within 167 nanoseconds.

The two most significant factors affecting accuracy are the geometric dilution of precision (GDOP) and the user equivalent range error (UERE). The GDOP, based on the geometric relationship of the satellites to the receiver, is a measurement of the spacing or spread of the satellites with the best situation being one nearly overhead and the other satellites equally spaced around the horizon. The worst case occurs when they are all nearly at the receiver's zenith and are spaced very close together.

UERE is based on several factors associated with the system: the stability of the satellite's clock, predictions of the satellite's orbit, errors in the 50-Hz transmission, precision of the correlation process, atmospheric distortion and the applied compensating calculations, and the satellite's signal quality. This error is considered to be random and is the result of the functionality of the satellite system and the user's receiver. The user should be aware of these errors associated with the system as potentially providing inaccurate position calculations and time variances.

The GPS system tries to account for these errors, particularly ionospheric delay errors. There are two methods employed for correcting this problem. The first is a dual-frequency correction technique where the receiving system compares the signal measurements received on both the L1 and L2 frequencies. Only government-authorized receivers have this capability. The second method is the ionospheric delay model. The value of the correction is determined from a mathematical model and then is included in the broadcast navigation message. While this method is not as accurate as the dual-frequency method, it provides some accuracy enhancement for the nonmilitary user community.

MILITARY APPLICATION

The Department of Defense is expecting extensive use of the GPS system in almost every military operation and mission area. The United States encouraged the North Atlantic Treaty Organization (NATO) participation in the development and deployment of GPS military equipment. In response, ten NATO nations signed a memorandum of understanding in June 1978 (updated in 1984) for participation in the development of GPS. These nations are Belgium, Canada, Denmark, France, Germany, Italy, the Netherlands, Norway, Spain, and the United Kingdom. Australia has signed a similar agreement.

The objective of this agreement is to establish a flow of information among the participating nations regarding all GPS program activities to facilitate national decisions supporting the application and use of GPS. To this end, personnel of participating nations are fully integrated within the GPS Joint Program Office to contribute to the U.S. development program and to coordinate NATO applications, development, and testing.

In addition to formal NATO involvement in the development of military GPS equipment, the U.S. DOD has working relationships with numerous nations and is sharing information designed to create interest in the expanded military use of GPS.

Widespread national and international civilian use of the GPS standard positioning service (SPS) is anticipated. Due to perceived national security considerations, the GPS precise positioning service (PPS) is restricted to the U.S. Armed Forces, U.S. federal agencies, and selected allied armed forces and governments. While GPS/PPS has been designed primarily for military radionavigation needs, it will nevertheless be made available on a very selective basis to U.S. and non-U.S. private-sector organizations. Access determinations will be made by the U.S. government on a case-by-case evaluation that is determined to be in the U.S. national interest. There are no other means reasonably available to the civilian user to obtain a capability equivalent to that provided by GPS/PPS. The U.S. government has a policy for submitting applications, granting approval for user access, and establishing operational procedures and compliance requirements for accessing the data from GPS/PPS.

In response to a DOD request, the U.S. Department of Transportation (DOT) has established the civilian GPS service (CGS), consisting of the GPS Information Center (GPSIC) and the PPS Program

Office (PPSPO). The GPSIC provides information to, and is the point of contact for, civilian users of the GPS system. The PPSPO administers GPS/PPS service to approved civilian users.

Any planned disruption of the SPS in peacetime will be subject to a minimum 48-hour advance notice provided by the DOD to GPSIC and the FAA Notice to Airmen (NOTAM) system. A disruption is defined as periods in which the GPS is not capable of providing SPS as specified. Unplanned system outages resulting from system malfunctions or unscheduled maintenance will be announced by the GPSIC and NOTAM systems as they become known.

Military users of the GPS system claim that the system has never been disrupted, although significant errors were witnessed by civilian users during the 1991 Gulf War. The errors were based upon a nonuniform constellation pattern. In nonmilitary parlance, this means that the satellites were moved for optimum coverage in the Gulf region. Since that time however, the complete satellite constellation has been returned to normal, and the need to break the planned orbital pattern should not be required.

CIVILIAN APPLICATION

With GPS fully operational, DOD is phasing out its requirements for and use of other radionavigation systems. Due to the system's high accuracy and the worldwide coverage and flexibility provided by GPS, nonmilitary use has grown rapidly and easily exceeds military use. Since the system is funded and operated by the military establishment, users must recognize the strategic importance of a system that provides such precise navigational information. Users are warned that if hostilities break out, the system could be disrupted substantially to nonselective users. The DOD can also restructure the constellation of satellites to increase accuracy in certain geographic areas. This ability can compromise accuracy of the system in those areas where satellites have been reoriented.

With the exception of overall system failures or intentional downgrading, GPS can be considered a reliable, fully available, user-friendly method of determining a vessel's position. It is expected that GPS and its Russian equivalent will become the primary navigation systems utilized by vessels worldwide.

GPS receivers are also very user friendly. Long gone are the days of carefully initializing SATNAV receivers. Because GPS is an on-demand system, it is always there for the user. Navigators need only read the operation manual of the device and look for the proper means of turning on the power. The receiving unit does the rest. In less than 2 minutes the GPS receiver will begin giving accurate positions.

Fig. 4-4. GPS user segment receiver units.
Courtesy of Trimble Navigation Ltd.

Currently, there are two types of GPS receivers available. These include the lower cost single-channel receiver, which can only track one satellite at a time, therefore lessening accuracy, and the higher quality and more expensive multichannel receiver, which locks onto four or five satellites at once, providing a more accurate fix without interrupting the navigation function. GPS receivers which also include a Kalman filtering computer program are able to determine the quality of signals received and weigh them against each other to provide a more accurate fix.

As with all radionavigation systems, caution should be exercised by the user in practical navigation. Dependence on a single fix from one source should always be avoided. Fixed errors in the system, variable errors resulting from severe weather conditions, and other unusual circumstances as well as overall system performance are still being discovered by the rapidly expanding user community.

GLONASS

GLONASS (global'naya navigatsionnaya sputnikovaya sistema, or global navigation satellite system) is the Russian equivalent of the U.S.-operated global positioning system. Designed to function in a similar manner as GPS, the system may ultimately use more satellites and thus result in greater accuracy than the western system.

GLONASS satellites are deployed in groups of eight in three orbital planes at an inclination to the equator of 65 degrees. While more than fifty satellites have been launched, the system currently has a completed constellation of twenty-one satellites, with three spares. Consideration is being given to increasing the system constellation to twenty-seven spacecraft, with eight active satellites and one spare satellite in each of three orbital planes. The orbits are semisynchronous and each unit broadcasts in the L-band on operational frequencies of 1,246 to 1,257 MHz or from 1,603 to 1,616 MHz. The spacecraft circle the earth at a mean altitude of 19,100 kilometers, with an orbital period of 676 minutes.

First promoted by the Soviet military in the early 1970s, deployment of the system began in the 1980s under the authority of the Soviet Ministry of Defense. The system is now operated by the Confederation of Independent States' Intergovernmental Radionavigation Program. The control segment of the system is handled by the quantum optical tracking stations located throughout the former U.S.S.R.

The system is considered to have a higher probability of accuracy than GPS in the civilian community, although its objectives for accuracy are 100 meters horizontal and 150 meters vertical positioning. In addition, there is no selective availability, and GLONASS receivers do more calculations for more precise ranging than GPS receivers. GPS provides access to a single P code where GLONASS provides access to dual-frequency P codes.

The coverage is also considered better because some of the GPS satellites are masked from receivers at higher altitudes, whereas more satellites in the GLONASS constellation prevent more frequent masking situations. The enhanced accuracy is becoming popular among the marine survey community, which depends on precision navigation to conduct its work. Commercially available GLONASS receivers will have the same capability as the more expensive military models, which have restricted use.

Similar to the federal radionavigation plan in the United States, a Russian radionavigation plan is now in place. This plan specifies user requirements for several radionavigational systems in addition to GLONASS. The GLONASS system, however, like its counterpart GPS, is considered to be the primary system operated by Russia and most fully meets the user requirements. This system is still being deployed and is expected to be fully operational and available to commercial users by the end of the decade.

Like GPS, there is a planned differential component for the GLONASS system. Because of the design and technology used, it is estimated that the potential accuracy for the differential GLONASS may be around one meter. Enhanced receivers that utilize dedicated data processors and phase carrier measurement may be able to achieve a level of accuracy that will be measured in centimeters.

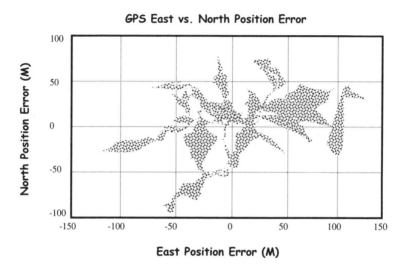

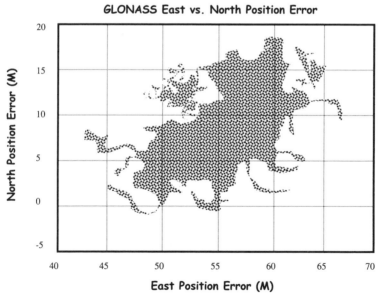

Fig. 4-5. GPS/GLONASS accuracy comparison.
Courtesy of Bell-Sea Navigation Systems

The Russian navigation plan contemplates the establishment of new radionavigation systems with even higher specifications for accuracy. It also includes provisions for integrating the Russian and U.S. radionavigation networks into the European and world infrastructure.

U.S. Coast Guard Differential GPS (DGPS)

By presidential proclamation in 1983, the U.S. global positioning system became available to nonmilitary users. A debate occurred regarding navigational accuracy. Initially, through selective availability, the U.S. Department of Defense proposed that nonmilitary users be permitted 500-meter accuracy. This was later changed to 100-meter accuracy. Even with this alteration, the available accuracy would not meet the dictated requirements of the federal radionavigation plan of 8 to 20 meters accuracy. This limited accuracy was deemed insufficient for safe approach to coastal areas and harbors, not to mention the aeronautical accuracy demands. In that same year, the Radio Technical Commission for Maritime Services (RTCMS) established a special committee to outline the requirements for a differential system.

Differential GPS (DGPS) was designed to provide the same information as GPS, except that an additional correction or differential signal was added to improve accuracy. This correction signal is broadcast over a specific frequency that covers particular geographic areas. Unlike the U.S. DOD-operated system, there is no limitation of accuracy due to selective availability (SA). The task of establishing and operating the system was turned over to the U.S. Coast Guard.

The process of deploying the system began with looking at the essential goals of meeting accuracy requirements as dictated in the federal radionavigation plan. Coastal and harbor areas were already covered by the popular loran C system, but the Coast Guard viewed the continued operation of the system as redundant to GPS. In addition, accuracy consistent with the federal radionavigation plan was not being achieved systemwide using the hyperbolic systems. It was determined that developing a system that corrected the intentional SA of GPS could achieve better accuracy than loran C and would be potentially less expensive to operate.

THEORY OF OPERATION

The Coast Guard established a series of reference stations that could serve as the basis of the correction factors. Since the national marine radio beacon system was already in place and covered similar areas to loran C, it was decided to couple the differential signals with the radio beacon broadcasts by attaching the correction factors to the modulated signal of the radio beacon transmission. In addition, a reorientation of some of the transmitting stations would correct any potential gaps in coverage.

Each reference station has a GPS receiving system, and the GPS position of the reference station is computed and compared to its surveyed geodetic position. The differential information, or error in fix position, satellite range error, or pseudo-range correction factor, is transmitted to the receivers being used in the geographical area near the reference station. By ranging computations, the receiver is capable of determining three-dimensional position.

Once the system was tested, it was determined that there was an improvement in accuracy to 10 meters or better, compared to 100 meters or better for the GPS/SPS. There was also an improvement in integrity due to the provision of an independent check of each GPS satellite's signal.

DGPS elements, normally integrated into a modified standard GPS receiver, collect navigational signals from all satellites in view, plus differential corrections from a DGPS station in the area. Most DGPS receivers consist of two units, one of which includes a GPS receiver with a data "port" for DGPS corrections. Another method is to

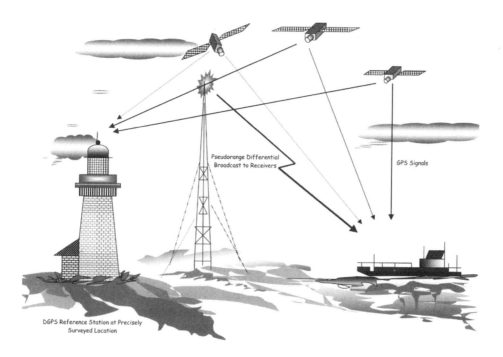

Fig. 4-6. Differential GPS. Drawing by Van Trong Nguyen.

integrate the DGPS element directly into a GPS receiver. DGPS receivers display position, velocity, time, and altitude as needed for marine, terrestrial, or aeronautical applications. The only disadvantages of the system are that additional receiver equipment is required and the coverage area is limited.

The Coast Guard DGPS service for public use in harbor and coastal approach areas of the United States includes the Great Lakes, Puerto Rico, and most of Alaska and Hawaii.

As mentioned, DGPS uses differential or pseudo-range corrections broadcast over the existing network of marine radio beacons. The corrections are broadcast using the RTCM SC104 version 2.0 data format. The SC104 format is very similar to the GPS navigation message and uses the GPS parity algorithm. The most significant difference is that SC104 uses variable-length messages instead of a fixed-length message. The Coast Guard system is flexible, providing signals that will be usable by marine, land, and air users as long as the receiver is within the coverage area.

The Coast Guard DGPS system consists of eight elements: GPS satellites, reference stations, broadcast transmitters, a broadcast standard, user equipment, a control station, data communications, and an integrity monitor. These elements work together to provide accurate information to the navigator.

The GPS satellites provide GPS navigation signals and messages. It is important to note that DGPS cannot operate without the GPS satellite signals and the information they provide. The signals are received by the reference station, where measurements of the errors contained in the received GPS signals are calculated and corrections generated. The reference station must be located in a surveyed location within the service area.

Data formatting is done in the reference station and real-time differential corrections are put in the RTCM SC104 format and sent through a broadcast transmitter by minimum shift keying (MSK) modulation of the medium-frequency radio beacon signal. The transmission conforms to a broadcast standard contained in a document describing the broadcast signal structure and data format. The signals are received by the receiver, which, as mentioned, is a GPS receiver capable of receiving and applying the differential corrections. DGPS receivers contain MSK detector elements.

The U.S. Coast Guard maintains a DGPS control center. This center is a radionavigation facility with computer-based control capability. The system is manned 24 hours a day and the control center's computer platform is connected to reference stations, monitoring stations, and broadcast sites through a data communications link with dedicated circuits.

Finally, contained within the system is an integrity monitor, a separate, independent station associated with a given reference station and broadcast transmitter. This station provides a check on the integrity of the GPS broadcast, DGPS correction data, and the MSK broadcast signal.

DGPS transmissions are broadcast in the 285 to 325 kHz medium-frequency band allocated for marine radio beacons. The marine radio beacons in DGPS service will simultaneously broadcast differential corrections and radio direction-finding (RDF) signals. The DGPS transmissions broadcast from a marine radio beacon may be either on the main carrier or, in very limited circumstances, on a dual carrier. RDFs will utilize only the main carrier and the subcarrier identification tone.

The U.S. Coast Guard DGPS navigation service is designed to provide coverage at the specified levels for all "harbor and harbor approach areas" and other "critical waterways" for which the Coast Guard provides aids to navigation. Due to the omnidirectional nature of the broadcasts, and the fact that high-power radio beacons may cover more than one harbor, coverage often extends into additional areas. As a result, complete coverage of the coastline of the continental United States is provided out to 20 NM. Final reorientation of the more powerful coastal radio beacons will extend this coverage to 50 NM, which will include the continental United States

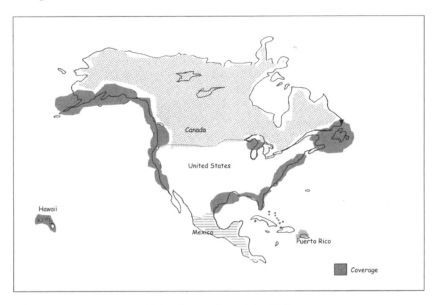

Fig. 4-7. U.S. Coast Guard DGPS coverage.
Drawing by Van Trong Nguyen.

(CONUS) coastal navigation zone. Though the accuracy of DGPS is much higher than needed in the coastal region, its integrity enhancement of GPS is more critical.

Additional areas that receive this coverage are all waters of the Great Lakes except portions of the Georgian Bay on Lake Huron and a considerable segment of the lower Saint Lawrence Seaway. Coverage for the western rivers (Mississippi, Missouri, Ohio, and Illinois) and Northern Alaska is not planned in the initial system but is under consideration for phase-in at a later time, as is coverage of the complete EEZ (exclusive economic zone) and the U.S. portion of the Saint Lawrence seaway. The network of radio beacons that composes the DGPS service will provide considerable portions of most areas with redundant coverage. Certain areas that require the movement of large vessels in severely constricted waterways will be provided with fully redundant coverage.

Although DGPS was only planned for optimum use averaging 150 miles offshore, reports from mariners indicate the DGPS signal is more resistant to attenuation then planned. Accurate DGPS fixes, as compared to GPS and loran C, have been reported nearly 1,000 miles off the East Coast of the United States. Although accuracy of ten meters is not needed at that range for navigational hazards, the mariner can be reassured that more than one system is available for position fixing.

GPS Information Services

The U.S. Coast Guard is the government interface for civilian users of GPS, and has established the Navigation Information Service (NIS) to meet the needs of the civilian user. The NIS is a Coast Guard facility located in Alexandria, Virginia. It provides voice broadcasts, data broadcasts, and an on-line computer-based information service, which are all available 24 hours a day. NIS watchstanders are also available 24 hours a day to handle telephone, fax, and mail inquiries. The information provided includes planned, current, or recent satellite outages and constellation changes, user instructions and tutorials, other GPS-related information, system status and information about other Coast Guard-provided radionavigation systems, and general information about federal radionavigation policy and systems.

GPS information is also available on NAVTEX and through other sources noted in appendix 1. Whenever possible, advance notice of when the GPS satellites should not be used will be provided by the U.S. Department of Defense and made available by the U.S. Coast Guard. Any planned disruption of the GPS/SPS in peacetime will be subject to a minimum 48-hour advance notice provided by the DOD to NIS. The NIS advisory services are updated

Station Number	Location	Range
801	Duluth, MN	40 NM
802	Eagle Harbor, MI	160 NM
803	Whitefish Point, MI	70 NM
804	Lookout 4., MI	40 NM
805	Seul Choix Pt., MI	120 NM
806	Sturgeon Bay, WI	60 NM
807	Milwaukee, WI	140 NM
808	Presque Isle, MI	100 NM
809	Saginaw Bay, MI	60 NM
810	Fort Gratiot, MI	140 NM
811	Belle Isle, MI	70 NM
812	Sandusky, OH	130 NM
813	Buffalo, NY	140 NM
814	Rochester, NY	100 NM
815	Tibbets Point, NY	70 NM
816	(Fairport Harbor, OH)	
817	(Chicago, IL)	
831	Aransas Pass, TX	180 NM
832	Galveston, TX	180 NM
833	Mobile Point, AL	170 NM
834	English Turn, LA	170 NM
835	Egmont Key, FL	210 NM
836	Key West, FL	150 NM
837	Puerto Rico	200 NM
838	Miami, FL	120 NM
839	Cape Canaveral, FL	250 NM
840	Charleston, SC	150 NM

Figure 4-8. Differential GPS station list. *Continued on next page.*

whenever new information is received. NIS services are described below.

The Department of Commerce transmits recorded time information on radio stations WWV/WWVH 2.5, 10, 15, and 20 MHz frequencies. During the 40-second interval between time ticks, navigation information is announced by voice. GPS status and current or forecasted outages are broadcast at minutes 14 and 15 on WWV and minutes 43 and 44 on WWVH.

The computer bulletin board system (BBS) provides GPS information such as GPS status messages, satellite almanacs, Notice Advisory to Navstar Users (NANU) policy, local Notices to Mariners, and general radionavigation information. Connections can be made

841	Fort Macon, GA	130 NM
Station Number	*Location*	*Range*
842	Cape Henry, VA	130 NM
843	Cape Henlopen, DE	180 NM
844	Ambrose Light, NY	100 NM
845	Montauk Point, NY	130 NM
846	Boston, MA	60 NM
847	Portsmouth, NH	100 NM
848	Manana Island, ME	170 NM
849	(St. Johns River, FL)	
850	(Cape San Blas, FL)	
870	Barbers Point, HI	170 NM
871	Upolo Point, HI	170 NM
872	Point Loma, CA	150 NM
873	Point Arguello, CA	190 NM
874	Pt. Blunt, CA	60 NM
875	Point Arena, CA	130 NM
876	Cape Blanco, OR	130 NM
877	Grays Harbor, WA	150 NM
878	Ediz Hook, WA	70 NM
879	Robinson Point, WA	60 NM
880	Guard Island, AK	200 NM
881	Cape Spencer, AK	260 NM
882	Cape Hinchenbrook, AK	120 NM
883	Potato Point, AK	100 NM
884	Cook Inlet, AK	200 NM
885	Kodiak, AK	200 NM
886	Cold Bay, AK	200 NM

Figure 4-8. *Continued.*

to the BBS either via phone, Sprint Net, or the Internet (public data networks).

The NIS disseminates GPS advisory broadcast messages through USCG broadcast stations using VHF FM voice, HF SSB voice, and NAVTEX broadcasts. The broadcasts provide the GPS user in the marine environment with the current status of the GPS satellite constellation, as well as any planned or unplanned system outages that could affect GPS navigational accuracy.

NIMA broadcasts navigation information concerning the high seas. Information is provided in message format via an established system of message dissemination. NIS provides the GPS operational advisory broadcast information to NIMA for broadcast in

NAVAREA, HYDROLANT, or HYDROPAC messages. These messages are generally geared to the deep-water mariner.

NIMA also publishes a weekly *Notice to Mariners* (NTM) containing Coast Guard marine information broadcasts and NIMA broadcast warnings for a 7-day period.

The NIS updates GPS information on the NIMA NAVINFONET database. The database is extensive and the GPS portion contains information such as recent satellite almanac and health parameters, scheduled outages, and administrative data. Users must register off-line before they are allowed to use NAVINFONET.

The Civilian GPS Service Interface Committee (CGSIC) was established to address issues and problems that relate to the civilian use of GPS. The CGSIC is the official interface between civilian GPS users and DOD GPS operators. The CGSIC consists of a general committee and three subcommittees (Reference Station Technology and Applications, incorporating the Read-time Carrier Phase and Surveying and Precise Positioning subcommittees; Timing Information; and International Information).

The CGSIC is jointly chaired by the U.S. Department of Transportation and U.S. Coast Guard. Computer programs are also available from commercial sources so that interested users can determine the availability and quality of GPS coverage at their particular location.

PRACTICAL APPLICATION OF
SATELLITE NAVIGATION SYSTEMS

Satellite navigation systems, while considered the most reliable and accurate of all radionavigation systems, are not intended to replace the skill, knowledge, and intuition of the navigator. The basic system and the many enhancements available through the incorporated microprocessing technology can provide excellent position information as well as course, speed, bearing, track error, and the like. However, it must never be forgotten that these systems are aids to navigation, and must be used as part of precise voyage planning and tracking methodology.

The stress or boredom of watchstanding will often cause mariners to become overly reliant on the information provided by advanced systems such as GPS or DGPS. The navigator may fail to take the precautions he or she recognizes should be part of proper navigation practice. Simple procedures such as backing up information or checking their positions with a second or even third method remain critical. Latitude, longitude, speed, and course made good can be done much more quickly within the context of instantaneous readouts, as opposed to terrestrial bearing, radar ranges off uncertain topographic features, or comparison to systems the operator knows are less accurate, but backup navigation must be done nonetheless.

In the practice of navigation, safety and confidence are built upon history and trend, as opposed to snapshots in time. Nothing remains more reliable than continual observance of a vessel's movements along a dead-reckoning track, with DR positions indicated based on presumed speed, and compared with positions obtained from multiple methods. This, coupled with a careful record of positions and a well-structured voyage plan, significantly reduces the chances of a serious error that may result in a grounding or other major marine casualty.

One should not become so dependent upon technology that improper operation by either the generator or the user assists in causing a "technology assisted grounding."

CHAPTER 5

MARINE COMMUNICATIONS AND BROADCAST INFORMATION

GENERAL

Marine communications has changed significantly over the last 40 years, from the days of radiotelegraph and signal lamps to systems utilizing satellites orbiting the earth. Aboard a vessel on the high seas or in a protected harbor communications are as fundamentally important as navigation. Proper communications has also been integrated in proper watchkeeping and collision avoidance. The intent is to allow the exchange or dissemination of information critical to the mariner. This chapter will focus on the systems and equipment employed and their effective use.

Equipment for communications in the maritime world is divided into several specific types. Interactive communication systems include short-range bridge-to-bridge voice, long-range, ship-to-ship/ship-to-shore, single-sideband (SSB) voice and telex, and satellite communications (SATCOM). Other kinds of systems include passive broadcast information systems such as radio time signals, weatherfax, and NAVTEX.

Aboard deep-sea ships, voice radio equipment has traditionally been available to the bridge officers, but equipment such as radiotelegraph and single-sideband equipment was usually under the responsibility of the radio operator. With the elimination of the long-used radiotelegraph system and the advent of new international calling and distress systems, more and more voice communica-

106

tion systems are becoming the responsibility of the ship's deck officers. This has been the situation for a number of years aboard smaller ships such as ocean tugs or research vessels. Technology is changing the way we deal with communications in the maritime profession and for that reason, this chapter and the next will be devoted to those systems. As in radionavigation, understanding basic radio theory will assist the operator in effectively using this equipment.

VHF BRIDGE-TO-BRIDGE RADIOTELEPHONY

Bridge-to-bridge radiotelephone, in its current form, utilizes frequencies in the very high frequency range. Designed to provide clear line-of-sight communications, the equipment uses a narrowband, frequency-modulated signal to carry information, normally in the form of voice transmissions. Unlike the more common broadcast FM, which utilizes a 200-kHz bandwidth, narrowband transmissions have a bandwidth allocation of between 10 and 30 kHz. The communications are clearer due to the fact that with frequency modulation, background noise and static do not affect signal amplitudes as in AM broadcasts.

Marine VHF is usually found in the frequency range between 156.00 MHz and 162.00 MHz. For the convenience of the user, the frequencies are broken down into a series of selective channels from 1 through 89. Depending on their use, the channels are classified either as simplex, transmitting and receiving on the same frequency; or as duplex, transmitting on one frequency and receiving on another frequency. VHF transceivers are equipped with a selector switch or are programmed for use in the appropriate mode.

Each VHF channel has a specific use and all marine frequencies are regulated in the United States by the Federal Communications Commission under 47 CFR 80.371(c) and 80.373(f). Uses for the various channels have been designated by international agreement. Some highlights from the regulations outlining designated channel usage follow.

Distress Safety and Calling: Channel 16 (156.750 MHz) and Channel 70 (156.525 MHz) are used to get the attention of another station (calling) or in emergencies (distress and safety). The U.S. Coast Guard and similar agencies throughout the world monitor these channels. Vessels navigating are required to maintain a radio watch on Channel 16 until 1999 when the global marine distress and safety system (GMDSS) requirements take effect. See chapter 6 for more details.

Intership Safety: Channel 6 is used for ship-to-ship safety messages and for search-and-rescue messages and ships and aircraft of the Coast Guard.

Coast Guard Liaison: Channel 22 is the designated channel for communications with the Coast Guard. Because channel 22 is considered a working frequency, the user needs to make contact initially on channel 16 then switch to this channel.

Noncommercial: Channels 9, 67, 68, 69, 71, 72, 78, 79, and 80. These channels are considered to be working channels for voluntary vessels. The communications must be about the needs of a vessel. Uses include fishing reports, rendezvous coordination, scheduling vessel repairs, or berthing information. Channels 67 and 72 are set aside for ship-to-ship messages.

Commercial: Channels 1, 7, 8, 9, 10, 11, 18, 19, 63, 67, 72, 79, 80, and 88. These channels are designated for working vessels only. Messages are about business or vessel needs. Channels 8, 67, 72, 88 are set aside for ship-to-ship messages.

Public Correspondence (marine operator): Channels 24, 25, 26, 27, 28, 84, 85, 86, 87, and 88 are used for communications through a marine operator at a public coast station. These operators can connect vessels to the telephone system ashore which, except in the case of distress calls, is a compensated service.

Port Operations: Channels 1, 5, 11, 12, 14, 20, 63, 65, 66, 73, 74, 77. These channels are used to direct the movement of ships in or near ports, harbors, waterways, and locks. Communications must be about the operational handling, movement and safety of ships. Channels 11 and 12 may not be available for this use in certain ports, Channel 20 is designated for ship-to-coast messages, and Channel 77 is designated for intership communications to and from pilots.

Navigation (bridge-to-bridge): Channels 13 and 67. Available to all vessels, these channels must be about navigation such as passing or meeting other vessels. There are some specific operational procedures associated with these channels including keeping messages brief and using low power (not exceeding 1 watt). These are also primary channels for working drawbridges and locks.

Maritime Control: Channel 17 is used by vessels to talk to other vessels and to coast and shore stations operated by state or local governments. Communication is for the purposes of exchanging information about regulations, controls, maritime activities, or assistance to vessels.

Digital Selective Calling (DSC): Channel 70. This is the channel designated for use with digital selective calling systems in distress, safety calling, or general-purpose circumstances. DSC systems are components of the GMDSS system or can be stand-alone systems.

Weather: Monitoring channels only; vessels cannot transmit on these channels. In the United States, the National Oceanographic and Atmospheric Administration broadcasts weather information on

Wx-1	162.55 MHz
Wx-2	162.40 MHz
Wx-3	162.475 mHz

Fig. 5-1. Weather frequencies

these channels. Most units have designated selector switches for weather channels.

Bridge-to-bridge radiotelephone is intended for intership communications and limited-range, authorized ship-to-shore communications. The system is designed to serve as an aid to navigation by personnel in control of a vessel while under way or at anchor. It is for this reason at least one VHF radio should be located at the primary conning position. The equipment is designed to transmit at low power (1 watt) for line-of-sight communications or high power (25 watts) for distress and safety calling and authorized ship-to-shore communications.

The operator should make sure that selected channels are used for their designated purpose. In addition to communications with other vessels, authorized uses for ship-to-shore include transmitting and receiving signals from government agencies, such as the Coast Guard, licensed commercial marine facilities, and commercial telecommunications companies providing marine operator services.

The designated calling and distress frequency for VHF is 156.80 MHz, or VHF Channel 16. This frequency must be monitored at all times and be ready for use on all vessels navigating on all waters, and when at anchor in most harbors.

VHF Radio

VHF equipment generally consists of a transceiver, a power supply, an antenna cable, and a vertical whip antenna. The transceiver is equipped with a channel selector that can be placed in simplex or duplex mode. In modern receivers, it is common to have the channel selector programmed with simplex or duplex operation designated and authorized for each particular channel if appropriate. Simplex is generally referred to as USA or A and duplex is referred to as international. This is because in the early stage of VHF there were only a small number of frequencies available and it was anticipated that they would fill up quickly. Allowing all channels to operate in either mode limited congestion. Ultimately, more VHF frequencies were made available for marine use.

The VHF transceiver also has several other features including power selection with high or low settings, squelch control to block out signals of lower power, and a Channel 16 watch monitor. Other features such as channel programming, scanning mode, and a safety channel "hot" button vary with manufacturers.

The power supply provides clean, filtered, constant low voltage, generally 12-V DC, to the transceiver. Commercial vessels are required to have a backup power system in case of emergency. These vessels are equipped with a transfer switch that can go from the power supply to a battery backup.

The antenna system consists of a coax cable, standing-wave ratio (SWR) meter or similar output indicator, and short vertical whip antenna. The cable should be kept separated from radionavigation, communication, or power lines. The output meter is required to allow the operator to be confident that the transceiver is transmitting.

VHF antennas are specifically designed for the short frequency band spread of marine systems. The antennas should be mounted as high up as possible to provide the best range of transmission and reception available. The antenna should be kept clear of other antennas and the vessel's structure.

As with every other piece of equipment used in the marine environment, these systems must be checked and maintained. The op-

Fig. 5-2. VHF radio location. Photograph by Forlivesi Photography.

erator should check power supply voltages, make sure that backup batteries are maintained and are operating correctly and power transfer switches are working properly. It is good practice to check backup supplies daily and operate the radio for a short time on backup power.

Antenna systems should also be checked frequently to ensure that connections are tight and free of corrosion and that the antenna and cable are properly secured. The entire system should be properly grounded and should be checked occasionally to ensure there is continuity between the cable shielding, the transceiver, and the vessel.

Some systems are equipped with DSC, which uses an identification code and an audible or visual alarm. Commercial marine operators have been equipped with DSC for a number of years, using it to contact vessels with traffic on designated frequencies. The vessel has a muted monitor with a designated DSC identity code. When a shore station has traffic for the vessel, they use the code to trigger an alarm aboard the vessel, which need only answer the signal. This method has eliminated having calls made over Channel 16 or having vessels monitor the marine operator channels. When GMDSS comes fully into effect, DSC will impact monitoring requirements on VHF and SSB safety and calling frequencies. More discussion on DSC can be found in the GMDSS section of this book.

SINGLE SIDEBAND (SSB), SHIP-TO-SHORE RADIOTELEPHONY

For long-range voice communications, single sideband is one of the most frequently used marine systems worldwide. The transmission system is based on basic amplitude modulation principles with a redistribution of power in the signal. In basic AM, intelligence is contained within an upper and lower sideband wrapped around a carrier wave. About two-thirds of the signal's power is contained within the carrier and a great deal of energy is wasted during the signal's transmission.

In single sideband, the RF carrier is suppressed and the power is redirected into transmitting the modulated signal in the sidebands. The fidelity of the signal is not affected because the carrier contains none of the modulated signal. Due to the fact that both of the sidebands contain the same modulated signal, one of the sidebands can be eliminated from the transmission. This also reduces the bandwidth required by one-half. Ultimately, the power can be reutilized to extend the range of the transmitted signal and the number of frequencies available can be increased by using upper and lower sideband signals separately.

Most units are capable of utilizing the upper sideband (USB) or lower sideband (LSB) for communications depending on the need of the user. There are still a few units with double-sideband capability (DSB), which is the same as AM. The AM ship-to-shore/ship-to-ship system was the first type of voice communication method used by mariners, but it has been almost completely replaced by single sideband.

Single sideband is primarily designed for long-range ship-to-shore communications. It is also designed to cover ship-to-ship communications beyond that which can practically be achieved with VHF. This type of equipment is very common in the towing and limited tonnage industry, where more expensive global satellite communication systems are generally not utilized. Many vessel operating companies have single-sideband systems installed at their shoreside operation centers for communications with their vessels. In addition, federal agencies throughout the world maintain shore stations for communications with vessels in time of distress or national emergency. Various large telecommunication companies also maintain shore stations for communications between vessels and land-based telephone networks. Single-sideband users can contact the high-seas marine radio operator in many nations throughout the world and (for a charge) connect with any phone number in any location.

The current international calling and distress frequency for SSB is 2,182 kHz. Most government agencies similar to the U.S. Coast Guard monitor the SSB calling and distress frequency in addition to handling routine communications on designated working frequencies. There are also high-seas radiotelephone services available on various frequencies.

The most common encounter a mariner has with ground waves and sky waves and how they impact radio signals is in single-sideband communications. Ground waves travel along the surface of the earth and tend to bend with the planet's natural geographic curvature. Short-range SSB communications, generally from 200 to 500 miles, travel in the form of ground waves. Sky waves, on the other hand, travel upward, and in some cases pass through the atmosphere. There are, however, a significant number of radio signals that are reflected back to earth. These signals can be picked up at great distances, normally thousands of miles.

As mentioned previously, single-sideband frequency spread is considered both medium frequency and high frequency. Signals transmitted between 2 and 3 MHz, medium frequency, will be more prominently received as ground waves with a general range of several hundred miles. Sky waves are more predominantly received in the frequencies above 3 MHz, or in the high-frequency range.

In the case of sky-wave propagation, the range of SSB signals will depend on the density of the ionospheric layers, the height of the ionospheric layers, the frequency used, the angle of transmission, and the power of the transmitter. During the day the ionosphere is spread out and tends to reflect fewer signals. The bottom layer of the ionosphere is also at a closer distance to the earth's surface. At night the ionosphere changes its structure, becoming denser and rising higher above the earth's surface. Sky-wave propagation travels shorter distances during the day and longer distances during the night.

Frequency is also critical as it has an impact on the wavelength of the transmitted signal. With sky waves, the higher the frequency, the shorter the wavelength, making the signal more reflective. Higher frequency signals will tend to bounce back off the ionosphere as opposed to passing through it. This signal bounce or hop can be used by the operator to extend the range of the signal.

The transmission angle of the signal is also critical. High-angle signals, close to perpendicular between the antenna and the ionosphere, tend to penetrate and not be reflected back to earth. Low-angle signals however, bounce back more readily. Unfortunately, the lower the angle the better the chance of having a skip zone. In most circumstances, however, it is difficult for the operator to ascertain transmission angles; he or she must rely on experience to determine where signals will be received.

The transmitter's peak power will also dictate how far a signal will be heard. SSB transceivers can be equipped with linear amplifiers that will increase output power to over 1,000 watts. The critical relationship is between wavelength and antenna length, however. Simply increasing the power may not achieve the desired results if the wavelength/antenna length relationship is incorrect. Even if this is achieved, huge power outputs may adversely impact shorter range communications. For this reason, most vessel SSB units have power outputs under 250 watts. For most communications, the ranges achieved with this power output can reach the nearest shore stations.

In the practical operation of single-sideband communications, the operator must keep the following concepts in mind. Low-frequency signals travel shorter distances in most circumstances, primarily because they travel as ground waves, and the signals that travel as sky waves tend to skip shorter distances. In addition, these low-frequency sky waves are absorbed in the lowest ionospheric layers during daylight hours. They will, however, travel a longer relative distance at night because of the increased density of the ionosphere.

Higher frequency signals will travel greater distances under most circumstances. They are not absorbed by the low ionospheric layers during the daylight and tend to skip greater distances. Some of the signals do penetrate and are lost to outer space.

The best approach is to begin with higher frequency signals and work your way to the lower frequency signals. You can sometimes hear a vessel with which you may wish to communicate, call them on a higher frequency, and find that they do not respond. The signal may be bouncing right over top of them. On the other hand, you may hear another station and try to call them on a lower frequency. This signal may not be able to reach them due to the fact that it is traveling in the form of a low-range ground wave. It is very difficult to develop a rule that will work effectively based on a frequency range relationship. For the most part, however, for communications during the day under 500 miles, 2 to 8 MHz should be effective. Above 500 miles to about 1,500 miles, 8 to 12 MHz should be effective. Above 12 MHz you can expect communications to 3,000 miles-plus, depending upon the output power of your transmitter.

The operator must keep in mind that the longer the distance he or she tries to communicate, the more the fidelity will be affected. Remember, you are only using a narrow sideband signal, which already reduces the quality of the communication. Although communications can continue to be effective, some operators have found it difficult to ascertain what is being said because people tend to sound like they have severe nasal congestion.

At night the operator has to keep in mind that because of the higher density of the ionosphere the same range can be achieved with a communication by utilizing a lower frequency. During the day a 15 MHz signal may effectively reach a receiver, where at night the same signal may bounce right over top of it and be picked up at twice that distance. Most of the time, you should be able to communicate with any station you can hear. Some operators note in their logbooks the frequencies and distances with which they have had experiences for future reference.

Signal reception can best be demonstrated in an example. During the day, while traveling in a car, you can pick up AM broadcasts from stations in your general geographic area. The driver will hear signals traveling in the form of ground waves with good fidelity. At night, however, that same driver will be able to pick up AM broadcasts from distant cities. Those signals travel in the form of sky waves and are reflected off the ionosphere, skipping greater distances. Using this concept, many a sailor at sea has tuned his or her radio at night trying to pick up some news or a distant ball game.

Fidelity becomes a significant issue here. Signals that travel in the form of ground waves are very steady and generally very clear. Signals that travel in the form of sky waves, however, tend to vary in strength or fade and will not be heard as clearly as ground-wave signals. This is a compromise that the operator must make, but where communications are limited to simple voice transmissions, for the most part, you can still get your message across. Single-sideband users must be familiar with designated frequencies for specific uses. Single-sideband frequencies are classified as medium frequency/high frequency, or MF/HF. Frequencies available for marine communications are between 2.0 MHz and 23.0 MHz. The frequencies now have specified channels associated with them called International Telecommunication Union (ITU) channels and, like VHF, they can be used in a simplex or duplex mode. ITU channels begin at 401 and go through 2,240, with the first one or two numbers of the channel corresponding to the frequency range in megahertz. Not every number in this range has a designated marine use. ITU channels cover the medium-frequency 2 to 3 MHz band and the high-frequency 4 to 23 MHz bands.

The most effective way to handle SSB traffic ship to ship or ship to shore is through scheduled communications. Selecting a specific UTC time for making contact on specific channels will limit the frustration of working with a system that is beyond the line of sight. Selecting specific frequencies based on estimated distance apart as well as time of day can be easily coordinated.

Single-Sideband Radio

Single-sideband equipment generally consists of a multichannel transceiver, an antenna coupler, a connecting cable, a power supply, and a vertical or horizontal whip antenna. Output power can vary depending on the make and model of the unit purchased. This will range from 25 to 150 watts. There is specialized equipment available that can have an output power of up to 1,000 watts. The frequency range of the system may also vary depending upon the operator's intended use. Manufacturers produce lower power limited frequency systems to try to contain the cost for the recreational boat market.

The power supply is designed to provide filtered, constant voltage to the SSB transceiver. The transceiver unit is connected to the antenna system with a heavier gauge coax cable. This protects the incoming and outgoing signals from interference. Between the transceiver and the antenna, an antenna coupler is usually installed. For every transmitted signal, there is an optimum antenna length based on the frequency/wavelength relationship. The antenna coupler varies the capacitance of the antenna system to try to match the wavelength of a transmitted signal at a specific frequency. In essence, this optimizes the transmission by varying the length of a fixed antenna through alteration of its electrical and magnetic characteristics.

SIMPLEX TELEPRINTER OVER RADIO (SITOR)

Simplex teleprinter over radio (SITOR) is a commercial version of narrow band direct printing (NBDP), which is a terrestrial-based telex system utilizing medium- and high-frequency transmissions. The system has become widespread in the maritime community for moving basic radioteletype information. SITOR is used to communicate from ship to ship, ship to shore, and shore to ship. It operates on specific frequencies designated as ITU channels.

Ship-to-ship SITOR communications are conducted over specified simplex frequencies between vessels. Operators must generally coordinate their schedules to move traffic back and forth. Ship-to-ship communications can be conducted between any vessels that have the proper equipment and reception and transmission capability.

Ship-to-shore communications are conducted between vessels and coastal radio stations using designated ITU channels in partial- or half-duplex modes. Unlike duplex radiotelephone communications, where the transmitting and receiving stations operate on different frequencies and can transmit and receive simultaneously, SITOR half-duplex systems use different frequencies for the ship

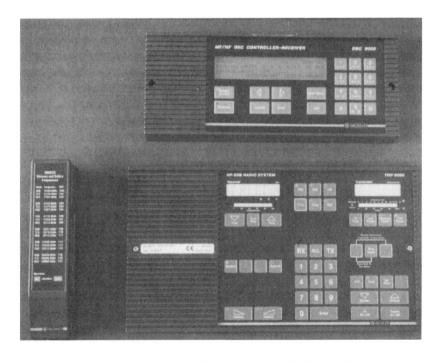

Fig. 5-3. SSB radio equipment. Photograph by Forlivesi Photography.

and coast station. The limitation is that only one station can transmit at a time. This, however, does not affect the efficiency of communications and is adequate for this type of transmitted and received signal. A list of coast station channels is available in several publications including U.S. and foreign government publications, as well as lists put out by the stations themselves.

Shore-to-ship communications are received aboard the vessel in the form of radio broadcasts containing traffic lists. If a message is available for a specific vessel, that vessel can contact the shore station to receive the message. Shore stations will also broadcast weather reports and safety information, which is available to all stations.

To assist in speeding up communications between ship and shore stations, selective calling numbers (SELCALs) are utilized. SELCALs are specific identity numbers assigned to both a vessel and a coast station in addition to the station's radio call sign. Five-digit numbers are assigned to vessel stations and four-digit numbers are assigned to coast stations. The ITU puts out a list of all SELCAL numbers and their assigned stations.

There are two basic modes to operations associated with SITOR: automatic repeat request (ARQ) and forward error correction (FEC). The ARQ mode reduces errors in the radio teletype text between a transmitting and a receiving station. The FEC mode is utilized for transmitting basic information from shore stations such as traffic lists. It is also utilized when stations are communicating with each other. ARQ cannot be used when broadcasting, while FEC can.

The ARQ mode tries to create real-time correction for detected errors during transmissions. Signals are received in small groups and the signal is analyzed to determine if there are any obvious errors. The system acknowledges receipt of the signal and either clears the signal or indicates whether an error has been detected. If an error has been detected, this will be indicated to the transmitting station for correction. Compared with modern computer systems, data transmission speed is relatively slow, with a baud rate of only about 100. However, in the ARQ mode, which on some units is indicated as the "A" mode, the baud rate can be cut in half.

The FEC mode works quite differently. In this method, text is transmitted on a continual basis but each individual byte is sent twice by the transmitting station, with a delay of about 250 milliseconds between bytes. The receiving station system will check the bytes twice when they are received. In most cases, it is able to detect one or both bytes and will produce a character in the message. If the byte's character cannot be determined, the system will produce an asterisk or other type of character in the message. It is left to the ability of the operator to try to interpret a message even if it is not received 100 percent correctly. In most cases the communications can be conducted quite adequately.

Once the messages are received, the information can be printed into hard copy. SITOR is utilized for safety messages and weather information received beyond the range of NAVTEX.

Equipment

SITOR uses a designated terminal with decoding equipment that converts the radio signals on the specific SITOR frequencies into visual alphabetical and numeric characters. The system can be connected to any standard MF/HF receiver or can use its own internal system receiver. The system uses the same type of antenna as an MF/HF system. Once the signals are received, they can be stored, viewed on a screen, or printed into hard copy.

SATELLITE COMMUNICATIONS (SATCOM)

Worldwide communications can also be achieved through use of satellite communications (SATCOM) utilizing the international mari-

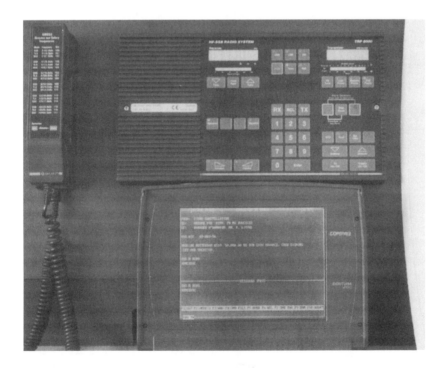

Fig. 5-4. SITOR equipment. Photograph by Forlivesi Photography.

time satellite system (INMARSAT). This network is operated as a joint effort by a group of international communication companies. The system utilizes a series of satellites that provide coverage in the major shipping areas of the world. INMARSAT is an organization with more than seventy-five nations participating in the operating agreement. The nations are represented by a public or private entity that invests in the overall system based on a specific percentage of anticipated use. The members also make policy decisions and plan investment and improvements for the overall system.

The purpose of INMARSAT, according to its charter, is "to make provision for the space segment necessary for improving maritime communications . . . thereby assisting and improving distress and safety of life at sea . . . and improving efficiency in the management of ship and maritime public correspondence services." The original convention that created INMARSAT limits use of the system to peaceful purposes and makes the system available to vessels of all nations. Membership in the organization is open to all countries that wish to participate. The system also services land-based mobile system users and aeronautical users.

The INMARSAT system provides direct-dial telephone service, telex messages, fax transmissions, electronic mail, electronic data interchange (EDI), emergency communications, and automated position/status reporting. Each participating nation or company maintains earth stations that link their particular normal telephone network with the satellite being used.

There are three basic segments in the system: the space segment, the ground segment, and the user segment. The equipment in each segment is maintained by the service provider with the exception of the user segment. SATCOM equipment is available in this segment from numerous commercial providers.

The space segment consists of a series of satellites in geosynchronous orbits in specific locations above the earth. Geosynchronous orbits permit the satellites to remain stationary in relation to a point on the earth. The satellites are placed at an altitude approximately equal to the earth's circumference of 21,300 nautical miles and are positioned over the equator. They provide coverage from about 70 degrees north latitude to about 70 degrees south latitude. The satellites cover the Atlantic, Pacific, and Indian oceans with one primary satellite and one back-up satellite per area. The system divides the marine segment into four ocean regions that include Atlantic Ocean region-east (AOR-E), Atlantic Ocean region-west (AOR-W), Pacific Ocean region (POR), and the Indian Ocean region (IOR). As technology improves, the satellites are supplemented or replaced by newer units with expanded capabilities.

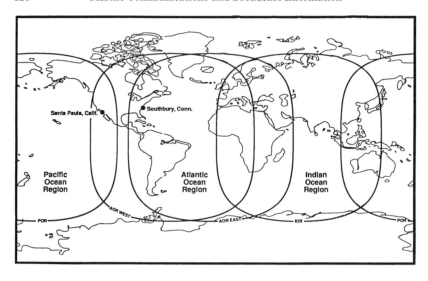

Fig. 5-5. SATCOM coverage. Courtesy of COMSAT Corp.

Satellite control is performed by four ground-based stations that handle the telemetry, tracking, and control (TTC) functions. The stations are located in Italy (AOR-E and IOR), China (POR), California (POR), and Connecticut (AOR-W). These stations are coordinated by and connected to the Satellite Control Center (SCC), which is located at the INMARSAT headquarters in London. All signals that handle the TTC functions of the satellites are independent from the communication frequencies utilized by system users.

The ground segment consists of a series of coast earth stations (CES), which handle such functions as interconnection to the ground-based telephone network. In addition to the CESs, a network coordination station and network operation centers handle each of the ocean regions. Message traffic control is handled by the CESs, with messages prioritized based on distress, urgency, safety, or routine communications. In the United States, Communications Satellite Corporation (COMSAT) generally is the prime operator for marine-based services.

The function of the network coordination stations is to monitor and control communications with each of the ocean regions. They are linked with a central network operations center in London. They also establish calls to and from mobile customers and connect ship and coast earth stations together. The network operations center monitors overall communications loads to and from mobile stations and tries to prevent system overloads by initiating specific actions within the system.

The user segment, in the case of shipboard stations, consists of an INMARSAT terminal and associated equipment. The terminal connects to telephones, telex units, fax machines, e-mail systems, and other types of data links. It is connected to a parabolic antenna generally placed within a protective dome high above the ship's structure. The terminal contains identification information and has the ability to track a satellite and adjust the antenna so that the communications link between the ship and the satellite is as direct as possible.

INMARSAT services include a series of different capabilities based on the technology available in both the satellites and ship station components. Services include INMARSAT A, B, C, and M.

INMARSAT A provides two-way direct-dial telephone and telex communications, interlinked to any location on earth. Voice circuits are used to transmit and receive electronic mail, computer data, or facsimile. INMARSAT A is based on analog technology. The system uses a large directional parabolic antenna.

INMARSAT B is based on digital technology and was designed to eventually replace INMARSAT A's systems. It provides the same basic functions as INMARSAT A; however, because of the digital application, communications are faster and less expensive.

INMARSAT C is designed to provide two-way store and forward messaging. The terminals used in this system are less expensive and smaller than the A or B systems. They have an increased baud rate for computer systems of more than 600 bytes. INMARSAT C is a key component of GMDSS, which will be described in the next chapter. In addition to general communications, INMARSAT C also provides distress notification and is used to provide marine safety information. Unlike standard A, the system uses a small omnidirectional antenna.

INMARSAT M offers telephone and low-speed fax and data interchange utilizing portable lightweight terminals. It uses a smaller antenna and can be utilized aboard smaller vessels or in other types of mobile service.

The system provides 339 channels to the user, transmitting between 1,636.5 and 1,645.0 MHz and received on frequencies between 1,535.0 and 1,543.5 MHz. The system is capable of multilink communications by voice, electronic data interchange (coded information relayed over voice communication lines), telex, and other forms.

The user selects the satellite to be used by the area in which they are located. The position of the user is then entered into the INMARSAT unit so the parabolic antenna can be oriented to the selected satellite. The user can select any earth station or system desired depending on where the communication link is required.

The ship earth station initiates a call into the INMARSAT system by selecting a specific earth coast station covering its ocean region. Once the station has been selected, and satellite tracking has been confirmed and stabilized, communication is as simple as dialing a shipboard phone or linking through a computer modem.

It is important to note that there must be a direct line-of-sight link between the ship's antenna and the satellite. If the antenna does not have a clear field of view, communications can be disrupted. This can also occur when, due to the vessel's motion, a mast or part of the vessel's structure blocks the signal.

The procedure for dialing varies somewhat depending upon the type of equipment aboard the vessel. An example of a typical dialing sequence for a U.S. telephone network using a COMSAT coastal earth station follows.

CES selection	Auto service country	Country code	Area code	Telephone number	Completes dialing
01#	00	1	508	8305000	#

Fig. 5-6. SATCOM dialing example

SATCOM is a very reliable and easy system to use. The communications are very clear and are comparable to land line reception. Only a nearly imperceptible "delay" can be sensed. Due to the tremendous expense to place and maintain the satellites, of all the systems integrated into land communication networks, SATCOM is the most expensive to use. Mariners should be aware that calling a CES can be very expensive, yet calling another SEC can cost twice as much.

Equipment

SATCOM uses a highly directional parabolic antenna to transmit and receive signals to and from INMARSAT satellites. The antennas are various sizes depending upon which INMARSAT service is being utilized. The largest shipboard antennas, however, are about 1 meter in diameter and are housed in a protective fiberglass covering. The housing can range from 1,400 millimeters high with a base of 1,300 millimeters to as little as 300 millimeters high with a base of 200 millimeters. Component weights range from about 100 kg to as little as 5 kg. Personnel working near the SATCOM antennas are warned of radiation hazards. Not only can they not see antenna direction, but transmission can occur automatically when the ship is being called.

The communications equipment, which is linked to the antenna by a specialized shielded cable, consists of a power supply and a system terminal. The terminal contains an antenna control unit, usually linked to the ship's master gyro system, access control and signaling equipment, the satellite transceiver, a telex terminal, telephones, a fax machine, a PC modem, and, if system-capable, a high-speed data link.

One key advantage of this system is that any number of phones, computers, or fax machines can be linked to the terminal. This provides telecommunications services throughout the vessel. On some vessels, pay phones have been installed and made available to passengers and crew. Once the principal operator of the equipment links to the desired satellite, service is available. The operator should monitor and change satellites during the voyage as necessary.

WATERWAY COMMUNICATIONS SYSTEM (WATERCOM)

The waterway communication system, or WATERCOM, is a communications network designed for use on inland rivers and intracoastal waterways of the United States. The system is operated by Waterway Communications System, Inc., a subsidiary of America Commercial Lines, Inc., which is a subsidiary of CSX Corporation. The system, constructed by Tracor Applied Sciences, Inc., consists of fifty-five shore stations providing rapid and microwave-based communications along the 4,000 miles of the Mississippi River system and the Gulf intracoastal waterway.

The system operates in the FM band allocated to mobile maritime communications by the FCC, between 216 and 220 MHz. There are forty assigned channels and users can directly connect into normal phone systems without going through the marine operator.

WATERCOM works in the same manner as a mobile telephone. Vessels have an identification number, which is used for accounting purposes. The operator can connect to the land-based telephone system by dialing the desired number. Charges are based on a system subscription, which includes connection charges to shore-based stations, and normal phone charges.

Communication units that consist of a radio transceiver with a microprocessor can be placed anywhere aboard the vessel, such as in the wheelhouse, and operate by using a simple touch-tone dialing system. There are extension telephones available for use in the crew spaces and other parts of the vessel. Each vessel is assigned its own separate operating number. Coded transmissions can be made from a vessel to its home office or other phone exchange. The system is designed to include non-voice data transmissions also.

COASTAL COMMUNICATIONS

As most people know, telephone communications are fully mobile to-day. The same systems that allow for automobile cell phones can be used by mariners. Cellular mobile phone systems are dependent upon shore-based cell antenna arrays within line of sight. Mariners can utilize these systems for relatively inexpensive telephone communications if cell signal strength exists. This range can extend to 50 or 60 miles from cell towers. Unfortunately, tower locations are not detailed on marine charts or radio communication reference materials; therefore, mariners must test the signal strength and can expect frequent interruptions.

Advances in cell technology have now moved to satellites. Many digital cell systems are serviced by satellite, particularly in Pacific Rim countries where hard-wire connections or cell towers are not effective. Presently a worldwide cellular system called Iridium is near capability. Once all 77 (iridium's atomic weight) low-orbit satellites are functional, mariners on the high seas can use relatively low-cost "telephone" service—as opposed to high-cost INMARSAT systems.

PRACTICAL COMMUNICATIONS

Excluding private communications that take place over closed link systems such as SATCOM or WATERCOM, following are some specific rules and regulations that dictate how ship-to-ship and ship-to-shore communications are to be made. As a person responsible for the operation of a vessel you are responsible for proper radio use and etiquette. If you are radio communications officer, you must obey and carry out the lawful orders of the master or person lawfully in charge of the vessel on which you are employed.

With the exception of broadcasts intended for public reception and distress messages, it is illegal to disclose the existence or content of any radio communications to anyone other than the party to whom the communication is addressed. You may not transmit false or deceptive signals or communications by radio or falsely identify a radio station by transmitting a call sign which has not been assigned by proper authority to your station. It is illegal to willfully or maliciously interfere with or cause interference to any radio communication or signals. It is also illegal to transmit unnecessary, unidentified, or superfluous radio communications or signals or tie up vital communications channels with idle discussions.

Any adjustments of transmitting equipment at any maritime coast or ship station that are made during the installation, servicing, or maintenance of that equipment, which may impact its proper operation, can only be made by a licensed individual. It is also illegal to

willfully damage or allow to be damaged any piece of radio equipment in a way that may affect its operation or transmitting parameters. You must stop using equipment immediately if you notice or
have been informed that your equipment is transmitting outside of
the technical parameters for your vessel's radio.

A vessel that is equipped with a radio station must allow government officials to examine the radio equipment and the station and
personnel licenses. Operators must maintain a station log for a period of 1 year from the date of last entry. If a station log contains a
distress message, the log must be retained for three years.

The only time an operator can make a general call, that is, one that
is not addressed to a particular station or a general group of stations, is
when the operator is making a distress call. All calls should be directed
to a specific station. When in sight of another station and the station
name or call sign is unknown, information such as type of vessel, color,
position, or other identifying parameters should be communicated. It
is also critical that when communications are established you confirm
that the station you are talking to is the intended party.

The most important thing that anyone operating a radio should
keep in mind is to monitor the channel you intend to use prior to
transmitting. Transmitting while another party is involved in communications can disrupt their signal and cause them to miss a portion of a message. When you begin communications, allow sufficient
time between calls if you have not reached the station you are calling. If you feel you need to make a call to see if your equipment is operating properly, do so to another ship station at a location where
you can get a good indication your system is working properly. Frequent requests for radio checks or calling on the distress and safety
channel is improper and illegal.

There are proper procedural words that should be employed in
communications. These include *over,* which is used when the transmission is completed and you are expecting a reply. *Roger* or *Charlie*
indicates an affirmative reply to a communication; *negative* means
the answer is no. When a communication is finished and no reply is
intended, *over and out* or *clear on channel (#).* Most operators will indicate that they are switching back to a working frequency or Channel 16 if further communications is required.

Under no circumstances may you use profanity when conducting
communications on any type of radio equipment. Although English has
been designated as the international language for communications, remember that dialects or accents may create a misunderstanding
when communicating. Speak slowly, use concise messages, and confirm that the other party has received and understood your message.
Communications between mariners with different languages or

dialects can be improved by using the international code of signals phonetic language. This code details the exact phonetic pronunication of all letters and numbers. Consult NIMA H.O. 102 for more details. If necessary, do not hesitate to employ the phonetic alphabet when communicating with another station.

CALLING AND DISTRESS FREQUENCY MONITORING

By international agreement all vessels under way are required to maintain a watch on certain designated calling and distress frequencies. These requirements will be superseded by the global marine distress and safety system (GMDSS), which is scheduled to be in place by February 1, 1999. Until that date a 24-hour watch on each of the following is required.

The VHF and SSB frequencies are required to be monitored by the person in control of the vessel at the principal operating station. In other words, if you are navigating your vessel, one of your responsibilities will be to monitor VHF Channel 16. You will also be required to monitor 2,182 kHz SSB if your vessel is required to carry this type of equipment. Channel 16 VHF should always be on and audible for incoming calls, distress or otherwise. For SSB there is a muted monitor that will activate upon receiving the two-tone distress alarm signal used on 2,182 kHz. The radiotelephone alarm consists of two high-pitched alternating tones, each one-quarter of a second in length. The tones will be transmitted for 30 to 60 seconds and will activate the monitor. The operator must pay attention to any incoming signals and should have a pencil and paper ready to write down any information. SSB equipment is required aboard all vessels on international voyages. The U.S. Coast Guard, in addition to other government agencies throughout the world, maintains a silent period on 2,182 kHz for 3 minutes immediately after the hour and half hour. During these time periods, no vessel may transmit any message other than distress or urgent communications.

Vessel operators should log all distress communications in their radiotelephone logbook. Any distress messages received, whether or not you can provide assistance, are required to be logged, as are any responses or assisting communications, such as relaying the message.

A.   Channel 16 (156.80 MHz), ship-to-ship VHF radio
B.   2,182 kHz (2.182 MHz), SSB radio

Fig. 5-7. Calling and distress frequencies

If a distress message is received, the officer should copy down all information and, if within range, act to render assistance and establish communications with the vessel in distress. The master should always be notified when a distress message is received, and if a radio officer is aboard, he or she should also be notified to render communications assistance. The vessel should always contact the U.S. Coast Guard or nearest coastal station and notify them the vessel is available to render assistance.

The deck officer needs to be well aware of the voice communication preambles used in marine voice radio communications. Each denotes a specific type of communications, with certain levels of priority. They are specifically designed to get the attention of personnel monitoring communications networks, recognizing that this is one of the many responsibilities a navigator may have. These preambles are used for the specified messages on both VHF and SSB voice systems.

A. "Mayday, mayday, mayday": Used to transmit distress messages
B. "Pan, pan, pan": Used to broadcast very urgent safety or navigation information
C. "Securité, securité, securité": Used to broadcast important navigational or safety information

---

Fig. 5-8. Radio preambles

The phonetic words are designed to be friendly to a variety of languages and alert the watchstander of important messages. "Securité" is used a great deal as its purpose is to be used for information that is not extremely important, but information that mariners in the area should be aware of to help them safely navigate their vessel. For example, a pilot bringing a large tanker into a congested harbor might transmit the following message before entering as notification to other vessels in the area that may be affected by the transit (often mariners will not verbally respond to the transmission, but the information is used in their navigation):

"Securité, securité, securité. The loaded tanker *Eagle* inbound New York Harbor, bound for 138th Street, any concerned traffic respond on channel 13 VHF."

The urgency call is used to transmit any critical information that might affect the safety of a vessel or lives. Examples of this type of message include vessel groundings, missing navigation aids, or man overboard:

"Pan, pan, pan. This is the passenger ship *Majestic Star*. We have a man overboard at position latitude 44 degrees 15.2 minutes north and longitude 72 degrees 36.1 minutes west. Person is not wearing a life jacket but a life ring with strobe light has been dropped near the suspected area. Any vessels in the area are requested to render assistance."

The final type of call is the distress call where a vessel or lives are in immediate danger. The distress signal "Mayday" is spoken clearly three times and all vessels that hear the call should stand by, stop any other communications, and prepare to render assistance. Information contained in a distress message is outlined below.

---

1. Distress call "Mayday, mayday, mayday" (spoken on VHF and preceded by the distress alarm on SSB)
2. The words "This is" and the name and call sign of the vessel
3. The distress message, consisting of:
   A. Nature of distress
   B. Location
   C. Type of vessel/size/color
   D. Number of persons aboard
   E. Other important information

Fig. 5-9. Distress data

You may be asked for additional information by rescue authorities, which you should try to provide if you are in a position to do so. Be sure to remain calm and provide the clearest and most concise information possible. Let the station you are talking to know what your problem is and where you are in latitude and longitude coordinates or loran C time delays, or provide a reference to land or a navigation aid. Tell them what they are looking for, how many people there are aboard, and whether anyone is injured. Finally, if you need to convey any additional information that can help others help you, do so, but also stop and listen to see whether you are being heard and whether anyone is in a position to help you. Here is a sample distress call: "Mayday, mayday, mayday. This is the fishing vessel *Lucky Lady*. We have an engine fire and are in danger of sinking, we are located two miles due west of buoy three in South Bay, the vessel is a 50-foot trawler with blue hull and white house, there are three persons aboard, one is badly burned, we are preparing to abandon ship, we are all wearing life jackets, I have put an EPIRB in the water, and have a portable VHF. Any vessels in the area respond."

VESSEL LICENSING AND REGULATION

All vessels that navigate on international waters or their associated tributaries, such as harbors, bays, or sounds, are required to carry a VHF bridge-to-bridge radiotelephone capable of monitoring Channel 16. All vessels that travel on international voyages are required to carry an SSB radiotelephone capable of monitoring 2.182 MHz. All U.S. vessels are required to have a station license issued by the Federal Communications Commission. The license is valid for a specific period of time and is subject to revocation if violation of any regulations regarding the use of marine radio equipment occurs, including VHF, SSB, radiotelephone, RDF, and marine radar equipment. In order to receive a license, an inspection must be conducted by the FCC or other appropriate government authority.

In the United States, a marine radio operator's permit is required for personnel who operate a voice radiotelephone at specific facilities. This permit provides for the use, but not the repair or adjustment, of marine radio equipment. Personnel who are authorized to make repairs or adjustments of radio equipment have a set of separate and much more stringent and technically oriented licensing requirements. Nations throughout the world have licensing requirements similar to those regulations in force in the United States.

Radio Station Requirements

1. on a cargo ship of 300 or more gross tons which is navigated on the open sea;

2. on a vessel sailing the Great Lakes which is more than 65 feet long, or carrying more than six passengers for hire;

3. on a vessel carrying more than six passengers for hire, regardless of size, which is navigated in the open sea or in any tidewaters adjacent to the open sea more than 1,000 feet from shore;

4. at a coast station, not located in Alaska, which uses frequencies lower than 30 MHz and which uses 250 watts or less of carrier power or 1,500 watts or less of peak envelope power; or

5. at a regional or local service (VHF) coast station which is located in Alaska and uses 250 watts or more of carrier power or 1,500 watts or more of peak envelope power.

Fig. 5-10. FCC requirements for carriage of
bridge-to-bridge radiotelephone

An individual with a general radiotelephone operator's license fulfills these requirements as well as meeting the needs of vessels carrying specific radiotelephone equipment. A holder of this license, along with a radar endorsement, may repair and adjust radios and radar in accordance with FCC regulations, specifications, and tolerances. Certification, like that for the marine operator's permit, is conducted by the FCC and requires a written examination.

Technology in shipboard communications has made several significant steps forward, as the reader may surmise. The technology involves more than radio advances, and includes equipment that is tremendously user-friendly in operation and offers highly reliable hardware electronics. The most dramatic application of the technology is still around the corner, however. The international global marine distress and safety system becomes fully operational in 1999. This system will essentially eliminate the shipboard radio operator position, and those duties will be shifted to the deck watch officers. As a corollary to their navigation duties, they will be required to possess the knowledge to operate high-seas radiotelephone equipment for both daily communications and emergencies. At least two GMDSS operator licenses are required by the FCC if a ship's radio station license is to be valid without a radio operator. GMDSS will be discussed in detail in the next chapter.

MARINE BROADCAST INFORMATION

It is important that the mariner maintain the ability to utilize up-to-date information in navigational planning and operations. Various government agencies have the responsibility to ensure that critical data for the mariner's use is broadcast on a frequent basis. While there are numerous systems available for providing information, the three most basic systems consist of radio time signals, marine weatherfax, and NAVTEX. There are additional information systems which are included within the GMDSS requirements.

Most maritime nations throughout the world offer nonscheduled marine broadcast information over VHF radio channels. These may be considered to augment the scheduled broadcasts, and may be more timely to circumstances and conditions in a particular area.

Use of the broadcast information is paramount to good seamanship for the oceangoing vessel. The watch officers must be attentive to both the scheduled and nonscheduled broadcasts. This information truly makes the oceans a safer place. Mariners should make every effort to comply with directives and participate in confirmation of information received. When notification of a vessel being overdue is received, it is the responsibility of the mariner to assist the nation's coastal defense or rescue agencies.

Radio Time Signals

In the United States, the National Bureau of Standards (NBS) operates two radio stations that provide constant time information that mariners can use for navigational work. The stations are WWV, located in Fort Collins, Colorado, and WWVH, located in Maui, Hawaii. The stations, in addition to providing continuous time signals, also provide marine storm warnings, geophysical alerts, and time corrections when required. There are additional services available; however, they are not generally used by the mariner.

Radio stations WWV and WWVH broadcast on frequencies of 2.5 MHz, 5.0 MHz, 10.0 MHz, and 15.0 MHz. In addition to their call sign announcement, the stations can be distinguished from each other because WWV utilizes a male announcer and WWVH utilizes a female announcer. The listener should use signals from the nearest station for time calibration. Additional information on National Bureau of Standards time services and formats can be found in NIMA Publication 117.

International time signals are also available from many other nations on the short-wave bands. Normally, however, you can pick up the stations operated by the NBS anywhere in the world. There are also stations broadcasting from India, France, Switzerland, Italy, Japan, Argentina, England, Czechoslovakia, Russia, South Africa, and Canada. Frequencies and periods of operation can be located in any general short-wave listener's guide. In some areas of the Western North Atlantic and Eastern Pacific radio station CHU, located in Ottawa, Canada, can be picked up with more ease than the NBS stations. CHU broadcasts eastern standard time in English and French at 3.33 MHz, 7.335 MHz, and 14.67 MHz continuously. The NBS stations broadcast coordinated universal time (UTC), which is the same as Greenwich mean time (GMT).

Weather Facsimile Broadcasts (Weatherfax)

For many years, deck officers had to create weather maps by hand with coded information available through radiotelegraph. The introduction of facsimile broadcasts has made this information more readily available to vessels at sea. Facsimile broadcasts involve the bit-mapping of a page of information, either symbols or verbiage, and the transmittal of this information. Today's fax machines have brought this relatively old system into common usage, although enhancements to equipment have produced superior-quality documents.

Weatherfax broadcasts are available on the medium- and high-frequency bands and originate from various stations throughout the world. These stations normally broadcast maps for the overall ocean areas near the country of origin. The transmitting station encodes

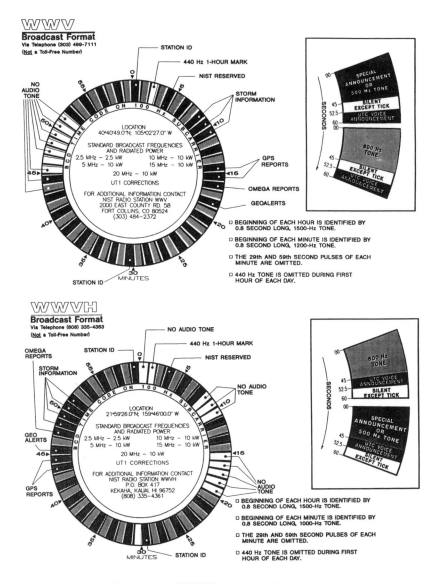

Fig. 5-11. WWV broadcast formats.
Courtesy of National Ocean Service/U.S. Government.

the area weather map and broadcasts the signals at high speed to receivers. The fax receiver in turn recreates the original map from the signals and prints it on paper. Weatherfax machines may be connected to general broadcast receivers or have separate receivers integrated in the individual unit.

Broadcasts are scheduled on specific frequencies for designated areas. The weatherfax system operates by using a 1,500 Hz and 2,300 Hz modulated signal to generate black-and-white traces on a reproduced map area. These modulated signals are carried on radio frequencies between 100 kHz and 29.9 MHz. Coverage areas include the North Atlantic, Mediterranean, South Pacific, Indian Ocean, Persian Gulf, and Antarctic. Specific frequencies, area coverage, and broadcast schedules are found in several U.S. government publications and in publications available from the World Meteorological Organization. Information concerning weatherfax broadcasts is also provided by equipment manufacturers.

NAVTEX

The International Maritime Organization has designated NAVTEX as the primary means for transmitting coastal urgent marine safety information to ships worldwide. NAVTEX is an international radio system of navigation and weather broadcasts providing updated *Notices to Mariners* to vessels in coastal waters. Vessels with NAVTEX receivers can obtain printed information on a preset programmed frequency within 100 to 500 miles of a transmitter, day or night.

All transmitters broadcast on 518 kHz for 10 minutes every 4 hours. Sufficient geographical distance between them as well as differences in broadcast time prevents stations from interfering with each other. For the purpose of simplifying broadcasts, the system divides the world into various specific geographic navigational areas called NAVAREAS. There are sixteen NAVAREAS, indicated by roman numerals. Each transmitter in a specific NAVAREA is assigned an identification letter from A to Z. When a message is received, the transmitting station will be indicated by this letter, which is included on the printed sheet produced by the NAVTEX receiver. A complete listing of NAVAREAS, transmitter station name, letter code, position, schedule of transmission times, language used, and operational remarks is found in NIMA Publication 117 and with most NAVTEX receiver instruction manuals.

The NAVTEX message is preceded by "ZC," to indicate the start of the message, followed by a four-character heading providing basic information on the message. The first character of the heading is the station identification letter, the second character indicates the type of message, and the third and fourth characters are the message's serial number, listed as 00–99.

A single letter is assigned to each transmitter. It is one of the criteria used to identify the broadcasts that are to be accepted by the receiver and those which are to be rejected. With only twenty-six possible identification characters available, it is necessary to ensure that two stations having the same identification character have a large geographical separation in order to avoid erroneous reception of transmissions from such stations. NAVTEX transmissions have a designed range of about 400 nautical miles.

The second character is the subject indicator, which is used by the receiver to identify the different classes of messages. Identification of the subject of the message is important, as this is used to re-

---

A.   Navigational Warnings *
B.   Meteorological Warnings *
C.   Ice Reports
D.   Search and Rescue Information *
E   Meteorological Forecasts
F.   Pilot Service Messages
G.   Decca Messages
H.   Loran C Messages
I.   Undefined
J.   SATNAV Messages
K.   Other Electronic Navigational Aid (NAVAID) System messages
L.   Additional Navigational Warnings
M.   Undefined
N.   Undefined
O.   Undefined
P.   Undefined
Q.   Undefined
R.   Undefined
S.   Undefined
T.   Undefined
U.   Undefined
V.   Notice to Fishermen (U.S. stations only)
W.   Environmental Notices (U.S. stations only)
X.   Special Trials
Y.   Special Trials
Z.   No Message on Hand (QRS)

*Cannot be locked out or rejected.

Fig. 5-12. NAVTEX subject indicators

ject messages concerning certain optional subjects not required by the ship (e.g., DECCA messages might be rejected in a ship not fitted with a DECCA receiver). More importantly, receivers use the subject indicator to identify messages which, because of their importance, may not be rejected.

The subject indicator characters B, F, and G are normally not used in the United States. The National Weather Service normally includes meteorological warnings in forecast messages; these are broadcast using the subject indicator character E. U.S. Coast Guard District Broadcast Notices to Mariners affecting ships outside the line of demarcation, and inside the line of demarcation in areas where deep draft vessels operate, use the subject indicator character A. Messages will include information based on very specific guidelines.

Type A:	Buoys out of position or missing, unlit buoys, new wrecks, floating debris hazardous to navigation, repositioning of rigs, military exercises, etc.
Type B:	Gales or severe weather warnings.
Type C:	Ice reports for specific areas (i.e., the Baltic area, Iceland, Norway).
Type D:	Distress alerts and search and rescue information. Initial information only with all distress traffic to take place on the international calling and distress frequencies. Messages of this type are numbered 00.
Type E:	General weather f0orecasts for coastal or other areas.
Type F:	Pilot service changes for offshore stations.
Types G–K:	Warnings regarding errors, irregularities, or failures in the Decca, loran C, or GPS systems.
Type L:	Indicates initial number series from 01-99 has been used up and an additional sequence has begun to be used. These messages should not be rejected by the receiver.
Types M–U:	No specific purpose for these types has been established to date.
Type V:	Notices to fishermen, from U.S. broadcast stations only.
Type W:	Environmental notices, from U.S. broadcast stations only.
Type X,Y:	Special trials or tests of different methods of broadcasting, such as messages not in English for a local nationality.
Type Z:	The transmitter has no message to broadcast at this time; indicated by the letters QRS.

Fig. 5-13. NAVTEX message types

The third and fourth characters are the serial numbers of the message, numbered from 00–99. After 99, the numbers repeat themselves. These four characters are followed by the date and time of the message (UTC) and the message text in abridged form. The end of the message is indicated by "NNNN." The system is designed to replace Notices to Mariners broadcast by radiotelegraph. Voice transmissions of this information for specific inshore or harbor areas remain in effect.

NAVTEX messages will generally be repeated for as long as their information remains current. It should be noted that the messages may not be broadcast consecutively. The receiver will generally reject signals too weak to be read properly. Undefined script may be the result of local interference or transmitter malfunction.

The NAVTEX system is currently being expanded and made operational in new areas. Users should refer to the weekly Notices to Mariners and the latest edition of NIMA Publication 117 for availability in specific areas. The system is very reliable and accurate in that it offers the latest information available to the transmitting station.

NAVTEX stations are operated by government stations throughout the world. In the United States, the broadcasts are made from U.S. Coast Guard facilities located in key geographical locations covering the East and West coasts, parts of the Caribbean Sea, and parts of the Pacific Ocean around U.S. territories and Hawaii.

The Coast Guard began operating NAVTEX from Boston in 1983, and completed its most recent installation in Adak, Alaska, in 1993. The U.S. Coast Guard provides no coverage in the Great

Boston, Massachusetts
Portsmouth, Virginia
Miami, Florida
New Orleans, Louisiana
San Juan, Puerto Rico
Cambria, California
San Francisco, California
Astoria, Oregon
Kodiak, Alaska
Adak, Alaska
Honolulu, Hawaii

Fig. 5-14. U.S. Coast Guard-operated NAVTEX stations

Lakes; however, coverage of much of the Great Lakes is provided by the Canadian Coast Guard. Since the U.S. Coast Guard has only installed NAVTEX at sites where Morse telegraphy transmissions were previously made, propagation analyses show some coverage gaps, particularly in the southeast United States, Guam, and Puerto Rico.

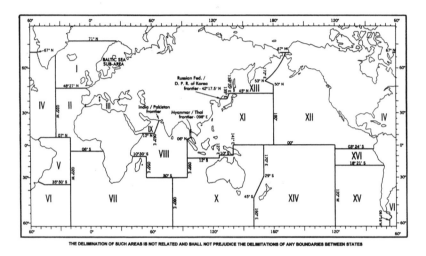

THE DELIMINATION OF SUCH AREAS IS NOT RELATED AND SHALL NOT PREJUDICE THE DELIMITATIONS OF ANY BOUNDARIES BETWEEN STATES

Fig. 5-15. NAVAREAS.
Courtesy of National Ocean Service/U.S. Government

CHAPTER 6

GLOBAL MARINE DISTRESS AND SAFETY SYSTEM

GENERAL

Since the sinking of various ships in the early part of this century, including the ocean liner *Titanic* in the North Atlantic in 1912, the need for ship and shore radio stations to monitor and utilize a common frequency for distress calls has been recognized as a serious shortcoming of ocean travel. Legislation enacted by the U.S. Congress shortly after the *Titanic*'s sinking required U.S. ships to use Morse code radiotelegraph equipment for distress calls. The call of S-O-S in Morse code has saved thousands of lives since that time, but the old Morse code distress procedures required trained radio operators who monitored distress frequencies 24 hours a day.

Until recently, 500 kHz medium frequency was the international calling and distress frequency for radiotelegraph. The frequency was heavily used, required 'round-the-clock monitoring by radio operators skilled in Morse code communication, was limited in range, and was found to be very congested. Although radiotelegraph still continues to be used by many nations, many governments have ceased to monitor the frequency due to advances in radiotelephony.

In the mid-1970s the International Maritime Organization (IMO), a U.N. agency that specialized in shipping safety and pollution prevention on the seas, began to investigate methods of improving maritime distress and safety communications. In 1979 the International Convention on Maritime Search and Rescue called for the development of a global search and rescue plan, which included the development of a global maritime distress and safety system (GMDSS). The primary objective of the system was to provide the communications necessary to meet the requirements of the new international search and rescue plan. The system was discussed at length by the various member nations and it was decided to implement the plan, which would cover all vessels at sea. That system is now being implemented by the participating nations and will be in full effect by the end of the century.

GMDSS is not a new communications system, but is a regulatory concept that incorporates a combination of terrestrial and satellite radio systems. GMDSS consists of several different systems, many of which have been in use for a number of years, including VHF bridge-to-bridge radiotelephone and SSB. It also incorporates new technology in the maritime world including satellite communications.

APPLICATION

GMDSS changes the concept of vessels in distress on the high seas, from looking for help from other vessels to seeking help from a shore-based rescue coordination center. The system links search and rescue (SAR) authorities ashore with vessel traffic in the immediate vicinity of a vessel in distress or requiring assistance. This approach improves emergency communications, automates some critical functions, decreases response time, and coordinates response operations. GMDSS incorporates existing systems and balances them with each other to remove geographical or other limitations.

GMDSS also changes the primary method of distress interactive communication from radiotelegraph (Morse code) to voice radiotelephony, which eliminates the need for Morse operators and opens distress messaging to virtually the entire maritime world using one system.

The IMO amended the Safety of Life at Sea (SOLAS) Convention in 1988, requiring vessels subject to SOLAS to begin outfitting with GMDSS equipment. These vessels began with the requirement to carry NAVTEX receivers and satellite EPIRBs (emergency position-indicating radio beacons) by 1993. In the United States, the Telecommunications Act of 1996 brought all U.S. ships into compliance. All vessels must be in full compliance with GMDSS requirements by 1999.

GMDSS incorporates faster automatic distress alerting and rapid determination of the position of vessels in trouble. It provides for the coordination of search and rescue operations, allows for short-range locating through homing, and incorporates general and bridge-to-bridge communications. It also addresses the need of vessels for up-to-date marine safety information and weather through full geographic coverage of areas with marine safety information broadcasts. The system also incorporates redundant or multiple means of distress alerting and emergency power backup systems.

Unlike earlier regulations, the requirement to carry GMDSS equipment is primarily dependent upon a vessel's area of operation, rather than its size or tonnage, although some smaller vessels are excluded. Any vessel subject to the requirements as defined by SOLAS or the Telecommunications Act must comply with GMDSS regulations. Those vessels include *all passenger ships regardless of size and cargo ships over 300 gross tons.*

A portion of the GMDSS requirements are based upon a ship's intended area of operation. The world's oceans are divided into four distinct communications areas that dictate what equipment is to be carried and how it is to be maintained.

PERSONNEL

GMDSS also impacts maritime personnel. The accepted certification for a GMDSS radio operator is the GMDSS radio operator license. This license is approved in the United States by the FCC, which did not permit existing licenses to cover GMDSS requirements. Additionally U.S. mariners must prove proficiency to the

---

Sea area A1: (approximately 25 NM from shore)
An area within radiotelephone coverage of at least one VHF coast station in which continuous digital selective calling (DSC) alerting is available.

Sea area A2: (up to approximately 150 NM from shore)
An area within MF radiotelephone coverage of at least one coast station at which continuous DSC is available. Area A2 excludes sea area A1.

Sea area A3: (ocean basins within INMARSAT coverage)
An area within the coverage of an INMARSAT satellite in which continuous alerting is available (approximately 70°N to 70°S). Area A3 excludes sea areas A1 and A2.

Sea area A4: (primarily polar regions above 70° latitude)
All areas outside of sea areas A1, A2, and A3. Sea area A4 relies primarily on HF communications.

Fig. 6-1. GMDSS coverage areas

U.S. Coast Guard and have their STCW certificate so noted. This license is issued separately by authorized agents and is not an endorsement attached to existing FCC or U.S. Coast Guard licenses. Similar license procedures are handled by national agencies throughout the world.

Vessels subject to the requirements must carry at least two persons holding GMDSS radio operator licenses who must be designated to perform distress, urgency, and safety communications. One of the qualified GMDSS radio operators must serve as the primary operator and the second serve as a backup during a distress situation. Carriage of a single GMDSS radio operator for distress and safety radio communications is not acceptable under the requirements, regardless of the vessel's intended area of operation.

INMARSAT-A	Distress Alerting
	voice channel communications
	TELEX communications
INMARSAT-C	Distress Alerting
	text messages
	low-speed data
VHF DSC	Distress Alerting
	digital selective calling
	voice communications
MF/DSC	Distress Alerting
	digital selective calling
COSPAS-SARSAT	Distress Alerting and Location
	Determination
	406 MHz EPIRBs
SART	Location Determination
	locating signals
SURVIVAL CRAFT VHF	On-Scene Communications
	VHF (voice)
MF/HF NBDP	Secondary Communications
	narrowband direct printing
	(SITOR)
MF/HF SSB	Secondary Communications
	single sideband (voice)

Fig. 6-2. GMDSS system capabilities

GMDSS EQUIPMENT

There is a scope of basic equipment that all vessels subject to GMDSS requirements must carry. Depending upon the vessel's intended area of operation, additional equipment will be required.

MAINTENANCE

GMDSS provides for three methods to maintain communications equipment. The system divides these methods into options depending on the sea area in which the vessel will operate. The options include duplication of equipment, shore-based maintenance, and at-sea maintenance.

> 1. Duplication of equipment
> 2. Shore-based maintenance
> 3. At-sea maintenance

Fig. 6-3. GMDSS maintenance options

Vessels operating in sea areas A1 and A2 must provide for at least *one* of the maintenance options. Vessels operating in sea areas A3 and A4 must provide for at least *two* of the maintenance options. If the vessel elects to conduct maintenance at sea, all adjustments, servicing, or maintenance that may affect the proper operation of the GMDSS radio station must be performed by a certified GMDSS radio maintainer, or under the immediate supervision and responsibility of a qualified GMDSS radio maintainer. These vessels must carry at least one person qualified as a GMDSS radio maintainer, who may also serve as one of the GMDSS operators.

The GMDSS radio maintainer's license is a separate certification from the GMDSS radio operator's license. The maintainer is responsible for preventive and corrective maintenance to equipment to make sure it is available in case of emergency. It should be noted that a GMDSS operator may perform "front cover" maintenance, such as fuse or bulb replacement. Under no circumstances, however, may an operator effect repairs to transmitting elements. Most shipping companies are opting to *not* use at-sea maintenance since the cost of spare parts is higher than duplication of equipment.

COMPONENT REQUIREMENTS

GMDSS consists of a group of required components that provide systematic coverage. These components consist of the satellite systems that incorporate INMARSAT A or C communications and the INMARSAT NET information system. Also required is the digital selective calling (DSC) on VHF/MF/HF surface-based RF systems for rapid and direct communications. For emergency search and rescue coverage there is COSPAS-SARSAT, which picks up EPIRB transmissions. Search and rescue transponders (SART) are used for surface vessels or low-flying aircraft units. Survival craft VHF radios are needed for at-scene communications between vessels in distress and rescue crafts. In addition, communications coverage is provided through MF/HF narrowband direct printing and MF/HF SSB.

INMARSAT A, INMARSAT C, INMARSAT SafetyNET

INMARSAT A was the first system to provide broad-based satellite communications and telex capabilities. The system has both direct-dial voice communications and send-and-receive telex. Safety messages can also be received as part of the GMDSS requirements although INMARSAT A equipment is not required as part of a GMDSS system. Based on analog technology, the system can be used to initiate a distress call on selected frequencies.

The INMARSAT C system is based on digital technology with expanded capabilities. Like INMARSAT A, the system can be used to initiate a distress call. Messages are routed directly to a rescue coordination center, which will acknowledge the message and begin assistance procedures. The coordination center can contact vessels using an enhanced group call (EGC), which allows broadcast messages to be made to selected groups of stations located anywhere within a satellite's coverage area. Information regarding vessels in need of assistance can be put out to vessels in a specified geographical area who may be able to render aid.

INMARSAT has two types of EGC services—SafetyNET and FleetNET. FleetNET is a commercial messaging service which is not recognized by the GMDSS requirements. SafetyNET, along with NAVTEX, is designated as the primary means for disseminating maritime safety information. Ships regulated by the SOLAS Convention traveling in areas not covered by NAVTEX must be equipped with an INMARSAT C SafetyNET receiver by February 1, 1999.

Virtually all the navigable waters of the world are in view of an INMARSAT satellite. Each satellite transmits EGC traffic on a designated channel at 1.5 GHz. Any ship within the coverage area of a satellite will be able to receive all SafetyNET messages broadcast by that satellite. Any ship with an INMARSAT C station can monitor the EGC channel. The EGC channel can also be monitored by dedicated receive-only equipment installed separately or as part of an INMARSAT A station.

Current INMARSAT C SafetyNET services available include urgency messages and navigational warnings to rectangular or circular areas, coastal warnings in place of NAVTEX (areas around Australia only), shore-to-ship distress alerts to circular areas, search and rescue coordination messages to rectangular or circular areas, and meteorological and navigational warnings and meteorological forecasts to a NAVAREA.

U.S. SafetyNET broadcasts include specific information covering U.S. territories and the coastal confluence zones. These broadcasts include NAVAREAS IV and XII navigational warning broadcasts from the U.S. National Imaging and Mapping Agency, NAVAREAS IV, XII, and XVI meteorological forecasts and warnings from the U.S. National Weather Service, distress alerts and search and rescue warnings from the U.S. Coast Guard, and Atlantic ice reports from the International Ice Patrol and the U.S. Coast Guard.

INMARSAT C units with a current position, either manually updated or updated by an installed GPS or other type of radionavigation receiver, will receive only messages pertinent to the circular or rectangular area which the ship is in, and will not receive a message addressed to other areas. If the terminal has no navigational information, then it will receive all such messages. A station will receive all messages addressed to a NAVAREA if the user has entered the NAVAREA number into the terminal, regardless of whether the station is in that area or not.

SafetyNET messages include a special header consisting of five "C" codes. These codes assist the operator in determining the type and urgency of the traffic being received.

C1	priority code	1 digit	distress, urgency, safety, routine
C2	service code	2 digits	type of message broadcast
C3	address code	12 characters	area broadcast instructions
C4	repetition rate	2 digits	number and frequency of broadcasts
C5	presentation code	2 digits	type of alphabet used

Fig. 6-4. SafetyNET C codes

Most INMARSAT C terminals are not able to receive a safety broadcast while transmitting a message, or while tuned to an INMARSAT ocean region not used for safety broadcasts in the area traveled. Most SafetyNET messages are rebroadcast after 6 minutes, to give transmitting terminals time to end their transmissions and receive missed messages. Lists of SafetyNET broadcast schedules and areas have been published by the World Meteorological Organization to assist ship operators in setting their terminals to the proper INMARSAT ocean region.

Although SafetyNET reception is automatic, the shipboard operator must set up the receiver properly at the start of the voyage or after the equipment has been shut down.

1. Select the appropriate broadcast channel. Log onto a land earth station in the ocean region for which needed broadcasts are made.
2. Select the NAVAREA identification code. If traveling near Australia, select the proper coastal area codes.
3. Manually update the ship's position every four hours during the vessel's voyage. Equipment can also be connected to a functional navigation receiver.

Fig. 6-5. SafetyNET setup

Updates regarding the vessel's position are critical. If the terminal does not have your position, it will collect all informational broadcasts, generating reams of unnecessary messages. Most equipment is capable of being connected to one of the global satellite navigation systems such as GPS or GLONASS. Loran C may also be used but the operator must remember to switch to manual imputs if the vessel leaves the loran C coverage area.

INMARSAT A terminals use a directional antenna that should receive heading and speed input either manually or from gyro/log equipment. INMARSAT C terminals use omnidirectional antennas and satellite tracking does not require a directional tracking link. These terminals are also equipped with interface to radionavigation receivers, such as GPS or loran C, for positional data.

VHF and MF/HF Digital Selective Calling (DSC)

The IMO introduced digital selective calling (DSC) on VHF, MF, and HF maritime radios as part of the GMDSS system. DSC is primarily intended to initiate ship-to-ship, ship-to-shore, and shore-to-ship radiotelephone and MF/HF radio telex calls. DSC calls can also be made to individual ships or groups of ships. DSC distress alerts, which consist of a preformatted distress message, are used to initiate emergency communications between other vessels and rescue coordination centers. DSC identifies the vessel by use of a mobile station identifier (MSI). This number is assigned to all DSC equipment by the manufacturer of the radio equipment.

When fully implemented, DSC will eliminate the need for persons on a ship's bridge or on shore to continuously guard radio receivers on voice radio channels, including VHF channel 16 (156.8 MHz) and 2,182 kHz now used for distress, safety, and calling. A listening watch aboard GMDSS-equipped ships is scheduled to end on 2,182 kHz on February 1, 1999. VHF channel 16, although planned for elimination, will likely remain viable for call and distress for years to come.

DSC-equipped VHF and MF/HF radios should be externally connected to a satellite navigation receiver. That connection will ensure that accurate location information is sent to a rescue coordination center if a distress alert is ever transmitted. FCC regulations require that a ship's position be manually entered into the radio every four hours on ships required to carry GMDSS equipment, while that ship is under way (47 CFR 80.1073).

Once SOLAS vessels are allowed to terminate watchkeeping on VHF and MF radiotelephone channels, other vessels are going to need DSC-equipped radios to contact them, particularly in close quarters situations. In the United States, the federal government is considering requiring that VHF, MF, and HF radiotelephone equipment carried on vessels include a DSC capability as a matter of safety. This would include a requirement that all newly manufactured maritime radiotelephones, VHF and MF/HF, have a basic DSC capability. Note: Bridge-to-bridge Channel 13 is still active, and Channel 16 will continue as a distress call frequency.

VHF digital selective calling also has other capabilities beyond those required for the GMDSS. The U.S. Coast Guard uses this system to track vessels in Prince William Sound, Alaska, through the local vessel traffic service. They are considering expanding this to include the Great Lakes and major U.S. ports. Tracking is possible through the "position integration" function, which was intended to aid in search and rescue. The International Maritime Organization is also considering using this system for ship-to-ship identification and tracking. DSC-equipped radios cannot be interrogated and tracked unless that option was included by the manufacturer, and unless the user configures it to allow tracking.

U.S. shore-based radio stations currently exist to support every element of the GMDSS, except for digital selective calling. The United States currently has no A1 or A2 sea areas, but does plan to have an

A2 sea area in place by the full implementation of the GMDSS. MF/HF digital selective calling facilities should be in place in the United States by February or March 1999, and VHF digital selective calling facilities (sea area A1) should be in place by 2002 to 2003.

COSPAS-SARSAT

COSPAS-SARSAT is a system established by participating members in the United States, Russia, Canada, and France. This international satellite system for search and rescue consists of a constellation of satellites in polar orbit and a network of ground receiving stations. The system provides distress alert and location information to appropriate rescue authorities via rescue coordination centers for maritime, aviation, and land users in distress. The system looks for distress alert and location data for 121.5-MHz beacons within the coverage area of COSPAS-SARSAT ground stations, and for 406-MHz beacons activated anywhere in the world.

The first actual use of COSPAS-SARSAT by SAR agencies was in September 1982. A small aircraft crashed in Canada, and through the use of the system, three people were rescued. Since then, the COSPAS-SARSAT system has been used for hundreds of SAR events and has been responsible for the saving of several thousands of lives worldwide. The COSPAS-SARSAT system is divided into three segments, which include radio beacons, the space segment, and the ground segment.

The radio beacon segment includes emergency beacons which are designed to transmit distress signals on 121.5 or 406 MHz. Most 406-MHz beacons also include a 121.5-MHz homing transmitter. Beacons can be activated either manually or automatically by immersion or shock. These beacons transmit signals that are detected by COSPAS-SARSAT polar-orbiting satellites. The signals are relayed by those satellites to COSPAS-SARSAT local user terminals (LUTs), which process the signals to determine the originating beacon's location. COSPAS-SARSAT satellites can store EPIRB messages until within reception range of CES if necessary.

121.5-MHz beacons are probably the most common units in use today, with more than an estimated half million in use worldwide. Transmission characteristics of 121.5-MHz beacons are given in ITU Radio Regulations Appendix 37-A, and are included in ITU Recommendation ITU-R M.690. Most of these units are used aboard aircraft and are required to meet national specifications based on International Civil Aeronautics Organization (ICAO) standards.

The initial ICAO standards were not established with the aim of satellite reception of 121.5-MHz signals. The 121.5-MHz COSPAS-SARSAT system was designed to serve the existing type of beacons, even though system performance would be constrained by their characteristics. Parameters such as system capacity, which is the number of simultaneous transmissions in the field of view of the satellite that can be processed by ground stations, and location accuracy are limited. No information is usually provided about the operator's identity, although a Morse coding of the signal is included in some models; however, this data is not processed by COSPAS-SARSAT local user terminals. The efficiency of 121.5-MHz beacons has been greatly enhanced by the use of satellite detection and Doppler location techniques.

406-MHz beacons are designed to be a new generation of beacons, transmitting at the beginning of the COSPAS-SARSAT project. The 406-MHz units were designed specifically for satellite detection and Doppler location, and provide improved location accuracy and ambiguity resolution, increased system capacity (capability to process a greater number of beacons transmitting simultaneously in field of view of a satellite), global coverage, and unique identification of each beacon. System performance is greatly enhanced both by the improved frequency stability of the 406-MHz units and by operation at a dedicated frequency.

Typical 121.5-MHz Beacon Characteristics
RF Signal
    Transmitted power: 50–100 megawatts peak radiated power
    Transmission life: 48 hours
    Frequency: 121.5 MHz ± 6 kHz
    Polarization: linear

Fig. 6-6. Beacon characteristics

These beacons transmit a 5-watt RF burst of approximately 0.5 second's duration every 50 seconds. The carrier frequency is very stable and the pulse is phase-modulated with a digital message. Frequency stability assures accurate location, while the high peak power increases the probability of detection. The low duty cycle provides a multiple-access capability of more than ninety beacons simultaneously operating in view of a polar orbiting satellite and low mean power consumption.

An important feature of 406-MHz emergency beacons is the addition of a digitally encoded message, which provides such information as the country of origin and the identification of the vessel or aircraft in distress and, optionally, position data from onboard navigation equipment. An auxiliary transmitter (homing transmitter) can be included in the 406-MHz beacon to enable suitably equipped SAR forces to home in on the distress beacon.

The COSPAS-SARSAT specifications for 406-MHz beacons and local user terminals (LUTs) were amended in 1995 to provide for optionally encoding position information in the transmitted message. At its seventeenth session, the COSPAS-SARSAT Council also approved amendments to the COSPAS-SARSAT type approval standard so that development and type approval of such beacons could be initiated prior to 1997.

The optional new coding schemes will be available to all user categories, including maritime EPIRBs, aviation, and land users. However, the adoption of new protocols does not affect the use of existing 406-MHz beacons, in particular the 406-MHz EPIRBs used in accordance with the IMO's GMDSS requirements.

New 406-MHz beacons encoded with the location protocols will become available by the time GMDSS requirements must be met. A number of prototypes of the new beacons with location protocols, which include integral receivers for global navigation satellite systems, are currently undergoing type approval testing, or are being used for trials with the 406-MHz COSPAS-SARSAT system and 406-MHz GeoSAR aircraft radar system.

Each EPIRB unit must be installed aboard the vessel in an easily accessible position, must be ready to be manually released, and must be capable of being carried on board a survival craft by one person. It must be mounted so it can float free from a depth of 4 meters in case of the vessel sinking and must be capable of automatic activation when afloat or be capable of manual activation. It must operate for a minimum of 48 hours once activated. Lithium battery expiration date must be clearly shown on the outer case.

The units must be tested on a monthly basis using a self-test mode control. Test signals broadcast a limited range using an internal artificial antenna. The signals can be heard on any radio capable of receiving a 100-MHz signal (i.e., FM standard broadcast radio).

EPIRBs are classified according to their functional capabilities, frequency broadcasts, and activation method. Specific classes are designated for certain types of vessels according to their areas of operation. Mariners should note that not all EPIRBs are suitable under GMDSS.

The space segment consists of the nominal system configuration, which is composed of four satellites. The United States provides two NOAA meteorological satellites for SARSAT (which stands for search and rescue satellite-aided tracking). These satellites are placed in

Type	Frequencies	Capabilities
Class A	121.5 and 243.0 MHz	Automatic activation Satellite/Aircraft detection Free floating Limited area of transmission
Class B	121.5 and 243.0 MHz	Manually activated Satellite/Aircraft detection Free floating Limited area of transmission
Class C	VHF Channel 15/16	Manually activated Vessel detection only
Class S	121.5 and 243.0 MHz	Manually activated Satellite/Aircraft detection Free floating Limited area of transmission Designed for survival craft
Category 1	121.5 and 400 MHz	**GMDSS approved** Automatic activation Satellite/Aircraft detection Free floating

Fig. 6-7. EPIRB classifications

sun-synchronous, near-polar orbits at an approximate altitude of 850 kilometers, and are equipped with SAR instrumentation at 121.5 MHz and 406 MHz supplied by Canada and France.

The remaining two satellites are provided by Russia for COSPAS (cosmicheskaya systyema poiska avariynyich sudov—space system for the search of distressed vessels). These satellites are placed in near-polar orbits at 1,000-km altitude and equipped with SAR instrumentation at 121.5 MHz and 406 MHz. The total satellite system is described in figure 6-8.

Each satellite makes a complete orbit of the earth around the poles in slightly more than 100 minutes, traveling at an average velocity of 7 km per second. The satellite maintains a footprint coverage of the earth that is more than 4,000 km wide as it orbits the globe. When viewed from the earth, the satellite crosses the sky in approximately 15 minutes, depending on the maximum elevation angle of the pass from the position of the observer.

COSPAS-SARSAT	Spacecraft	Launch Date	Status	Payload
COSPAS-4	Nadezhda-1	July 1989	In operation	(see note 1)
COSPAS-6	Nadezhda-3	March 1991	In operation	
COSPAS-7	Nadezhda-4	July 1994	In operation	(see note 2)
COSPAS-8	Nadezhda-5	As required	In operation	
SARSAT-2	NOAA-9	December 1984	In operation	(see note 2)
SARSAT-3	NOAA-10	September 1986	In operation	(see note 2)
SARSAT-4	NOAA-11	September 1988	In operation	
SARSAT-6	NOAA-14	December 1994	In operation	(see note 2)
SARSAT-7	NOAA-K	July 1998	In operation	

Notes:
   (1) Limited availability in Southern Hemisphere due to unstable orientation
   (2) 406-MHz on-board processor (SARP) not operational
Nominal System: 4-satellite constellation in polar orbit

Fig. 6-8. COSPAS-SARSAT spacecraft availability

The ground segment is composed of local user terminals and mission control centers (MCCs). The LUT processes relayed distress signals to provide a beacon location, then transmits alert messages to its associated MCC. Mission control center functions include the validation and exchange of alert data and system (technical) information, both within the COSPAS-SARSAT system and with the SAR networks. MCCs are established in most of the countries that have LUTs. Specifically, they collect distress alert data from LUTs and other MCCs, then geographically sort and redistribute them to appropriate SAR authorities.

The configuration and capabilities of each local user terminal (LUT) may vary to meet the specific requirements of the participating countries. The COSPAS and SARSAT spacecraft downlink signal formats ensure interoperability between the various spacecraft and all LUTs meeting COSPAS-SARSAT specifications. For the 121.5-MHz signals, each transmission is detected and the Doppler information calculated. A beacon position is then determined using these data.

Processing of 2,400-BPS data (i.e., those generated from 406-MHz transmissions) is relatively straightforward since the Doppler frequency is measured and time-tagged on board the spacecraft. All 406-MHz data received from the satellite memory on each pass can be processed within a few minutes of pass completion.

To improve location accuracy, a correction of the satellite ephemeris (orbital pattern) is produced each time the LUT receives a satellite signal. The downlink carrier is monitored to provide a Doppler signal using the LUT location as a reference, or highly stable 406-MHz calibration beacons at accurately known locations are used to update the ephemeris data. The second method only applies to LUTs processing 406-MHz data.

LUT operators are expected to provide the SAR community with reliable alert and location data, without restriction on use and distribution. The COSPAS-SARSAT parties providing and operating the space segment supply LUT operators with system data required to operate their LUT. To ensure that data provided by a LUT are reliable and can be used by the SAR community on an operational basis, COSPAS-SARSAT has developed LUT performance specifications (document C/S T.002) and LUT commissioning procedures (document C/S T.005). LUT operators provide regular reports on their LUT operation for review during COSPAS-SARSAT meetings.

Mission control centers have been set up in most countries operating at least one LUT. The main functions of an MCC are to collect, store, and sort the data from LUTs and other MCCs, to provide data exchange within the COSPAS-SARSAT system, and to distribute alert and location data to associated regional rescue coordination centers. Most of the data falls into two general categories: alert data and system information.

Alert data is the generic term for COSPAS-SARSAT 406-MHz and 121.5-MHz data received from distress beacons. For 406-MHz beacons, alert data contains the beacon's location and coded data. System data is used to keep the COSPAS-SARSAT system operating at peak effectiveness and to provide users with accurate and timely alert data. It consists of satellite ephemeris and time calibration data that are used to determine beacon locations, the current status of the space and ground segments, and coordination messages required to operate the COSPAS-SARSAT system.

All MCCs in the system are interconnected through appropriate networks for the distribution of system information and alert data. To ensure data distribution, reliability, and integrity, COSPAS-SARSAT has developed MCC performance specifications (document C/S A.005) and MCC commissioning procedures (document C/S A.006). Regular reports on MCC operations are provided by MCC operators annually. Worldwide exercises are performed from time to time to check the operational status and performance of all LUTs and MCCs and to review data exchange procedures.

COSPAS-SARSAT LUTs and MCCs are being modified to accommodate the new location protocols; the COSPAS-SARSAT Council at its seventeenth session in October 1996 decided that the

COSPAS-SARSAT ground segment would start processing the new location protocols in a preoperational mode starting January 1, 1997.

Further modifications to the COSPAS-SARSAT MCCs will be necessary before implementing the new alert data distribution procedures designed to enhance the processing of both low earth orbit search and rescue (LEOSAR) and GEOSAR alerts, which were agreed upon at the October 1996 session of the council. These new procedures were phased into the COSPAS-SARSAT MCC network in early 1998.

Search and Rescue Transponder (SART)

A GMDSS search and rescue transponder (SART) is a device designed to transmit locating signals which can be picked up by 3-cm, X band, 9-gHz marine radars. The signal emitted from the transponder appears as a series of equally spaced dots radiating outward from the vessel's position on the radar display on a line of bearing toward the transponder unit. SARTs are the primary method for providing locating signals within the immediate area of a vessel in distress, on scene.

GMDSS installation on ships includes one or more SARTs. The detection range between these devices and ships, depending on the height of the ship's radar mast and the height of the SART, is required to be at least 5 miles and is normally less than about 10 miles, based on the transponder's antenna being at least 1 meter off the sea surface and clear of obstructions. An aircraft at about 3,000 feet, using 3-cm radar, should be able to trigger the unit at around 40 miles.

SART units are waterproof, can be carried off the vessel in distress into survival craft, and are manually activated and deactivated. Units are equipped with a visual and audible indicator to let personnel using them know that they are functioning and that they have been triggered, or interrogated by a marine radar. The units are designed to float but work best when elevated above the surface of the water. For this reason SARTs are capable of being mounted on extension poles. SARTs will best respond to 3 cm interrogation when the unit is supported vertically above the water. They should hold their watertight integrity to a depth of 10 meters for at least 5 minutes and should sustain a drop of 20 meters without damage.

The units have internal batteries which must last for a minimum of 96 hours in standby mode and 8 hours in transponder mode. SART units should be tested regularly to ensure they are working properly. They are labeled to indicate battery date and activation instructions.

Survival Craft VHF

GMDSS-required survival craft transceivers (SCT) are small portable waterproof units designed for use after a vessel has been abandoned and personnel are afloat in survival craft. These units are regular VHF transceivers capable of broadcasting on VHF Channel 16 (156.8 MHz) and one additional channel, usually Channel 6. This equipment is designed for communications between survival craft and rescue units on scene and between survival craft and vessels in distress.

SCTs are not significantly different from a portable VHF unit except that they have been designed to be shock-resistant and waterproof. Shock resistant means that they can withstand hitting a hard surface after being dropped from a height of at least 1 meter. To be waterproof they must maintain watertight integrity to a depth of at least 1 meter for a period of at least 5 minutes. In addition to Channel 16, these units are required to operate with one additional communications channel which is normally VHF Channel 6 (156.3 MHz). Channel 6 is the designated on-scene search and rescue frequency. In addition, some manufacturers equip these units with additional working frequencies for use aboard ship. All frequencies must comply with those allotted in the VHF marine band.

Each unit has a built-in nonrechargeable lithium battery for application under GMDSS requirements. Many units are also equipped with rechargeable nickel-cadmium batteries for other applications. A GMDSS-approved survival craft transceiver must have sufficient battery power to operate a minimum of 8 hours at the unit's highest RF power output. It must broadcast with a minimum of 0.25 watts (250 Mw). The unit must also have a built-in extended vertically polarized antenna.

GMDSS requirements dictate that at least three survival craft transceivers must be carried on every passenger ship regardless of size, and on cargo ships of 500 gross tons and above. For cargo ships between 300 and 500 gross tons, two units are required.

These units must be placed in locations aboard a vessel where they can be rapidly and easily put into any survival craft. They can also be installed in survival craft. It should be noted, however, that survival craft are generally of the rigid type such as lifeboats, rather than life rafts. Most vessels' masters will issue the SCT to designated officers responsible for survival craft duties. These units must be tested annually (instructions are printed clearly on the front of the units) and are generally brightly colored and and are equipped with wrist straps and reflective tape.

MF/HF Narrowband Direct Printing (NBDP)

The GMDSS includes HF radiotelephone and narrowband direct printing (NBDP) radio telex equipment. NBDP equipment such as SITOR provides direct links to information services worldwide on designated HF narrowband direct printing channels.

To meet these GMDSS requirements, many nations including the United States, under authority of the U.S. Coast Guard, have begun to improve high-frequency (HF) ship-to-shore radio safety services from their communication stations to the maritime community. These improvements include DSC as well as narrowband direct printing broadcasts.

MF/HF SSB

Single sideband will continue to be utilized in GMDSS for primary and secondary communications in both radiotelephony and radio telex modes. The monitoring requirements will change once DSC is required.

Band	Radiotelephone	DSC	Radiotelex
MF	2,182 kHz	2,187.5 kHz	2,174.5 kHz
HF	4,125 kHz	4,207.5 kHz	4,177.5 kHz
HF	6,215 kHz	6,312.0 kHz	6,268.0 kHz
HF	8,291 kHz	8,414.5 kHz	8,376.5 kHz
HF	12,290 kHz	12,577.0 kHz	12,520.0 kHz
HF	16,420 kHz	16,804.5 kHz	16,695.0 kHz

Fig. 6-9. MF/HF distress communication frequencies

MARITIME SAFETY INFORMATION

GMDSS vessels are required to copy maritime safety information (MSI) at all times while under way. If a ship sails outside of a NAVTEX coverage area and is within the coverage of an INMARSAT satellite, an INMARSAT C terminal must be used to receive SafetyNET broadcasts. The SafetyNET system can provide an automated service in coastal waters where it may not be feasible to establish the NAVTEX service or where shipping density is too low to warrant its implementation.

The requirement to receive MSI may also be met on ships where HF NBDP is available and the vessel is suitably fitted with equipment to receive these broadcasts.

The frequency 4,209.6 kHz is used to promulgate NAVTEX-style messages internationally. Due to good coverage in its coastal confluence zones, the United States will not use 4,209.5 kHz for this purpose.

Band	Frequency
HF 4 MHz	4,209.6 kHz (non-U.S.)
HF 4 MHz	4,210.0 kHz
HF 6 MHz	6,314.0 kHz
HF 8 MHz	8,416.5 kHz
HF 12 MHz	12,579.0 kHz
HF 16 MHz	16,806.5 kHz
HF 19 MHz	19,680.5 kHz
HF 22 MHz	22,376.0 kHz
HF 26 MHz	26,100.5 kHz

Fig. 6-10. MSI HF/NBDP frequencies

GMDSS IMPLEMENTATION DATES

The GMDSS regulations apply to cargo ships of 300 gross tons and over on international voyages or in the open sea, and to passenger ships regardless of size carrying more than twelve passengers when traveling on international voyages or in the open sea. These ships required to comply with GMDSS regulations are termed compulsory ships. The following is a summary of the implementation dates for the GMDSS in the United States.

February 1, 1992: GMDSS provisions of SOLAS Convention enter into force. Ships may begin voluntarily fitting GMDSS equipment. Until the Telecommunications Act of 1996 is amended, carriage of the current distress and safety radio equipment remains mandatory for U.S. ships. 47 CFR 80.1065(b)(5).

February 1, 1992: New passenger ships and new cargo ships of 500 gross tons and over constructed on or after this date must carry at least two 9-GHz radar transponders (one on each side of the ship) and at least three two-way VHF radiotelephones for use in survival craft. New cargo ships of 300 to 500 gross tons constructed on or after this date must carry at least one 9-GHz radar transponder and at least two two-way VHF radiotelephones. 47 CFR 80.1095.

August 1, 1993: All compulsory ships are required to carry a NAVTEX receiver and a 406-MHz EPIRB. Ships will no longer be required to carry a Class S EPIRB for survival crafts after equipping with the 406-MHz EPIRB. 47 CFR 80.1065(b)(1) and SOLAS Convention, Resolution 4.

February 1, 1995: New compulsory ships constructed on or after this date must comply with all GMDSS requirements. 47 CFR 80.1065(b)(3).

February 1, 1995: All passenger ships and cargo ships of 500 tons gross tonnage must carry at least two 9-GHz radar transponders (one on each side of the ship) and at least three two-way VHF radiotelephones for use in survival craft. All cargo ships of 300 to 500 gross tons must carry at least one 9-GHz radar transponder and at least two two-way VHF radiotelephones. 47 CFR 80.1095.

February 8, 1996: The Telecommunications Act of 1996 was signed into law, eliminating the radiotelegraph carriage requirement for GMDSS vessels.

February 1, 1999: All compulsory ships must meet all GMDSS requirements. 47 CFR 80.1065(b)(4).

OPERATIONS

GMDSS vessels are required to have equipment capable of transmitting ship-to-shore distress alerts by at least two separate and independent systems. Distress alerts identify the vessel in distress and its position, and may include information regarding the nature of the distress, the type of assistance required, the course and speed of the vessel, and the time this information was transmitted. Ship-to-ship and ship-to-shore distress alerts are not used to alert other ships of navigational hazards or bad weather.

When a vessel is under way on the high seas, it must be able to receive shore-to-ship distress alerts, communicate with search and rescue units, communicate at the scene, transmit/receive locating signals, transmit/receive maritime safety information, transmit/receive bridge-to-bridge communications, maintain general communications with shore-based facilities, transmit/receive distress alerts

1. Receive shore-to-ship distress alerts
2. Transmit and receive search and rescue coordinating communications
3. Transmit and receive on-scene communications
4. Transmit and receive locating signals
5. Transmit and receive maritime safety information
6. Transmit and receive bridge-to-bridge communication
7. Transmit and receive general communications with shore-based facilities
8. Transmit and receive distress alerts by two separate, independent means using different radio communication services

Fig. 6-11. GMDSS operational functions

by two separate and independent means and transmit/receive ship-to-ship distress alerts.

The GMDSS radio operator is responsible for radio communications during distress incidents. He or she is also responsible for ensuring that GMDSS watches are properly maintained, that DSC equipment is properly programmed with appropriate guard channels, and that the vessel's position is properly entered into DSC equipment.

As mentioned in the previous chapter, voice communications are classified as distress traffic, urgency traffic, and safety traffic. Distress traffic includes all communications relating to a vessel in distress that requires immediate assistance. It also includes communications on scene and search and rescue communications. It has the highest priority and is recognized by the prefix "Mayday."

Urgency traffic is the second highest priority in communication. It is utilized when the safety of a vessel or a person is threatened. In voice radiotelephone this type of traffic is prefixed by "Pan pan."

Safety traffic is the third priority of communications and the most frequently used. It indicates important safety information such as vessel traffic, navigational dangers, and other circumstances impacting the safe navigation of vessels. Important weather information is also broadcast as part of safety traffic. In voice R/T transmission, use the prefix "securité."

In VHF or single-sideband radiotelephone, the above prefixes are used when dealing with important messages not considered routine traffic. Once GMDSS is fully instituted, the requirement to monitor the international calling and distress frequencies, for both types of systems, will be covered by the use of digital selective calling. The most critical element of this system is distress traffic. These communications are considered emergency traffic, and there are some specific procedures associated with the transmission of a distress message.

To begin with, GMDSS provides operating guidance for vessel masters facing a distress situation. These guidelines must be taken into account when deciding whether it is necessary to initiate distress communications.

Remember that the EPIRB should float free and activate automatically if the vessel sinks, and if it is taken into a survival craft, it will not function well unless it is tethered into the ocean since proper grounding is required. Also keep in mind that if necessary a vessel should use any appropriate means to alert another vessel and that GMDSS is not intended to preclude the use of any and all available means of distress alerting.

When transmitting a distress alert, make sure your vessel is identified and that an accurate position is transmitted. Try to in-

1. Vessel is sinking or is to be abandoned.
   a. Transmit distress call by VHF, medium-frequency or high-frequency SSB, digital selective calling (DSC), or INMARSAT (if situation and time permit).
   b. Embark in survival craft with VHF, search and rescue transponder (SART), and emergency position-indicating radio beacon (EPIRB).
   c. Turn on SART and EPIRB and leave units on transmitting mode.
2. Vessel is in danger and immediate help is needed.
   a. Transmit distress call by VHF, medium-frequency or high-frequency SSB, DSC, or INMARSAT.
   b. Await response.
   c. Once response is received, communicate on VHF, MF/HF SSB, or INMARSAT to regional coordination center and other vessels.
   d. If no response is received, turn on EPIRB and SART manually on board your vessel.
3. A potential problem exists but the vessel is not in imminent danger of sinking.
   a. Notify regional coordination center by VHF, MF/HF SSB, DSC, or INMARSAT.
   b. If no response is received immediately, continue trying to make contact.
   c. Once response is received, communicate on VHF, MF/HF SSB, or INMARSAT to regional coordination center and other vessels.

Fig. 6-12. GMDSS procedures

clude as much additional information as required, such as the type of distress and assistance required, vessel type and cargo, vessel course and speed, and any other key information. Once the information is transmitted, it should be relayed to a regional rescue coordination center (RCC) for appropriate action. It may also be picked up by other vessels that can respond to your emergency. The rescue coordination center will contact vessels in the area as well as search and rescue agencies and will coordinate rendering assistance.

If you become aware of a vessel in distress, you may be required to initiate and transmit a distress relay message. This may occur when a vessel in distress is not in a position to transmit its own alert or when the master of a vessel not in distress determines that further assistance is needed. If a vessel initiates a distress relay for another vessel, it must indicate that it is not the one in distress.

Once the distress message is sent, it should be acknowledged by any station receiving it. If a message is sent via INMARSAT, it will be acknowledged by a regional RCC.

If a person aboard a vessel receives a distress alert, that person must inform the master regarding the contents of the distress alert message as soon as possible. It will be the responsibility of the master in coordination with the regional RCC, if possible, to render any assistance.

A vessel receiving a digital selective calling distress alert should wait a few minutes before responding on follow-on communications frequencies to allow the signal to be received and acknowledged by a coast station. If the vessel does not hear an acknowledgment, and informs the vessel in distress that it has received the message, it should try to inform a regional RCC through a coastal station or by using INMARSAT as soon as possible. Any vessel receiving a DSC distress alert on medium-frequency or high-frequency SSB should try to relay the information, if it is not acknowledged by a coast station, within 3 to 5 minutes. DSC distress alerts on medium frequency will be broadcast on 2,187.5 kHz. Acknowledgment of receipt of the alert should be made on 2,182 kHz. If acknowledgment of the distress alert is unsuccessful on 2,182 kHz, the acknowledgment should be tried with a DSC call on 2,187.5 kHz.

A vessel receiving a DSC distress alert on VHF Channel 70 (156.525 MHz) should acknowledge receipt of the alert, if it is not acknowledged by a coast station, within 3 to 5 minutes. Acknowledgment is made on follow-on communication VHF Channel 16 (156.8 MHz) and, like SSB, if the acknowledgment is not received it can be attempted with DSC on Channel 70. When the distress traffic is heard, all stations are prohibited from utilizing the frequencies for other traffic upon the RCC directive "Silence." This does not preclude providing other distress or safety information not related to the initial distress situation. A vessel listening to distress traffic may continue normal traffic when it can be determined that their traffic does not interfere with the distress communications. Once the situation has been resolved, the shore station coordinating search and rescue efforts uses the term *"Silence fini"* (pronounced "Seelonce feenee").

If a vessel is in a position to render aid, the master must now deal with on-scene communications. The first task a vessel providing assistance must face is to accurately locate the vessel. Search and rescue transponders and visual identification will be critical. Extra look-outs should be posted and once the vessel is located, this information should be relayed immediately to the RCC. You should also provide any information regarding the circumstances that have been found, as well as your exact location, so the RCC can assist other vessels in reaching your location if their assistance is necessary. The RCC may also employ aircraft that will extend their search parameters looking for EPIRB signals and using marine 3-cm radar.

Once your vessel is on scene, you should try to contact the vessel in distress or its survival craft using VHF Channel 16. Control of all communications at the scene is the responsibility of any unit coordinating the search and rescue operations—which may be your vessel if the RCC designates you. As part of the procedure to render assistance, your GMDSS radio operators should be prepared to handle traffic on all communications equipment and maintain a constant radio watch until the situation has been cleared. NBDP equipment can also be used for on-scene communications, but must be utilized in the FEC mode.

Short-range communications as mentioned can be conducted on VHF Channel 16 and also on 2,182 kHz MF. The coordinating SAR unit will designate any working frequencies on which a continuous watch must be maintained.

GMDSS is a system that is only to be utilized in case of emergency, and vessel masters and equipment operators should not become complacent about the system or its associated equipment. Regular testing of equipment is required. Training and the proficient use of the equipment is critical. Commercial companies should avail themselves of every opportunity to ensure that their personnel are well trained and receive frequent refresher training in many of the simulation programs run worldwide.

One of the biggest problems that has been encountered in the initial stages of GMDSS is the large number of false alerts being produced by EPIRBs or through INMARSAT and DSC. This may be attributable to curiosity by unknowing mariners. GMDSS radio operators should make every effort and institute any appropriate procedures to ensure that unintended alerts are not transmitted. If a false alert is sent, the operator should make every effort to cancel the alert immediately and let all stations know that the alert was unintended. Probably the best method a vessel can use to disclose a false alert is through INMARSAT A. Simply call the CES and request connection to an RCC. Upon contact with the RCC identify your vessel and mobile marine station identifier (MMSI) and explain the circumstances of the false alert.

The automated mutual assistance vessel rescue system (AMVER) is the principal system utilized throughout the world for rendering aid to vessels in distress through coordinated international efforts. The system is operated by the U.S. Coast Guard and utilizes a computerized database tracking more than fifteen thousand voyages annually and more than twenty-five hundred vessels daily. AMVER, a

Fig. 6-13. GMDSS station. Photograph by Forlivesi Photography.

voluntary program endorsed by the IMO, set the standard that GMDSS will follow. There are many agencies worldwide like AMVER that already operate or will operate coast stations and rescue coordination centers as part of GMDSS. All these efforts are dedicated to the safety of life at sea and the protection of property and the environment. Every person who follows the profession of the sea should embrace and thoroughly understand how GMDSS works.

In the United States GMDSS operators are required to have completed a 70-hour course of study with proficiency testing. Although a comprehensive understanding will exist at course completion, time can erase skills. When joining a vessel, and if assigned GMDSS duties, do not wait to familiarize yourself with the equipment and proper procedures. Do not wait until your life or another seaman's life is at stake to "refresh" your memory.

GMDSS has changed the face of emergencies at sea. In the past, if your vessel became involved in a situation that required abandoning ship, the survivors were relegated to waiting to see if their departing message, emergency radio broadcasts, or EPIRB transmissions were received. In a way, that hasn't changed, yet by a coordinated worldwide effort, it has.

Upon recognition of an emergency either VHF/MF/HF or INMARSAT C distress alerts can be made by merely pushing two buttons simultaneously or by holding one down for a prescribed number of seconds. In moments, vessels and RCCs worldwide are alerted to your situation and you may expect calls on follow-on frequencies. If your situation deteriorates to abandon ship, EPIRBs, SARTs, and SCT are brought along with you to the survival craft. Once deployed after safely away from the sinking ship, these devices will be relaying your ship's identifier via satellites to RCCs. Vessels navigating nearby may be receiving SART information about your location, and the SCT may receive a call from a search and rescue vessel.

How long might a distressed crew have to wait for rescue? There is no definitive expectation, but if navigating in normal shipping lanes, it is fair to say you will be aware of rescue efforts within twenty-four hours. The GMDSS international cooperation can save many lives, but only if the mariners accept the need to know how to use it effectively!

CHAPTER 7

HYDROSONIC NAVIGATION SYSTEMS

GENERAL

The development of radionavigation systems has contributed to the evolution of electronic systems that are designed to determine water depth and vessel speed. Based on a principle similar to radio, the equipment associated with these systems is designed to generate sound waves that are directed through the water medium and are reflected off the seabed to provide the required information. For this reason they are referred to as hydrosonic systems. Hydrosonic systems include two general classifications of equipment—depth sounders and speed logs.

Depth sounders, also referred to as echo sounders or fathometers, are specifically designed to generate sonic pulses that are directed toward the ocean floor. The system then measures the amount of time it takes for the echo to be received and, based on an average velocity of sound through water, calculates depth. The broader term for this type of equipment is "depth sounder" because modern equipment can provide indications in fathoms, meters, or feet. Speed logs utilize similar hydrosonic signals to determine speed over the ground or through the water.

DEPTH SOUNDERS

All depth sounding, echo sounding, and fathometer systems, whether they are indicating or recording, work on the principle of producing short pulses of sound vibrations. These pulses are transmitted nearly vertically down to the ocean floor, where they echo back toward the surface. When the pulses are received by the ship's depth sounder, it calculates the difference in time between transmission and reception. This is based on the principle that sound travels at a near-constant speed of 4,800 feet per second, 800 fathoms per seconds, or 1,500 meters per second, or about four and a half times sound's speed through air.

The depth sounder measures the time interval between the signal transmission and echo return. This principle is very similar to that of radar. The time interval divided by two, when translated to distance, is the depth of water below the ship's keel. For example, if the elapsed time period between a generated signal and its return

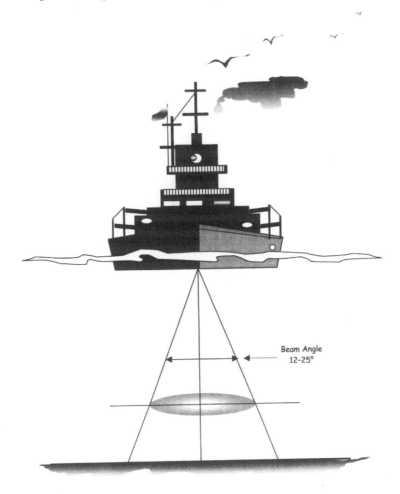

Beam Angle
12-25°

Fig. 7-1. Sonic wave. Drawing by Van Trong Nguyen.

echo is 1 second, the depth of water would be approximately 2,400 feet, 400 fathoms, or 750 meters.

The operator needs to remember that the depth sounder indicates the depth of the water below the keel, which is in the same approximate plane as the transducer, rather than the actual depth of the water. Adding the vessel's draft to the reading produces the approximate depth of the water.

Sound vibrations travel in a beam pattern that has an angle of about 12 to 25 degrees in width, perpendicular to the vessel's bottom. This beam pattern travels downward, with the wave front striking the ocean bottom, where the signals are reflected back. This is called specular reflection. When the waves reflect back at various angles, diffuse reflection occurs. The bottom topography is usually not per-

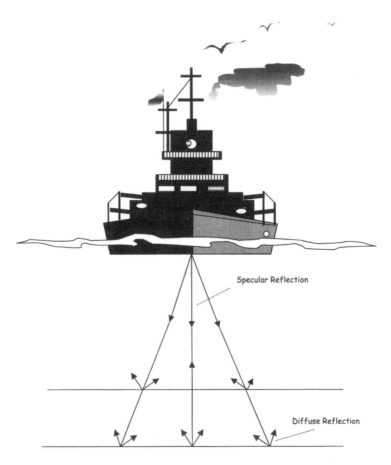

Fig. 7-2. Depth sounder waves. Drawing by Van Trong Nguyen.

fectly flat, thus signal return varies with the contours. It is important to understand that the depth sounder is dependent on both specular and diffuse reflection of a signal to function properly. It is imperative to keep this in mind when a vessel is rolling and signals are returning at different angles at different times.

The depth sounder incorporates some general corrections for random variations of the speed of sound through water. Although the system can make approximate corrections for these variations, sound waves will move faster than the built-in speed of calibration for the depth sounder. This is to provide a small margin of safety for the operator, who should keep in mind that the normal or calculated variation between the actual depth of water and the indicated depth will tend to appear shallower than the actual depth. This variation is very small and the calibration can be easily compromised when the water is very saline or extremely warm, or when the vessel is in brackish or fresh water.

Like radio waves in the atmosphere, density differences in the ocean cause the depth sounder signal to be absorbed, scattered, or reflected. The effects of the different densities of the water cause the signal to be attenuated. This effect occurs not only on the transmitted signal but also on the returning signal. The depth sounder can

Fig. 7-3. Indicating/recording echo sounder units.
Photographs by Forlivesi Photography.

compensate for this attenuated signal by utilizing a swept gain circuit. This essentially increases the amplification of the signal at a rate dependent upon the amount of time the signal takes to return. The further the signal travels, the more it is absorbed. This absorption can be decreased by lowering the frequency of the signal. Depth sounder signal frequencies vary from about 55 kHz for shallow depth to about 10 kHz for greater depths. Since the signals are above the audible range they are classified as ultrasonic. This is done specifically so the transducer will not be confused by any noise being generated by the vessel.

Most depth sounders have a range of between 1.5 and 4,500 feet. They emit between 10 to 600 sound pulses per minute, depending on the depth.

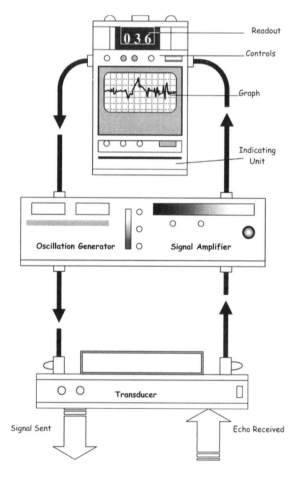

Fig. 7-4. Echo sounder components. Drawing by Van Trong Nguyen.

System Components

Most depth sounding systems are made up of the same basic components. This includes an indicator unit, which provides the depth indication; an oscillator, which creates the electrical signal at the desired frequency; and a transducer, which converts the electrical signal into ultrasonic vibrations for transmission. The transducer also converts the returning echo back into an electrical signal, which then passes to an amplifier. The amplifier boosts the signal to a usable level, where it can be read on the indicator or on a recording graph. The indicator unit is essentially the controlling element of the system, coordinating the transmission and reception of signals. It also controls the timing and the frequency of the signals.

There are two types of transducers used in commercial application today. The first is the electrostrictive type, which functions by converting the electrical signals to sound vibrations by passing the current through two plates that sandwich a nonconductive material. The electrically induced magnetic field causes the plates to vibrate, thus creating the sound vibrations. The second type of transducer is the magnetostrictive type. This uses a form of electromagnetics, creating vibrations in a diaphragm and thus producing the ultrasonic signal. Most transducers are installed in special hull openings and are in direct contact with the water. The operator should be aware of where the transducer is located to prevent damage to the unit when dry-docking, hull blasting, or hull painting, as well as for proper interpretation of data from the unit. The face of the transducer should not be sanded or painted in any way. Refer to the specific unit's owner's manual for proper maintenance and care of the transducer face.

Operation

The two types of depth sounder are the indicating depth sounder and the recording depth sounder. The indicating depth sounder provides some form of visual representation of depth using one of a variety of methods of presenting information. These include a rotating neon light, a digital readout, or a cathode ray tube presentation. Most indicating depth sounders are capable of indicating depth in fathoms, feet, or meters.

Recording depth sounders produce a graphic record of depth against a time base. The recording unit has special graph paper that moves over the top of a metal plate or desk. When an electrical current signal is sent for transmission, a stylus conducts an electric current through the paper to the metal desk. The electrical charge burns a nonconductive coating off the special paper, leaving a trace on the graph. When the signal returns, the stylus once again passes an

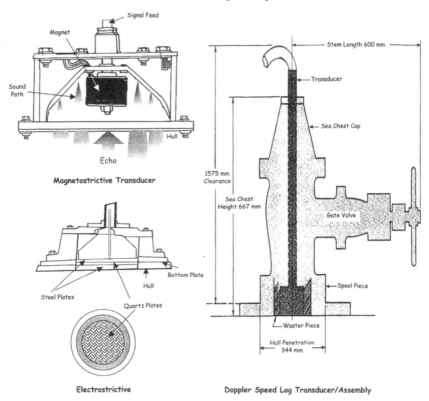

Fig. 7-5. Transducer types/assemblies. Drawing by Van Trong Nguyen; Doppler courtesy Litton/Sperry Marine Systems.

electrical charge through the paper to the metal desk, leaving a second trace on the graph. By properly reading the graph's preprinted scale, the operator has an indication of depth below keel.

Depending on the way the signal is heard upon its return, the presentation can show the bottom characteristics to the trained eye. A clear dark line indicates a hard bottom and a wider less distinct line is a soft bottom. When the bottom is very soft, the unit may actually appear to give several depth readings, called multiple traces. This is due to echoes returning not only from the bottom surface but from hard levels in the subbottom. Operators should use the shallower reading when multiple traces exist since the prudent choice in navigation would be to be conservative in "best-guessing" electronic equipment.

It is essential that the user select the same depth soundings on the depth sounder as the navigational chart in use. This process will

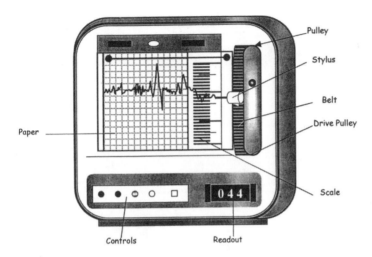

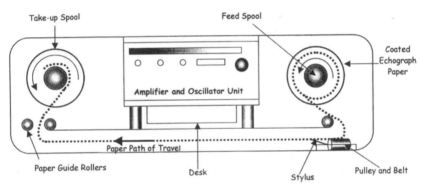

Fig. 7-6. Paper path in recording echo sounder display unit.
Drawing by Van Trong Nguyen.

alleviate simple errors of conversion between different types of soundings and potentially dangerous navigation. This also ensures that the signal timing and frequency are properly set for the appropriate depth, thereby allowing the system to function properly and efficiently. The depth information recorded on the graph paper of a recording fathometer will usually display several scales. Be sure to read the scale that is indicated on the unit's selector switch. The trace is essentially a profile of the seabed along the course traveled by the ship. Incorrect scale settings can result in additional tracings on the graph that appear as overamplified signals in shallow depths or false echoes from echoes that have bounced off the ship's bottom.

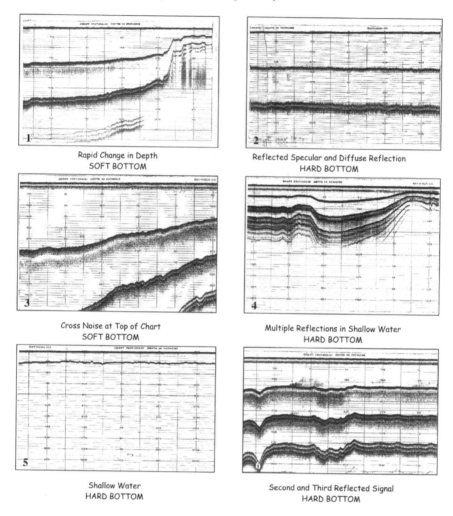

Fig. 7-7. Echographs.
Courtesy of the State University of New York Maritime College.

Most depth sounders have manual gain. If turned up too high the unit will pick up noise from vibrations created by the vessel's movement through the water. The type of sea bottom will have the greatest effect on the amount of gain required to obtain a depth reading. The harder the bottom, the less the amount of gain that will be required.

Different temperatures and varying water densities caused by salinity content can also effect the proper functioning of the depth sounding system. Colder, denser water will permit the signal to travel faster, presenting a depth indication that is shallower than the real water depth. Warmer water will slow the passage of the signal and may compromise your safety limits by indicating a greater depth of water than may actually be present. Depth indications may also be compromised when operating in harbors or rivers where the water is brackish or fresh. The user should keep these factors in mind when the vessel encounters extreme water temperatures and salinity changes other than those of normal seawater.

Colder or denser layers may also return the signal before it reaches the bottom. This thermocline or deep scattering layer can actually give an indication of water depth far less than is the case, and a dual trace may appear on a graph. This, however, does not usually compromise the vessel's safety because it indicates a shallower depth than is actually present. The easiest way to determine whether you are getting echoes off a thermocline is to look at the trace on a graph, which will most likely appear continuous and at a relatively constant depth, even when charts indicate otherwise. This is common in water depth of over 100 to 200 fathoms. Even in areas where the water is very deep, the operator may receive indications around 200 fathoms during the day and even less at night, as the sun's heating of the seawater changes.

Most modern digital indicator units allow the operator to program the vessel's draft into the depth sounder operation. This means that the digital readout indicating depth does not require the addition of vessel's draft. The user must always be aware of whether this adjusted depth-reading information feature is functioning or not. If the user thinks the unit is displaying depth below the keel, but the unit is really displaying corrected depth, the incorrect interpretation could lead to a grounding casualty.

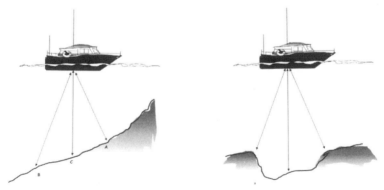

Fig. 7-8. Topographic signal errors list.
Drawings by Van Trong Nguyen.

Each indicating and recording unit has specific methods of operation established by the manufacturer. The operator must consult the manual for that unit to determine proper operation.

BATHYMETRIC NAVIGATION

The easiest method of navigating with a depth sounder is the simple comparison of charted depth to indicated depth corrected for draft. Navigational charts show carefully surveyed depth points and contour curves, which can be used for comparison. This provides the navigator more navigational information to check against position information. Tidal information, if available, can also be employed to further increase the accuracy of the readings. It is surprising that this easy-to-use piece of equipment is often least utilized. In determining position information, depth readings are often overlooked unless bottom clearance becomes suspect. With new regulations regarding minimal bottom clearances being contemplated, the practice of utilizing depth sounders will no doubt intensify.

Another common method of checking position information using the depth sounder is to carefully check the chart for bottom topographic features that are prominent and easily identified by depth. A common practice employed regularly by Pacific Ocean navigators is to plot a track over a seamount when approaching island chains and record the time of passage when the topographic feature is indicated on the depth sounder. This offers the navigator another line of position useful in navigation. Recording depth sounders can very precisely show when this type of bottom feature is approached and passed.

A chain of soundings can also be utilized to determine a vessel's track with reasonable accuracy. A transparent piece of material is used and depth readings are taken at specific time intervals. The navigator uses speed along a projected track to determine the distance traveled, and the depth indications are marked with a grease pencil on the transparent sheet along a track line. The depth readings and the distance between them are then compared to the charted contours near the vessel's DR position. Where they match the contours indicates the vessel's most probable track and approximate position. The navigator must always remember to apply the vessel's draft to the readings to compare them with water depths shown on the chart, if no draft correction function exists.

SPEED MEASUREMENT SYSTEMS

A device used to determine a vessel's velocity while under way is generally referred to as a speed log. The earliest type of speed log em-

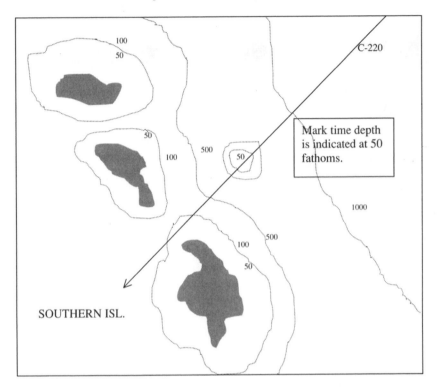

Fig. 7-9. Navigation by seamounts. Drawing by Thomas Bushy.

ployed was a device called a chip log that was trailed astern of a vessel to measure the distance traveled through the water over a specific period of time. The measurement of nautical miles per hour, or knots, was actually derived from the practice of paying out a knotted line with a drag on the end from a spool for 30 seconds. When the time was up, the numbers of "knots" payed out was measured and the vessel's approximate speed determined.

Patent logs were next in the evolution of speed logs. They had a small tubular finned device attached to the end of the drag line that would spin as the vessel moved through the water. This in turn would spin the drag line, which was attached to a meter that gave a reading of distance calibrated to the motion of the line. After a period of time elapsed, the meter would be read and a speed estimation made.

Another type of speed log that was developed was the pitot-static log or pitometer log. This device worked on the principle of comparative measurements between static and dynamic pressures introduced

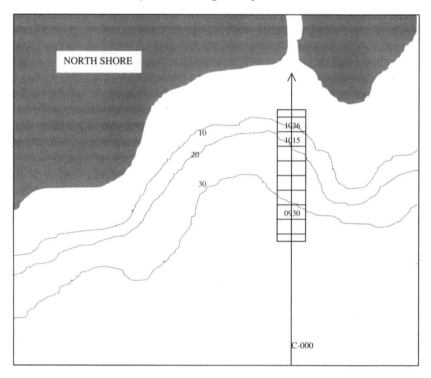

Fig. 7-10. Navigation by line of soundings.
Drawing by Thomas Bushy.

into a pitot tube contained within a device extending from the vessel's hull, called a rodmeter. The information was provided to an indicator that displayed velocity.

An electromechanical device introduced in the marine world was the impeller log, which used a small propeller to drive a geared mechanism that produced a measurable electrical impulse. This was converted to a speed measurement. Once the application of electronics worked its way into the marine environment, very accurate speed logs started to be installed aboard vessels. This new type of equipment not only proved itself to be useful in navigation, but would evolve to become an integral part of advanced collision avoidance and docking systems.

Currently there are two types of speed logs employed aboard modern vessels. The first is the electromagnetic speed log, which is still found on some ships. This is found more often in small-vessel instrumentation. The second type is the more widely used Doppler speed log. Due to its accuracy and small number of limitations, Doppler has become the mainstay in large vessel application. This type of equipment is designed to provide speed information as well as calculate distance traveled over a period of time.

Electromagnetic Speed Logs

The electromagnetic speed log was the first method of determining the velocity of a vessel through the water using modern electronic technology. This system utilizes a flow probe, or rodmeter, that extends out beyond the ship's hull. The probe contains a coil through which an electric current is passed, producing a magnetic field around the probe. As water moves past the probe, the magnetic field becomes altered, producing a variation in the signal voltage. The measurement of this variation can be utilized to indicate the vessel's speed through the water.

As mentioned in chapter 1, a conductor produces a magnetic field when a current passes through it. The consequence is a magnetic field inducing a current in a conductor when it passes through an electromagnetic field. The flow probe generates a magnetic field and the water passing around the probe serves as a conductor. The induced current in the water varies due to its velocity as it passes by the probe. The varying voltage of the induced current is measured by a separate unit in the probe and is used to calculate the velocity of the water moving past the probe.

The probes are sometimes retractable into the hull, where they can be protected when not in use or to service as necessary. Generally, the probe must be cleaned of biological growth as routine maintenance when the vessel is dry-docked.

The operator must understand that the system is designed only to measure speed through the water. The unit cannot compensate for any current, which, when present, introduces a positive or negative error into the speed readings. Errors indicating a higher speed than actual can also be introduced into the measurements when the vessel is pitching or rolling. Most logs of this type have compensating adjustments that can be employed to reduce this type of error.

Errors can also be introduced into the measurements if the water does not move in a linear fashion past the probe. This can occur if the vessel is experiencing yaw or extensive set and drift. In addition, errors can occur when the temperature, density, or salinity varies from the standard at which the device was calibrated.

The system's limitation of being able to measure only speed through the water is the primary reason this type of speed log has become less common since the introduction of the Doppler speed log. Doppler systems can calculate the speed of the vessel over ground and over the sea bottom and are considered to be more accurate.

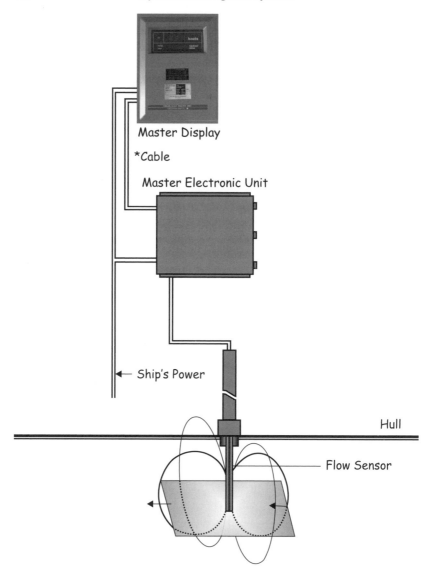

Fig. 7-11. Electromagnetic speed log. Drawing by Van Trong Nguyen.

Doppler Speed Logs

Doppler speed logs work on the principle of the Doppler effect, which is a shift in frequency between a transmitted signal and a received signal caused by the motion of a vessel over the bottom or through the water. A transducer broadcasts a continuous beam of sound vibration ahead of the vessel at about a 60-degree angle from the keel. A second transducer receives the diffusely reflected signal returning from the seabed. Unlike the depth sounders, which time the returning signal, the Doppler speed log registers the change in frequency between the transmitted and received signal, then calculates the speed of the vessel based on the amount of the frequency shift.

There are several differences between Doppler beams and depth-sounder beams. Doppler beams are continuous, narrower, and higher in frequency. In addition, one transducer is set facing forward along with a second transducer set facing aft. This dual transducer configuration is called the Janus configuration (named for the two-faced Greek god) and allows the system to calculate frequency shift in two directions. This ensures a more accurate speed measurement.

The fore-and-aft direction of the Janus configuration is known as the single-axis system, and is used to calculate speed over ground in the forward and aft direction. The longitudinal beam width for ahead and astern speed is between 3 and 6 degrees. A dual-axis system places a second grouping of Janus-configured transducers in the athwartships or transverse direction. This allows for the calculation of a vessel's speed when moving laterally through the water, as is experienced during docking and undocking. The beam width in the athwartships position is between 8 and 16 degrees. This width is larger than that of the fore-and-aft grouping to account for the rolling motion of the vessel.

Normally, the Doppler system can calculate speed with an accuracy to within 0.5 percent of the total distance traveled. This system will function well for all modern vessels that can travel in water with a minimum depth of about 1.5 feet. The maximum depth where the system will function efficiently is about 600 feet, although signals can penetrate and return to about three times that depth. Frequencies of the beam pattern employed by this system range from 100 kHz to 600 kHz, with a pulse transmission power of approximately 25 to 30 watts.

The Doppler system normally measures speed over ground in depths of 600 feet or less. Deeper than 600 feet the signals may be returned by a colder layer of water located throughout the oceans called the deep scattering layer (DSL). Signals returned off the DSL are not as accurate as those reflected directly off the bottom. However, these reflected signals can still represent a useful indication of vessel speed. It is important to remember that signals reflected off the DSL do not give speed over ground but speed through the water. The mariner must take into account the rate of any current that may be present. Some units have either a manual or automatic system, which will switch from bottom tracking to deep-water tracking.

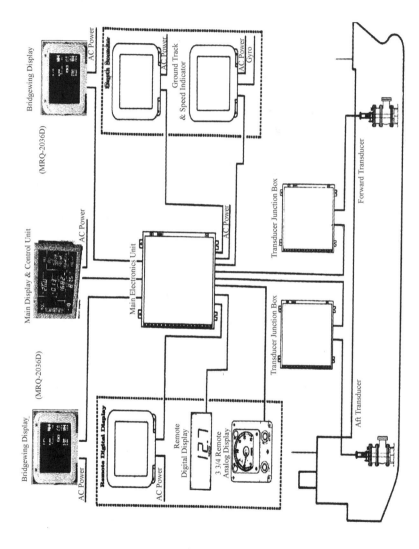

Fig. 7-12. Doppler system diagram. Courtesy of Litton/Sperry Marine Systems.

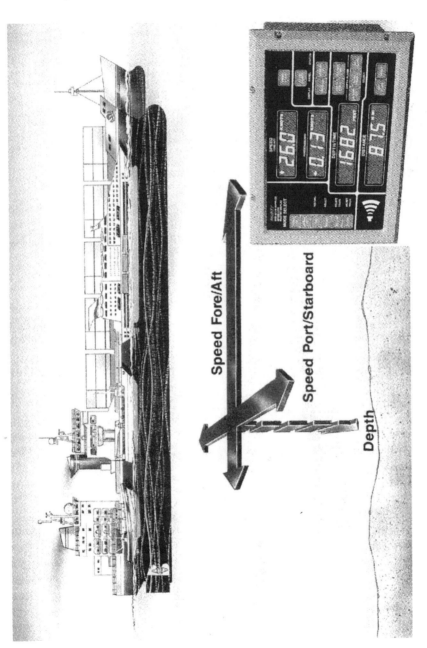

Fig. 7-13. Doppler dual-axis speed log equipment. Courtesy of Litton/Sperry Marine Systems.

In most cases the operator can select the mode that will either use bottom signals or DSL signals for the determination of speed. If the system is in the bottom return mode or bottom track, the readings will indicate speed over the ground. When the system is placed in the volume reverberation mode or water track, the readings will indicate speed through the water. In this mode, the signals are returned from the deep scattering layer. The operator can assume for the purposes of practical operation that the unit's readings will be given in speed through the water.

There are four primary errors associated with the use of Doppler speed log systems. The first is transducer orientation error, which is caused when the pitching or rolling of the vessel becomes excessive. This problem can also be noticed with a change in trim. Variations in draft do not normally create transducer orientation errors.

The second type of error is vessel motion error, created by excessive vibration of the vessel as it moves through the water. This is most common when a vessel is laboring in a rough sea or because of variances of draft or trim due to loaded or ballast conditions, creating propeller-induced shaking. This type of error is also noticeable when backing, which not only causes vibration, but induces air bubbles passing below the vessel.

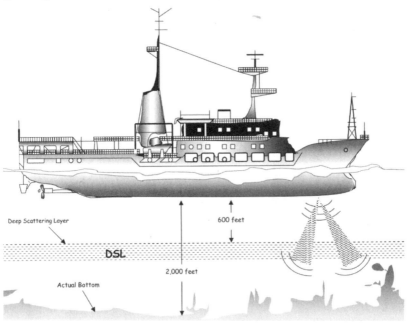

Deep Scattering Layer

600 feet

DSL

2,000 feet

Actual Bottom

Fig. 7-14. Deep scattering layer impact on Doppler speed logs.
Drawing by Van Trong Nguyen.

When there is a change in water temperature or salinity, velocity of sound errors can be created. This possibility exists when a vessel enters a harbor containing fresh water, or when passing through ocean currents where salinity and temperature vary. Bodies of water that have a high particle content, such as rivers with high sediment content, can also cause this type of error. In this case, the speed of sound through water may vary from the normal calibration at which the system is adjusted. Most systems are equipped with a device

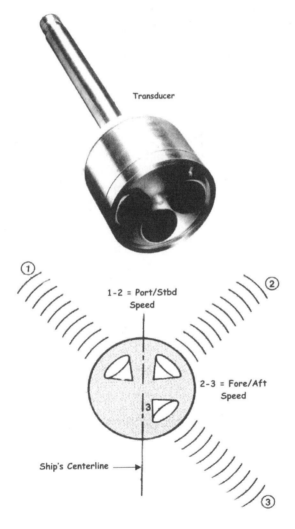

Fig. 7-15. Doppler transducer.
Courtesy of Litton/Sperry Marine Systems.

called a thermistor that measures water temperature and adjusts for this type of variation.

The final error is signal loss error, caused by the attenuation of the vibrations during transit of the signal through the water or upon reflection from the bottom. The system compensates for normal attenuation in circumstances when water temperature or density conditions are constant. Errors can also be introduced in shallow water such as a river or when the seabed is very soft and muddy. Harder bottoms will produce better reflections and return stronger signals.

The Doppler system can be interfaced with other navigational equipment to provide generally accurate speed input. The navigator should be cautioned, however, that precise speed should be determined not only by using the Doppler system but also by calculating speed between accurate fixes.

OUTLOOK

Speed logs, especially Doppler-based systems, have gained widespread use in vessel operations today. While they are expensive to acquire and install, they are critical to the application of speed data in normal navigation and through automatic radar plotting aids and integrated bridge systems. They also have widespread use in vessel docking systems, which require very precise, localized data for maneuvering.

It has been suggested that new, highly accurate satellite navigation systems like GPS render speed log information antiquated and therefore useless. Satellite velocity information also remains historical, even if the history file is only 10 seconds old. Speed log information is still based on real-time observation. Satellite systems, while providing excellent velocity information for navigation or collision avoidance, have not been utilized in commercial applications for determining precision docking speeds. This is primarily due to selective availability in the systems, which is discussed in chapter 4. Military vessels do not have this restriction and utilize satellite systems for all applications requiring precise velocity information.

It must be remembered that speed logs, particularly Doppler systems, provide very accurate information that can be utilized as a primary velocity measurement system. This will always be useful as a check against observed speed from any form of navigation, or even as a backup system to satellites. As long as manufacturers continue to make speed logs, it is anticipated that their widespread use will continue.

CHAPTER 8

VESSEL CONTROL SYSTEMS

INTRODUCTION

The determination of a vessel's course has changed considerably since the days when sailors from Asia used a magnetized piece of metal floating in a bowl of water. For centuries, the magnetic compass was, and still remains, a critical piece of equipment aboard ship. Technology allowed for a new mechanical compass to be incorporated, giving a more accurate method of determining a vessel's course. It also allowed for integration with other navigational equipment. This led to the development of the electromechanical gyrocompass in the early part of the twentieth century.

Ship control systems have become very sophisticated, and this chapter will focus on three types of technology used in the modern maritime world. The first system is the flux gate magnetic compass, which is simply a magnetic compass with an add-on system that can be integrated into other vessel equipment. The second type of system is the master gyro system, which is the mainstay for course determination on most modern vessels today. Finally, there is the autopilot system, which not only utilizes input information from one of the first two systems mentioned, but also incorporates information from very accurate radionavigation systems.

The addition of repeating systems to both flux gate and gyro systems has enabled navigators to get accurate bearing information from bearing repeaters installed on bridge wings. That same information has been used to provide course heading data to autopilots that maintain a ship's course when under way. Additional utilization of this information includes dead reckoning calculations in radio-navigation equipment, heading information in radars and automatic radar plotting aides, heading information for navigation plotters, and even input into highly advanced integrated bridge systems.

Modern autopilots not only utilize heading information but now integrate that information with data received from the global positioning system or other radionavigation aides. It is critical to understand that these systems are subject to the accuracy and condition of each individual component.

FLUX GATE MAGNETIC COMPASSES

The integration of various navigation and vessel control systems led to the development of a method that could translate practical heading information from a magnetic compass into other vessel systems. System design strove to incorporate end-user systems such as radars, automatic steering controls, and various types of navigation equipment and plotters. While gyro systems are ideal for this type of integration, the industry needed to find a lower-cost method of accomplishing the same goal. This led to the development of the magnetic repeating compass.

Magnetic compasses can be made into repeating compasses through the utilization of a flux gate unit, which produces electronic pulses for integration into equipment requiring heading information. Flux gate units are magnetometers that detect the intensity and direction of magnetic fields. The corresponding assembly uses a series of thin wires contained within a tube and surrounded by a coil. The assemblies are mounted so that they are parallel and side by side. Low-frequency alternating current runs through the wires, creating an opposing magnetic field in each of them.

An additional coil is wrapped around the entire assembly, interacting with the first set of coils to detect when the flux gate's magnetic field is out of alignment. This coil produces the output voltage necessary to drive a separate platform located under the compass card. In addition, it drives the repeating system.

The entire assembly is contained within the compass bowl of the unit. The system is driven by the magnetic field produced by the compass card assembly. As the compass card moves to seek magnetic north, the flux gate assembly senses the compass card movement, and develops a corresponding signal which drives a servomotor keeping the flux gate assembly in alignment with the compass card. As the assembly moves, it generates a corresponding repeater signal which is amplified and distributed to the units integrated in the

Fig. 8-1. Flux gate compass and indicator unit.
Courtesy of Ritchie Navigation.

system. Because magnetic compasses can move very easily, a dampening system is incorporated to slow repeater movement.

It is critical that the flux gate system incorporates deviation and variation corrections so that a more accurate geographical north indication may be obtained. The information obtained from the flux gate compass, with these corrections applied, tends to be more accurate on true north. These systems have been employed on supply boats, offshore service vessels, ferries, and a multitude of other limited-tonnage vessels with great success. They have enabled the installation of automatic steering systems and automatic radar plotting aids and have been used to provide heading information to radionavigation equipment.

The use of flux gate magnetic compasses heightens the sensitivity of vessel operators to compass deviation and variation associated with all magnetic compasses. The system has proven to be effective and very useful in the commercial world.

MARINE GYROCOMPASS SYSTEMS

Perhaps no other piece of equipment is utilized or depended upon more than the gyrocompass. Since its first applications on commercial vessels right after World War I, the master gyro has been the mainstay for navigation on the high seas. Master gyros and their associated systems have gone through only one major evolution since first being introduced. The application of computers and electronic technology in the 1970s brought about a change from electromechanical technology to microprocessed electronic technology. Even still, the basic component of the gyro system, the master compass, remains electromechanical in nature. A gyro installed aboard a vessel to indicate direction is commonly referred to as a gyrocompass, and is classified as an electromechanical device.

To understand how a gyrocompass works, it is important to recognize the problems that had to be overcome in developing a system that was more accurate and less susceptible to error than the magnetic compass. It was recognized that the most effective method would be to develop a system that would line up with the geographical meridians of the earth, which could then be utilized to indicate true north.

The designers that developed and engineered the gyrocompass took advantage of four elements of natural physics to make their device work. These include the properties of gyroscopic inertia, precession, gravity, and the rotation of the earth.

Anything that spins rapidly enough to render stability of motion can technically be considered a gyro. The small toy top a child plays with is a gyro and demonstrates for us the first of the fundamental properties that must be understood. Sir Isaac Newton's first law of motion dictates that a body will remain in its state of rest or uniform motion in a straight line unless a force is applied to change that state. In other words, if a body is spinning, it will remain in the same plane of rotation until an external force is applied to change the plane of rotation.

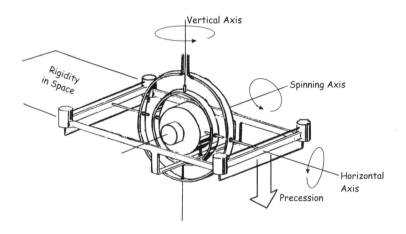

Fig. 8-2. Gyroscopic axis of freedom forces.
Drawing by Van Trong Nguyen/Donna Manoli.

Taking advantage of the stability of a spinning object was critical to final application in the master compass. Engineers were trying to develop a unit that would give a steady course heading and not fluctuate due to external forces. This would be the central basis for designing a stabilized electromechanical device.

The property that causes the gyro to remain in the same plane of rotation is called gyroscopic inertia, or rigidity in space. Gyroscopic inertia causes the spinning element of a gyro to remain stable and in its initial plane of rotation. Even if the gyro is moved across the surface of the earth, or if it remains stationary, the plane of rotation will not change as long as it continues to spin. Viewing the gyro, it would appear to tilt as the earth moves. In addition, the gyro appears to move relative to the observer, which is referred to as drift. In reality, however, it is the observer who is moving, not the gyro. This rigidity in space permits us to begin utilizing this spinning gyro for a directional compass.

The second property, precession, is the external force that is applied to the gyro to change its plane of rotation. Precession causes the body to move in a direction nearly perpendicular to the application of the applied force. Once again, envision the spinning top. If a force were applied down on one side, one would expect the top to turn away from the applied force. Instead, it turns at a right angle to the outside force.

At this point, it was understood that if a consistent applied force could be maintained on the axis of rotation of the spinning gyro, it would precess in a manner perpendicular to the applied force. It was determined that if a weight could be added which was acted upon by gravity (the third property), and the resulting force could be applied to the axis of the gyro, it would seek the geographic meridian.

To make the gyro direction-seeking, a weight was attached to the frame supporting the spinning element of the gyro. As the earth rotated (the fourth property), the gyro had a tendency to remain in its original plane of rotation. However, as the force of gravity acted upon the weight, the axis of the spinning element was forced to precess. Due to the fact that gravity pulls on the weight toward the earth's center, the gyro precessed until it became aligned with a geographic meridian, approximately north and south.

Master Gyrocompass Components

The functionality of the gyrocompass is dependent on having three axes of freedom: spinning, vertical, and horizontal. These freedoms allow the gyro to move in any manner without interference. The spinning function must be constant, to avoid upsetting the inertia, and the vertical and horizontal freedoms allow the device to be acted upon by the motions of the ship.

The construction of the gyro varies by manufacturer, but generally all gyrocompasses have five major parts, which may also have slightly different names. For ease of identification, we will refer to the names employed by the Sperry gyrocompass system. Each manufacturer produces a manual for its own gyro and corresponding names can be easily identified in these publications.

The first and central part of the gyro is called the sensitive element. This contains the spinning gyro, called the rotor, an electric motor that drives the rotor, the rotor housing, and the supportive frame. The rotor can turn anywhere from 6,000 to 12,000 rpm, depending upon the manufacturer and the size of the unit. The smaller the unit, the faster the rotor is designed to spin to enhance stability. The electric motor that drives the rotor operates on a filtered voltage, generally AC, at a reduced hertz to reduce any variations in the current.

The second part, the controlling element, contains the ballistic or pendulous weight. It should be noted that gyros are not necessarily north-seeking. Depending on the manufacturer, gyros can use one of several methods to apply a weight that creates the precessive forces toward a particular direction. One way is to utilize a ballistic, or a liquid leveling system, that uses a free-flowing heavy liquid such as mercury or silicone within the element. This is known as a ballistic gyro. Another method is to use a solid weight suspended from the gyro frame. This is called the pendulous-style gyro.

The third element of the gyro comprises the frames and mechanisms that shadow the movement of the sensitive element without interfering with it. This element, known as the phantom element, also contains the compass card off of which we read the ship's heading. The phantom element is not directly connected to the sensitive element but instead mimics the motion of the sensitive element in a fashion similar to the flux gate magnetic compass. A magnetic field is set up between coils that are attached to both elements and are parallel and next to each other. When the field is disrupted by the movement of the sensitive element, an indication is sent to a control unit that will drive the phantom element and keep it in alignment with the sensitive element.

The fourth element is a support component that contains the motor, which drives the phantom element to follow the movement of the sensitive element, and a transmission system, which sends compass signals to the heading indicators throughout the ship's bridge. This element is known as the spider element.

Finally, there is the binnacle housing, which contains all the previously mentioned components of the master gyrocompass. Vessel personnel were required to handle routine maintenance on the various components of older units, which were less critical and more

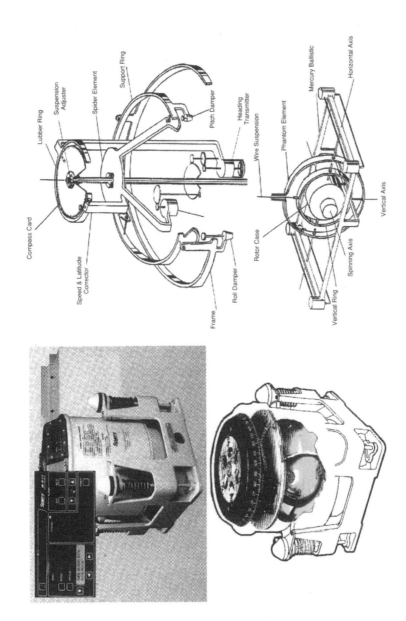

Fig. 8-3. Master gyrocompass. Courtesy of Litton/Sperry Marine Systems; drawing by Donna Manoli.

accessible. Today, modern binnacle housings are sealed to prevent tampering. The gyro is set into a shockproof support and is contained in an inert atmosphere to reduce rotor friction. Binnacle housings are also equipped with locking mechanisms or caging devices to prevent motion of the sensitive element when the unit is not activated.

The master gyro is operated by an electronic control device that regulates the electrical power that operates the various elements of the master gyro, including the rotor, azimuth, phantom, and transmission systems. Most modern vessels carry two master gyros, thus providing a backup should one of the units fail. Output from the two master units goes to a selector switch, which can be operated by the deck officer to alternate between units. Normally, they are rotated daily to ensure the repeater system works correctly on both master gyros.

Gyrorepeater System

A separate transmission amplifier and distribution control system receives signals from the master gyro transmitter and distributes this signal. This distribution system is called the repeater system, and each unit designed to give indication of ship's heading is called a gyrorepeater.

From the master gyro's spider element, the transmitter signals go to the transmission amplifier/distribution control. This unit allocates a single electrical circuit for each repeater within the system, each having separate on/off control and equipped with protection fuses. The distribution control system maintains sufficient power to drive all the vessel's repeaters. Repeaters are provided throughout the bridge to allow convenient indications of the vessel's heading. A repeater positioned near the ship's steering stand is called a steering repeater. Bearing repeaters are usually located on the wings of the bridge to aid the mariner in taking true direction visual bearings or for compass comparisons. Gyro information is also currently interfaced into various navigational equipment. Radar display units, radio direction finders, automatic steering systems, course recorders, loran C systems, and GPS units are all capable of being interfaced with gyro information.

There are two common types of repeater systems. The step system produces segmented signals driving a repeater motor in three separate "steps." This system is generally associated with older types of gyroscopes. The second type of system is the newer synchronous motor or system. This uses a different voltage requirement than the step system, with a syncronous-style operating motor. The movement of this type of repeater is truer to the movement of the master compass.

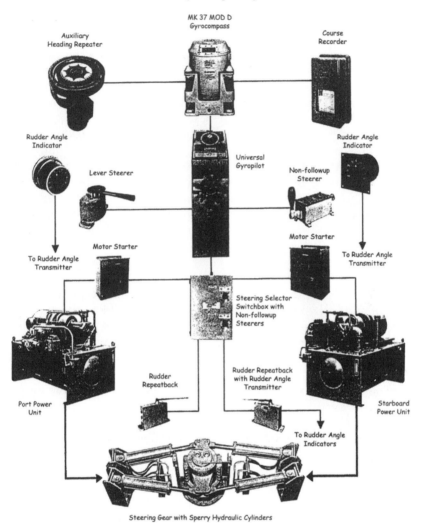

MK 37 MOD D
Gyrocompass

Auxiliary
Heading Repeater

Course
Recorder

Rudder Angle
Indicator

Universal
Gyropilot

Lever Steerer

Non-followup
Steerer

Rudder Angle
Indicator

Motor Starter

To Rudder Angle
Transmitter

Motor Starter

To Rudder Angle
Transmitter

Steering Selector
Switchbox with
Non-followup
Steerers

Rudder
Repeatback

Rudder Repeatback
with Rudder Angle
Transmitter

Port Power
Unit

Starboard
Power Unit

To Rudder Angle
Indicators

Steering Gear with Sperry Hydraulic Cylinders

Fig. 8-4. Gyrorepeater and steering system.
Courtesy of Litton/Sperry Marine Systems.

These repeaters are found in various forms, including the standard repeater, which exhibits the entire azimuth ring, or the open scale repeater, which shows a larger but only partial section of the azimuth ring. The open scale repeater is most commonly used as a steering repeater.

Course recorders are often considered separate navigational bridge equipment, but in reality they are merely recording repeaters.

There are two types of course recorders. The older style uses an 8-day windup clock mechanism with two ink stylus pens. The more common modern type uses an electronically driven clock mechanism with two electric stylus pens. This graph mechanism works similarly to the fathometer in that special graph paper is drawn over a metal desk and an electrical signal scores the graph paper to show the quadrant and course. In both types, as a means of decreasing paper size, the two-pen stylus system is utilized. One pen indicates which quadrant of the compass the record is showing, and the other indicates the precise course based upon the quadrant. As an example, a quadrant labeled 0 to 90 degrees would represent the northeast quadrant, and although the course pen might be pointing to 225 degrees, closer examination would indicate the course was actually 045 degrees. Multiple gradients therefore require the mariner to be careful in recording information.

Practical Gyro Systems Operation

There are several important points that the watchstander should keep in mind when using the gyro system. Navigators should make every effort to avoid becoming complacent about this key system. In addition, frequent checks through terrestrial bearings and with the magnetic compass are an easy way to determine whether your unit is working properly.

The navigator should ensure that all repeaters are aligned with the master gyro; if there is a dual gyro system aboard, ensure that any difference in their readings are constantly noted. Dual systems are equipped with a transfer switch that allows the operator to go from one master compass to another. Transfer should be made daily to determine that both systems are working correctly. This can be easily accomplished by transferring systems when the master compass to be utilized settles onto the heading on all the repeaters. When switching from one gyro system to another, be sure all the repeaters are lined up with each other and with the master gyro you are switching to and from.

Azimuths for determining compass error should be taken as frequently as permissible, and the information applied to both master compasses if a dual gyro system is installed. The difference in master compass readings should also be noted. If errors between the systems are constant over a long period of time, the units may be aligned through a slight adjustment in the lubber line on the compass.

All master gyros are equipped with speed and latitude correctors. These are necessary because the directive force of the gyro decreases as you get nearer the poles. There is also an error introduced in the master gyro by the vessel's motion along its track. Each master gyro

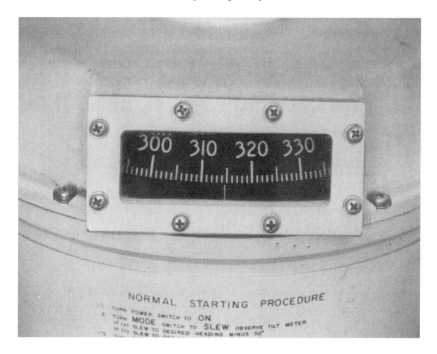

Fig. 8-5. Lubber's line. Photograph by Forlivesi Photography.

has specific parameters for setting these correctors, but generally they should be kept within 3 degrees of latitude and 3 knots of speed.

Every system has a manual that dictates its specific maintenance requirements. Be sure to follow these maintenance plans as required. Inspect all equipment frequently, particularly external repeaters, which frequently develop problems due to moisture. Remember, an electrical short in one repeater could affect the entire system. Each repeater is usually equipped with a fuse to avoid this problem. Also remember to check units that are located in remote parts of the vessel, such as the steering gear room or master's stateroom.

Errors in the gyro system can be introduced by a ship's fluctuating power supply. The gyro system should be on emergency circuits and if extensive variations in the power source are noted, be sure to inform the vessel's engineer so that the problem can be corrected as soon as possible.

Although most manufacturers recommend starting a gyro within only a few hours of getting underway, the prudent operator will bring the system on-line as early as possible to provide a maximum time for problems to become noticeable. The gyro will hunt or oscillate prior to

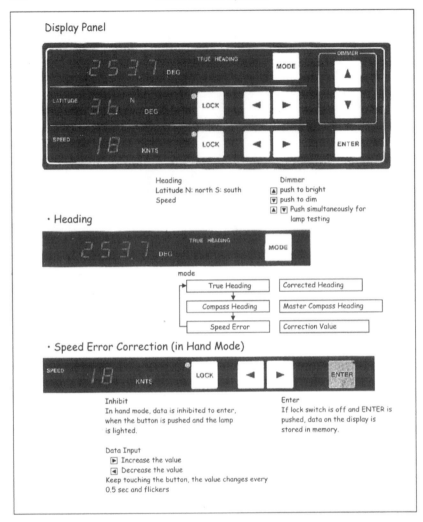

Fig. 8-6. Gyro speed-latitude connectors.
Courtesy of Litton/Sperry Marine Systems.

its settling out, therefore your gyro should be started as close to the vessel's present heading as possible to minimize this settling time. If the vessel is located at the dock, you can get the vessel's heading from a nautical chart. Be sure to set the speed corrector at zero when tied up and remember to change it after you are underway. In the event of starting the gyro at sea, it should be done as close to the heading as possible, with the speed corrector set accordingly.

Remember that the axis of the rotor aligns itself with the geographic meridian and the gyro is not necessarily north-seeking. If you start the gyro up 90 degrees or more from the vessel's heading, your gyro may have a 180-degree error after setting out. Every gyro has a specified startup and shutdown procedure that should be followed. This information is available in the unit's operating manual.

Be sure to remove the gyro's locking system or uncage the unit as specified by the manufacturer. This step may be unnecessary on modern sealed units equipped with automatic caging systems. Set the unit's controls in the proper operating mode and be sure that the repeater system is off until the unit has been started and been allowed to settle out.

All gyro systems have a failure alarm. Be capable of recognizing this alarm by sound or sight and know the procedures required to properly respond to a system failure. Some guidelines related to gyro failure, as recommended by the IMO, are contained in the last section of this chapter.

STEERING SYSTEMS

The need to eliminate long tricks at the helm and the desire to redistribute man-hours on vessels with decreasing crews brought about the development of automatic steering systems. Because these systems take input from the master gyrocompass through the repeater system they are often referred to as gyropilots. No matter what the technical designation may be, seamen have always referred to the automatic steering system as the "iron mike." Automatic steering systems can also be used in conjunction with flux gate compasses or radionavigation systems in a similar manner.

Magnetic repeating compasses and gyrocompasses have been adapted to provide a directional signal for use with automatic steering systems. Automatic steering systems have been adapted for use on small-tonnage vessels, which use these types of compasses to provide basic helm control. Automatic steering systems for shipboard use, however, have become very sophisticated. These units not only can be used to steer a ship but can also be used to plan voyages, maintain tracks, and take into account the change in vessel characteristics in loaded or ballast conditions.

The autopilot may be a separate system, as found on many smaller vessels, or it may be integrated into an electric steering unit. Electric steering units provide a single helm with redundant operational systems for the rudder. They may be the primary steering system aboard a ship or, in the case of older vessels outfitted with hydraulic telemotors, may serve as a supplement to the hydraulic system.

Electric steering has become the mainstay on modern vessels. Where regulations in the United States dictated that there must be redundancy in regard to rudder control, hydraulic and electric systems were installed. Electric steering systems became the primary method of rudder control when separate and independently powered electric systems could be employed, even if operated through a single steering stand. This eliminated the need for hydraulic systems, which were more expensive to maintain.

The use of electric steering has broadened the methodology employed in controlling vessels; new integrated bridge systems are util-

Fig. 8-7. Steering stand. Courtesy of Litton/Sperry Marine Systems.

izing computer-controlled track maintenance software to keep vessels on their intended course. At the heart of any system however, is the basic autopilot, which manages some primary functions that will be discussed here.

Components

Every automatic steering system has a power control switch to turn the system off and on. If the system is installed as a secondary system to a hydraulic system, there will be a deactivation control on the

Fig. 8-8. Steering system performance controls.
Photograph by Forlivesi Photography.

telemotor steering stand that will automatically shut down the electric steering if the telemotor is engaged.

A system selector is also installed on the steering system to switch between the port and starboard rudder control systems. Each rudder control system is fully redundant to the other and is powered from a separate source. The systems should be switched over daily when under way to ensure both are working correctly. In addition, both systems should be checked as part of the predeparture and prearrival test procedures.

Steering controls vary depending on the manufacturer and the specifications of the vessel operator. In most cases, vessels have been equipped with a small steering wheel for use as the primary helm. Some gyropilots have a "joy stick" or control lever in the form of a non-follow-up control system (NFU) or full follow-up control system (FFU). This allows direct control of the rudder without use of the wheel. This unit is designed as the primary steering station or as a remote station that can be placed anywhere on the vessel. NFU systems allow the operator to move the rudder into any position and leave it where placed. FFU systems, on the other hand, automatically return the rudder to amidships when the control lever is released. Both have their own unique applications depending upon the preference of the operator and the type of vessel.

Remote controls in the form of NFU or FFU systems can be used as the emergency steering control on most vessels since the rudder actuation process can be directly connected to the rudder control system, bypassing the steering stand. A selector switch on the steering stand allows the operator to transfer steering control to another unit in the bridge or to a bridge wing. A control at the emergency steering station may be utilized to bypass the steering stand completely.

All main steering stands have rudder direction, rudder order, and rudder angle indicators. In addition, rudder angle indicators are placed in key locations throughout the bridge deck, including wings, and at the emergency steering station. The helmsman should always use the rudder order indicator to adjust the helm, but should always rely on the rudder angle indicator as the true determination of the rudder's position. Small remote-control mechanisms generally have only left/right markings, and the operator must rely on the rudder angle indicator for proper execution of rudder commands.

There are various course indicators employed on modern steering stands. These may be in the form of a standard 360-degree repeater, an open-scale repeater showing only an enlarged portion of the compass scale, a graphic scale, or a digital course heading.

In addition, most units are equipped with a rate of turn indicator that allows the operator to determine the vessel's rate of turn when the

rudder is applied. Rate of turn indicators are very useful when maneuvering and allow the person controlling the maneuver to see the effect
of various rudder angles. Although the systems are quiet, some produce audible clicks to allow the person maneuvering to hear the rate of
turn, as was the case with the familiar old click of step repeaters.

When in automatic mode, the steering system accepts signals
from the repeater network and compensates for the difference between the required course and the actual heading. The automatic
steering control will react to the difference within the parameters set

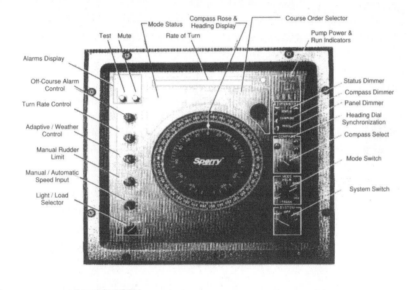

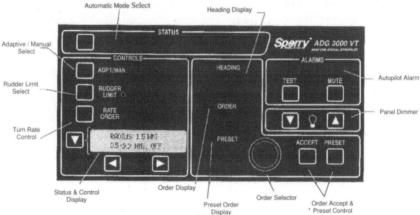

Fig. 8-9. Steering system controls.
Courtesy of Litton/Sperry Marine Systems.

by the operator. The operator sets those parameters through the utilization of performance controls. Most automatic steering units have the same range of performance controls, which include a rudder adjustment, weather adjustment, speed adjustment, and loaded/light condition adjustment.

Most basic steering systems contain a rudder adjustment to control the amount of rudder used in returning the vessel to course. Rudder adjustments are designed to allow the operator to use a "seaman's eye" to determine how the vessel is acting in a seaway. Depending on any number of factors, the rudder adjustment allows the system to use a small amount of rudder or a larger amount of rudder, depending on prevailing conditions. If a vessel is properly trimmed and adequately loaded, and is running in a calm sea, only a small amount of rudder may be needed to keep the vessel on track. If the opposite is true, larger amounts may be required.

The second control, the weather adjustment, is designed to slow the response of the rudder by reducing the reaction time of the rudder in heavy seas. Conversely, if the seas are calm, the unit can be set to react faster. The proper use of the weather adjustment will prevent the system from being overworked in heavier seas. The operator should keep in mind that in extreme weather or very heavy seas, it is prudent to use manual steering.

All vessels react differently depending on their speed through the water. A vessel moving at sea speed will change direction faster than one on a slow bell. For this reason, a speed adjustment has been included on most automatic steering systems. Many vessels operate at reduced speed for any number of reasons, and when the vessel is slowed, the steering system must apply more rudder. The system may not need to react as often. The speed adjustment compensates for these variances.

Finally, depending on whether a vessel is in a loaded or light condition, the vessel will again react differently. This is most noticeable in vessels such as tankers. Loaded vessels will react more slowly and will require larger rudder movements. Vessels in a ballast condition will react faster and require less rudder.

The operator must balance these controls properly to optimize the use of the automatic steering system. These controls should be checked frequently and adjusted as necessary to fit the prevailing conditions. If improperly used, one adjustment could negate the intended effect of another. Watchkeepers should make every effort to note settings and change them when required. It is also important to understand how the controls are set, based on the scales utilized by each manufacturer. Proper use of an automatic steering system not only can save lives, but also can produce greater fuel economy.

Advanced steering systems have claimed 10 percent fuel savings over most manual helmsmen.

Automatic steering systems are required to be outfitted with various alarms to give the operator an indication of trouble. These include power failure alarms for the steering unit and rudder control systems; a course alarm that activates when the vessel varies beyond a set parameter for the intended course; and, if outfitted with radionavigation inputs, a track alarm for when the vessel is outside of stated parameters for an intended track.

Due to the integration of radionavigation and speed log information into steering systems and the ability of the operator to set departure, destination, and waypoints into the system, more sophisticated units are referred to as ship control systems. These systems utilize not only gyro information, but input from speed logs and radionavigation systems, to maintain the vessel's course as well as its intended track. The units can be used to calculate courses and distances, set a vessel on the calculated track, and maintain that track by analyzing all of the data. The ship control system has the capability of assisting the vessel operator in maintaining the most efficient performance along an intended track, thus optimizing the watch officer's time and maximizing efficient fuel consumption.

Ship control units, however, do not possess the intuition of a thinking individual. The computer adage "garbage in, garbage out" is very relevant to these systems. Only proper monitoring of the system will guarantee that it is not responsible for bringing the ship into dangerous situations.

IMO REQUIREMENTS FOR SHIP CONTROL SYSTEMS

The International Maritime Organization has promulgated recommendations for predeparture inspections and watchkeeping regarding compass systems and steering systems. These recommendations apply to gyro and magnetic compasses, including magnetic compass

---

Steering and Compasses
1. Gyros and repeaters on and heading checked with berth heading
2. Gyro system transfer switch tested
3. Steering gear, telemotor, and electric tested
4. Compass binnacle light, standard, and steering checked
5. Compass record books ready and initial entry made

Fig. 8-10. Presailing bridge checklist

repeating systems (flux gate compasses). Excerpts from those recommendations follow.

It is preferable to leave the gyro compass running continuously. Should it have been stopped for any reason, it should be started and later checked to ensure it has "settled" and is reading correctly in sufficient time before use.

Latitude and speed corrections should be applied to the gyro compass, as appropriate. Repeaters should be synchronized with the gyro at least once in a watch. The gyro alarm should be checked daily. As a safeguard against the gyro and gyro repeaters wandering, frequent checks should be made between the magnetic and gyro compasses. Compass errors should be ascertained each watch, if practicable, either by azimuth or transit bearing.

All liquid magnetic compasses should be checked weekly for air bubbles. They should be covered at all times when not in use. Where fitted as a standby system, magnetic compass control of the automatic pilot should be tested and exercised weekly in clear weather.

There are also recommendations in the case of gyro or steering failure.

In regard to steering failure, "The automatic pilot should only be used when safe and practicable. All methods of change-over between alternative means of steering should be displayed prominently on the bridge, demonstrated and exercised.

"The off-course alarm, when fitted, should be adjusted depending on weather conditions. The alarm should be in use at all times when under automatic steering. If it becomes unserviceable, consideration should be given to changing to hand steering. The use of an alarm does not in any way relieve the Officer of the Watch from checking the course being steered."

---

1. Magnetic compass or any alternative means used as heading
2. Master informed
3. Person responsible for gyro maintenance informed
4. Engine room informed
5. Effect of failure on other navigational aids considered

Fig. 8-11. Gyro failure procedures

There is no doubt that vessel control equipment has made the lives of seafarers easier. The capabilities and applications available

1. Engine room informed and alternative/emergency steering engaged
2. Master informed
3. "Not under command" shapes or lights exhibited
4. Appropriate sound signal made
5. If necessary, take way off ship

Fig. 8-12. Steering failure procedures

have increased the efficiency of watchstanders. With this new equipment, however, has come the need for expanded vigilance, new consideration, and due diligence. Human nature compels us to become complacent about how we depend on these systems. Many marine casualties have proven to us that there must be a proper understanding of how these systems are used and the potential problems associated with their use. Every manufacturer engineers in a little difference and each time you are a shipmate with this equipment, you should review the manufacturer's instructions and note the system's performance. Due diligence is the key to avoiding casualties with this and all other equipment.

CHAPTER 9

MARINE RADAR SYSTEMS

THEORY OF RADAR SYSTEMS

"Radar" is an acronym for radio detecting and ranging. Radar is used to determine range, bearing, and sometimes height. Originally an aid for detecting other ships in poor visibility, it evolved to become the most important electronic device on the bridge. While radar's main purpose was for manual plotting and navigation, it has become the linchpin of modern collision-avoidance computers.

The U.S. Naval Research Laboratory noticed in 1922 that passing ships near the lab interfered with a 60-megacycle radio signal that was being transmitted between two stations. This anomaly was, at the time, considered a simple annoyance; it was not until 1930 that science was applied to the phenomenon.

The U.S. Navy installed a prototype radar unit on the USS *Leary* in 1937. The British were also working on developing radar and, with the possibility of war threatening Europe, began to work with the Americans in 1940. Early radar units played a major role in warning the British of oncoming raids from Germany during the Battle of Britain. Radar development no doubt saved thousands of lives in its early years.

On December 7, 1941, the U.S. Army radar station in Hawaii picked up approaching Japanese aircraft before they began their attack. The information was forwarded to the island defense command center, but was thought to be insignificant. As the war progressed, the development of radar proceeded by leaps and bounds, and the installation of radar aboard U.S. Navy ships played an important role in several major battles.

The first commercial application on U.S. merchant ships began to take place in the late 1940s. Radar was generally regarded by the 1950s as standard equipment aboard ships. Radar has since become a baseline device on ships throughout the world. Many nations of the world require at least one radar device aboard their ships. Although it is constantly changing with technology, its basic theory has never changed. And although first designed as a collision avoidance tool, today nearly every maritime fix taken within 15 miles of a coastline includes information derived from radar.

The application of microprocessor computers for collision avoidance was introduced in the 1970s. Radar coupled with computer-aided collision avoidance systems is standard equipment aboard ships in the 1990s. These, too, are being required by many governments involved in international safety standards.

FUNDAMENTALS OF RADAR

Radar systems used in marine applications are pulse-modulated. Pulse modulation is a transmission system where the frequency and amplitude are modulated and transmitted in short, relatively power-ful bursts. The system sends out a short burst of energy under strict time control from a directional antenna and notes when an echo or reflection is returned. The radar unit merely has to know the speed of radar waves in the atmosphere, the time it takes for an echo to re-turn, and basic time-rate-distance computations. Since the antenna is directional, it also allows for the determination of the direction to the echo.

Like all radio waves, radar waves travel at the speed of light, 161,830 nautical miles per second. Radar pulses are measured in mi-croseconds because of the exceptional speed. A microsecond is one mil-lionth of a second. In one microsecond, a radar pulse can travel 0.162 nautical miles, 328 yards, or 300 meters. In more relative terms, in one second a pulse of RF energy will travel around the earth seven times. When a radar unit transmits a pulse, and then receives the echo of that pulse in one microsecond, then the target would have to be half the distance the radar energy traveled, since the radar energy had to reverse direction when it bounced off a solid object. In one mi-crosecond the energy travels 328 yards. Dividing this time distance by two reveals the actual distance to the object that caused the echo to be 164 yards. This computation model is referred to as a radar nautical mile per second. It is determined by dividing radio energy of 161,830 NM per second in half, or 80,915 NM per second.

Radar wave pulses are one microsecond or less in duration with longer separations between them. The length in microseconds of a

Fig. 9-1. Standard radar unit with reflector plotter.
Photograph by Forlivesi Photography.

particular burst of radar energy is called the pulse length. The pulse
length is used as the single determination in minimum detection
range, but is also important to maximum detection range. A compromise must be found where the desired minimum detection range is
balanced against the maximum detection range.

If it is desired to receive target information at 100 yards, the
pulse length must be short enough to allow complete pulse transmission before any echoes are returned. Since the radar energy must
travel two directions—out to contact and back to receiver—the pulse
can be no longer than 0.6 microseconds. At the same time it is desired
to receive echoes from targets out to 24 NM. This means the listening
period between pulses must be long enough for radar energy to travel
48 NM. Therefore the listening period must be 296.3 microseconds.
The total time for transmission of pulse and receiving period is 296.9
microseconds. This means the radar will transmit 3,368 pulses per
second.

The number of pulses per second is the pulse repetition rate
(PRR), pulse repetition frequency, or pulse recurrence. PRR will be

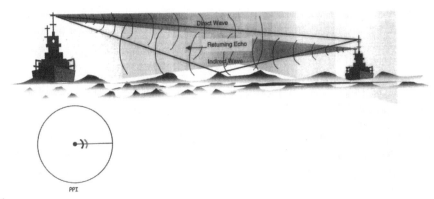

Fig. 9-2. Reflected radar wave. Drawing by Van Trong Nguyen.

used in this text. The PRR is used to determine the maximum detectable range of contacts by dividing the radar nautical miles per second by the PRR. In the above example, divide 80,915 by 3,368.

These transmission and receiving windows allow for the use of one antenna. Since the antenna is rotating, and radar waves are so fast, a single pulse can be broadcast, hit an object, and bounce back before any significant rotation of the antenna occurs. The radar has the ability to provide the user with direction to the object with slightly less accuracy than range (hence the name, radio detecting and ranging).

The pulse length is very important to the data the radar is providing the mariner. As discussed in the previous paragraph, simple arithmetic solves for the distance to contacts. But what if two ships were close together, and on the same bearing from the radar unit? If they were so close that the pulses of radar energy overlapped each other, then the radar really wouldn't know two targets were out there. This concept is known as range resolution, and is dependent upon the pulse length.

Radar can therefore detect solid objects that are a specific distance and direction from the vessel. This is critical when determining whether objects are moving in such a fashion as to create a risk of collision, to be at close quarters, or to be navigation hazards or aids.

CHARACTERISTICS OF RADAR PROPAGATION

Radar waves are radio waves comprised of electromagnetic energy, with power output expressed in watts. They are considered electromagnetic because they have both electric and magnetic fields. The electric field is at a right angle to the magnetic field and these are in turn at a right angle to the direction of propagation. The orientation of the electric axis establishes the polarization of the wave. Radar waves are horizontally polarized, which means the electric axis is in the horizontal space. Radar waves are emitted in a highly directional pattern, in a full circle around the horizon corresponding to the motion of the antenna. These waves are transmitted in the form of a radar beam, which is formed by the construction of the antenna. The beam consists of short pulses of high-frequency energy created in the transmitter and sent up to the antenna through the wave guide.

Radar waves are emitted on carrier frequencies between the 3,000- and 10,000-MHz band. The FCC allows a tolerance of plus or minus 50 MHz for a radar transmitter on a designated frequency that falls into this area. There are two common types of marine radars on modern vessels. The X band radar operates at 9,375 MHz with a wavelength of 3.2 centimeters, and the S band radar operates on 3,070 MHz with a wavelength of 10.0 centimeters.

The pulses of RF energy transmitted from a radar antenna form a single-lobe shaped pattern of radiation. The directional antenna also focuses the radiated energy into a relatively narrow beam very similar to the beam of light from a searchlight. This pattern also includes undesirable minor lobes called side lobes, which are formed due to the shape of the antenna.

Beam energy is concentrated along the axis of the beam. The strength of the energy attenuates as the distance from the source becomes greater. The strength of the energy attenuates in directions away from and perpendicular to the beam axis. This decrease in energy is very rapid and is proportional to distance, and predetermined points along the beam can be established where the power has decreased by between 25 and 50 percent. These points are known as quarter-power points and half-power points, respectively.

The radar beam is dimensional and is normally defined by horizontal and vertical beam widths. The beam width is determined by

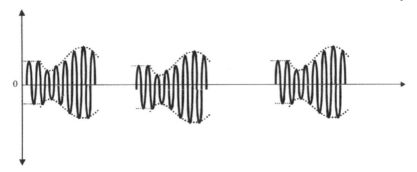

Fig 9-3. Pulse modulated signal. Drawing by Van Trong Nguyen.

calculating the angle of emission from the antenna. The vertical beam width is the angular distance perpendicular to the earth's surface and is relatively broad, ranging between 15 and 30 degrees. The horizontal beam width is the angular distance parallel to the earth's surface and is relatively narrow, measuring between 0.65 to 2 degrees. Beam width is dependent upon four factors: the frequency of the transmitted energy, the wavelength of the transmitted energy, the antenna design, and the dimension of the antenna.

Narrower beam widths for a given antenna size are obtained by employing shorter wavelengths with higher frequency. Narrower beam widths for a given wavelength are created by using a longer antenna. The narrower the beam width, the greater the concentration will be for a given amount of transmitted power. This greater concentration of power will allow the beam to travel a greater distance.

Beam widths play a vital role in the performance of a radar unit. Obviously, a vessel under way in the ocean is subjected to motion, particularly rolling and pitching. The vessel rolls through greater angles than those at which it pitches. By having a large vertical beam width, the radar unit is more prone to detect contacts at close range as the vessel rolls in the opposite direction, and to detect contacts that are at greater ranges when it rolls toward the contact. Although no specific limitations are created by smaller vertical beam widths, the concept should be understood, since stable vessel minimum range may be less than possible when computed using pulse length.

Horizontal beam width plays an important part in the viability of radar information. Because the radar antenna is rotating to provide directional information, it may pulse on a target many times before it rotates to the next degree. It is therefore logical that the narrower the horizontal beam width, the fewer pulses that will hit a contact during rotation. Although this may appear a detriment, it is in fact a benefit. The narrower the beam, the more precisely the radar can display information. If two ships are at equal range from a radar unit and are separated by a relatively small angle, then the narrower the beam,

Fig. 9-4. Radar beam. Drawing by Van Trong Nguyen.

the more capable the unit is of discerning between the two. This principle is called bearing resolution and is primarily dependent upon the horizontal beam width. Oceangoing vessels are required to have radar units which do not exceed 2 degrees of horizontal beam width, but smaller vessels often have units installed with relatively large horizontal beam width, as large as 6 degrees. Frequently a small radar unit for boats may make claims of greater bearing resolution than the short antenna can possibly support. In this case the manufacturer is basing bearing resolution information on close ranges and maximizing half-power points.

Propagation of RF Energy

The same factors that affect radio waves will affect radar waves. This includes refraction, trapping or ducting, diffraction, and, most importantly, reflection. If a radio wave traveled in a straight line along the surface of the earth, the distance it would travel would depend on the height of the antenna. This means that the distance to the horizon would be limited by antenna height in the same way visual distance is limited by the height of the observer. Radio waves, however, bend as they move along the surface of the earth due to refraction. Although the visible horizon may be at a limited distance, the radio waves travel well beyond the visible horizon. The horizon the radar waves reach is called the radar horizon and extends beyond the geometrical and optical horizon.

To express the mathematical relationship: the distance to the geometrical horizon is equal to 1.06 times the square root of the height of the antenna. The distance to the optical horizon is equal to 1.15 times the square root of the height of the antenna, and the distance to the radar horizon is equal to 1.22 times the square root of the height of the antenna, all above the surface of the water. It must be noted, however, that this is based on calculations using a standard atmosphere, which assumes an equal distribution of temperature,

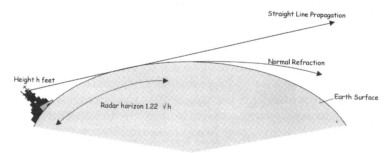

Fig. 9-5. Radar horizon. Drawing by Van Trong Nguyen.

pressure, and density at varying vertical levels. In actuality, this may vary quite differently from true conditions, so these relationships should be considered only as general rules.

For the most part the radar horizon exceeds the geometrical horizon by 15 percent and the optical horizon by 6 percent. It is important to understand that the distance to the radar horizon does not in itself limit the distance from which returning echoes may be received from a target. If you have sufficient power, echoes may be received from well-elevated targets well beyond the radar horizon, particularly if they have good reflecting surfaces.

There are two additional forms of refraction of which the user should be aware. These are the superrefraction and the subrefraction. Superrefraction occurs in normally calm weather when there is an upper layer of warm dry air over the surface layer of cold moist air. This increases the downward bending of the radar waves and thus increases the ranges at which targets may be detected. This normally occurs in the tropics when warm land wind blows over the cooler ocean currents.

Subrefraction occurs when the opposite conditions exist, or when cooler moist air has moved over a shallow layer of warm dry air. This bends the radar waves upward and thus decreases the maximum range at which targets may be detected. Subrefraction also affects minimum ranges and the radar may fail to detect low-lying targets at short range. This condition occurs in polar regions or in cases of temperature inversions within harbors surrounded by large land masses. This is critical because visibility is normally reduced with a temperature inversion and, when under way, the radar may fail to display contacts and create potentially serious situations.

Ducting, which is the same as trapping, occurs during extreme cases of superrefraction. A tunnel or channel is created when a layer of warm dry air moves over the top of cooler moist air. The effect greatly increases the range the radar wave can travel and allows the radar to pick up targets at a much greater range. It should be noted that in these extreme cases targets normally will not be detected when the antenna is above the duct and surface targets are below the duct.

The radar observer should clearly understand the difference between ducting and superrefraction. Superrefraction is a circumstance of exceptional useful radar information. Where most shipboard radars display targets between 15 and 20 miles, under superrefraction conditions, good radar information may be displayed on range scales not normally used, such as 48 or 60 miles.

Ducting, on the other hand, is often considered an interference. This is because the target information of the radar scope is basically useless, and may even be an unnerving distraction. The circumstances

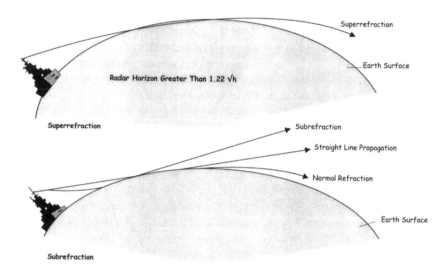

Fig. 9-6. Super- and subrefraction. Drawing by Van Trong Nguyen.

and conditions that allow for ducting to be noticed by the radar observer are very remote. Remember basic theory from chapter 1, where radio ducts can significantly increase radio reception ranges. The same is true for radar waves in a duct, but in this circumstance the radar wave travels a significant distance in the duct, then finds its way out. Once out of the duct, it may hit a contact and reflect right back into the duct. What occurs then is that the echo sneaks back into the radar after a subsequent pulse. So the radar observer may have a strong target being displayed on the radar, but not be able to visualize the contact. As stated, it can be rather unnerving to have a definitive echo displayed on the radar, yet when looking out for the ship causing the echo, there just isn't anything there. Thankfully, ducting usually occurs in relatively clear weather conditions, and the specific areas of the world in which it occurs are known.

There are several areas of the world and certain times of the year when ducting can occur frequently. These include the northern part of the Atlantic Coast of the United States in the summer, the coasts of Florida in the winter, the eastern Atlantic, British Isles, and North Sea in the summer, and any area within the Mediterranean in the summer, particularly when winds blow from the south. The winter season in the Arabian Sea, particularly during the dry period, will produce significant ducting.

In the Arabian Sea-Persian Gulf area there is an exception. During the rainy monsoon season, when strong northwesterly wind is present in the Strait of Hormuz, the monsoon from the southwest mixes with the dry, northwesterly wind over the humid monsoon and very extensive ducts occur. Conditions in the Bay of Bengal and the northern Indian Ocean are normally the same as for the Arabian Sea during the dry winter season.

In the Pacific Ocean, expect ducting in the South China Sea in the winter and in the Yellow Sea and Sea of Japan, particularly around the island of Honshu, during the summer. Ducting also occurs at any time around Guadalcanal, along the east coast of Australia, near New Guinea and Korea, and along the Pacific Coast of the United States. Sometimes it occurs in the open ocean when strong trade winds are present.

Diffraction normally occurs with radar waves in the same manner as it does with all other radio waves. Diffraction of the knife edge of radio waves allows radar to bend around solid objects. Of particular interest is the pattern of radar signals on a scope when the radar antenna is located in front of a mast. A blank area appears, called a shadow, and can be quite noticeable. Once the signal has traveled away from the mast, it appears to fill back around the mast to some extent. Objects within the shadow of the obstruction cannot be detected by the radar at close range, but may become visible at greater range.

Diffraction will eliminate most shadows if the antenna and the interfering object have a relatively large horizontal separation. However, when antennas are located very close to a solid object, diffraction may compensate for the signal loss area. The user need note physical object interference and be aware of the limits it places on the detection capability of the radar. The sector beyond the intervening shipboard obstruction is called a known shadow area, and mariners must not expect the best radar echoes within them.

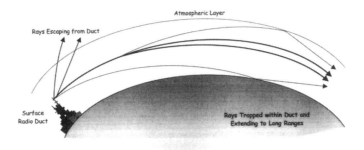

Fig. 9-7. Radar ducting. Drawing by Van Trong Nguyen.

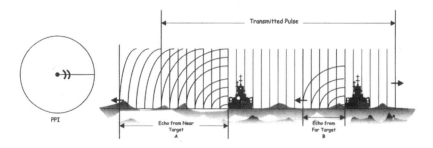

Fig. 9-8. Range resolution. Drawing by Van Trong Nguyen.

   Reflection of radar signals is the key element in the functioning of the radar system. Reflection is both specular and diffuse, depending upon the angle of the surface that the radar beam strikes. That is, when the echo returns directly from the object off of which it is reflected, it is specular. An echo returned by a reflection in other than a direct perpendicular angle is diffuse. Reflected echoes are much weaker than the transmitted pulses because of attenuation and reflective surface area. The characteristics of the returned signal are similar to the transmitted signal and thus are affected by all the forces that affected the original emitted signal.

   The strength of the echo is dependent upon the amount of transmitted energy striking the target and upon the size and reflecting property of the target. Keep in mind that both the transmitted and received signal are subject to attenuation, which is the decrease in the signal strength with distance. This is due to scattering and absorption of RF energy as it passes through the atmosphere. Attenuation is greater at higher frequencies or shorter wavelengths.

   Contact height, size, aspect, shape, texture, and composition all are significant factors contributing to radar's usefulness. Height has

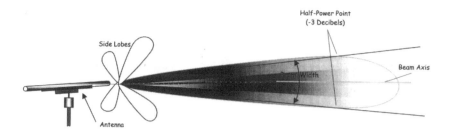

Fig. 9-9. Radar beam horizontal power level.
Drawing by Van Trong Nguyen.

been previously discussed. Obviously the larger the size of the contact, the greater the amount of radar energy that will be reflected. Aspect refers to the angle at which the radar energy hits the contact. With this in mind, the radar observer will understand that less radar energy will be returned from the bow of a ship than from beam ends. Shape is similar to aspect but refers more to objects other than ships, such as navigational hazards or aids. A nun buoy, for example, is a convex surface to the radar energy, and tends to diffuse the energy upon reflection. But observers may note that in most cases, the conical shape of the top part has been removed, offering an almost concave surface that focuses radar waves back to the transmitter. Texture has to do with the surface itself. Rough surfaces may tend to diffuse radar waves and lessen return, whereas smooth surfaces offer excellent reflection. But texture has a relationship with shape and aspect. The nun or spherical buoy may have a rough texture, which may assist radar energy being returned to the transmitter. If the surface were very smooth, then very little energy could escape diffusion and return. Composition relates to the basic electrical properties of the contact's surface. Steel offers an excellent composition, whereas wood or fiberglass offer very little reflective composition.

Sea Surface Effect

The surface of the sea has an effect on the radar beam. The radiation pattern has been explained as the pattern for radar waves in free space. The radar beam is composed of a number of lobes emitting in a wide pattern. During normal transmission, radar waves will travel not only outward but also downward toward the sea. These waves, known as direct waves, will travel outward in a straight manner or will be reflected off the surface of the water. The resulting reflection off the sea surface causes a pattern of indirect waves to reflect upward and mix with the direct waves in the outward path of travel. This can cause an effect similar to simultaneous reception of sky waves and ground waves, namely a form of fading. Because of this phenomenon, there are areas where targets may be physically visible but are not picked up by radar, or the strength of the echo will vary greatly. Every radar has a calculated area of target loss based on vertical beam width and antenna height. This calculated pattern is often provided in the radar manual for users and service technicians.

Sea surface can also create unwanted returns to the receiver. Radar waves that strike the wave action of the ocean's surface are returned and displayed at close ranges. This clutter around the center of the indicator screen is sea return. Sea return is never detected at greater ranges from the vessel, since the returning echo is too weak to reach the antenna.

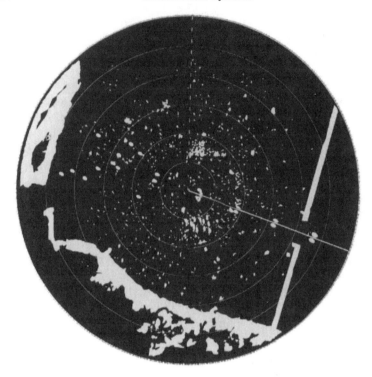

Fig. 9-10. Sea clutter. Courtesy of Raytheon Marine Company.

BASIC COMPONENTS OF THE RADAR SYSTEM

All radar systems, while differing greatly at times, maintain the same general principles of operation and components. There are six major components in the radar system: the power supply, the modulator, the transmitter, the antenna, the receiver, and the indicator.

In most normal radar units, the modulator, transmitter, and receiver power supply are contained in the same chassis. This unit is known as the transceiver, and it is usually separate from the indicator. The unit may also be called an MTR unit for modulator, transmitter, and receiver. Although six components are noted, most modern units will only show three separate parts: the MTR, the indicator, and the antenna. Small-vessel radar units are compacted even more, with the MTR unit installed within the antenna housing.

The power supply provides all AC and DC voltages necessary for the operation of the entire system. In virtually all cases the radar unit takes raw power from the ship's electrical service and conditions it to the demands required by the manufacturer. Power systems on

U.S. ships are generally 115 to 120 volts AC with a 10 percent variance factor. Radar systems should be supplied by vital ship's power or have emergency power backup. The power supply also provides for the operation of the indicator and associated components, as well as the antenna, also known as the scanner.

The modulator produces the synchronizing signals that trigger the transmitter to the number of times per second a pulse is emitted and that also trigger the indicator sweep. It also ensures that all circuits connected within the radar system operate in a definite, coordinated time relationship with each other. The modulator should be considered the timekeeping device of the radar unit. Since radar is based entirely upon accurate time measurements in all phases of operation, the modulator has a special importance, acting in a manner similar to the human brain.

The transmitter is an oscillator that generates RF energy in the form of high-frequency, short, powerful pulses. These are produced by a magnetron or klystron within the transmitter. A system will have either one or the other.

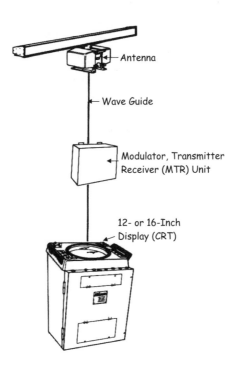

Fig. 9-11. Basic radar system.
Courtesy of Raytheon Marine Company.

The antenna system converts RF energy to radar waves and radiates the energy in a highly directional beam. The antenna also receives echoes and passes the signal to the receiver. There are generally two types of common radar antennas. The first and older type is the parabolic reflector antenna, which utilizes a feedhorn at the center of a directional reflector. The feedhorn splashes the radar signal against the reflector and the waves travel outward. The second type is a slotted wave-guide antenna. Also known as a scanner or array, this type of antenna utilizes slots in the side of a hollow tube to emit radar signals. The advantage of the slotted wave-guide antenna over the parabolic reflector is that many of the emitted side lobes are eliminated. The powerful radar signals move to and from the antenna through a wave guide, which is a hollow tube that can be either rigid or flexible. Its dimensions are based upon the wavelength or carrier frequency of the signals. Wave guide is used because it is more efficient than other types of antenna cable, particularly with high power.

To allow a common wave guide and antenna to receive and transmit signals, a transmit-receive (TR) tube is used. The TR tube rapidly switches from transmitting to receiving functions and vice versa. This prevents damage to the receiver from energy emitted by the transmitter. The TR tube protects the receiver and a second unit called an anti-transmit-receive (ATR) tube is used to block the passage of echoes to the transmitter.

The function of the receiver is to accept and amplify the weak received echoes using a crystal mixer and klystron. Once amplified, the receiver reproduces the echoes as video signals for use by the indicator, also known as the plan position indicator (PPI) because of the way the received signals are presented on the screen. The PPI uses a polar diagram with the transmitting ship's position located at the center. Images of target echoes are displayed in either their true or relative bearings at their distances from the PPI center. The indicator cabinet provides a means for operating the various controls associated with the radar system and the video presentation. More modern terminology may refer to the PPI cabinet as the radar display unit (RDU).

The indicator cabinet contains a cathode ray tube (CRT) that is used for the video display. The CRT screen, which is the PPI, is coated with a film of phosphorescent material. A cathode draws electrons from a filament and forms them into a narrow beam that travels past a series of anodes that shape and accelerate the beam. The beam also passes by a series of coils that focus and deflect the beam.

Because the PPI uses phosphorescent glow, it may be dim in daylight. PPIs are often fitted with hoods that allow just the eyes of

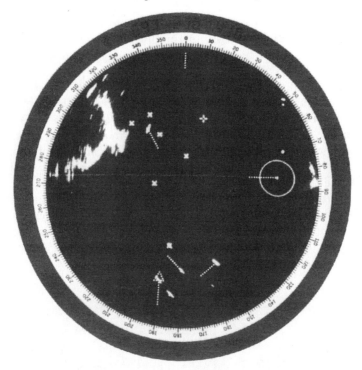

Fig. 9-12. Radar display. Courtesy of Raytheon Marine Company.

the observer to view the screen. The electron beam is rapidly and repeatedly moved back and forth from the center point of the PPI. The bright line formed is called the trace. Because the electron beam reacts with the phosphorescent material on the screen when the beam is shut off, the trace continues to glow. This glow is called persistence, and it decreases in strength when the electron beam is not present. At the instant the modulator triggers the transmitter, it sends a timing signal to the indicator from the center of the PPI to form the trace. The trace moves at the same rate as the antenna, in a clockwise direction called the sweep. The timing signal also establishes the production of range rings on the PPI scope.

The deflection of the electron beam forming the sweep is tied to the pulse repetition rate and the set range on the unit. As the signals are transmitted the sweep is formed. When an echo is returned during the nonoperating time of transmission, the echo is transformed to video pulse and displayed on the sweep, indicating a target. The sweep is rotated electromagnetically and synchronized with the antenna every time it passes the heading point on the radar.

Newer radar units now display radar information using high-resolution rasterscan displays. In this form of radar, the electrons are not emitted from the center of the screen but horizontally, in thousands of dots called pixels. Radar display requires the traditional radar echoes be transformed into video signals, but also passed through a microprocessor for proper display. The indicator and image seen by the radar observer is similar to a television screen or computer monitor. Since the radar information is usually displayed as a circle to assist in determining bearings, additional areas of the rectangular screen are used to display information such as range scale in use, variable range, and bearing lines. The circular PPI simulation done by the rasterscan also has a sweep programmed in to give the radar observer the feel of using a radar. This type of display is not required, however. These indicator displays are naturally preferred for modern automatic radar plotting aids (ARPA), as will be discussed in chapter 10.

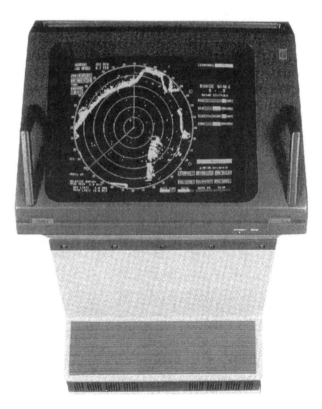

Fig. 9-13. Rasterscan radar screen.
Courtesy of Litton/Sperry Marine Systems.

The rasterscan unit presentation appears to contain sharper rectangles in the displayed target image. Some observers feel they are losing an accurate view of objects, particularly topographic features. After an acclimation period, extended experience with the rasterscan's performance overcomes most of these doubts. One of their prime advantages is the ability to offer color in the presentation and superimpose target designations and information right on the screen. New "day bright" units, which do not require the use of a screen or hood to reduce glare, also use this system.

COMMON OPERATIONAL CONSTANTS

There are certain operational constants associated with every radar system. These include carrier frequency, pulse repetition rate, pulse length, and power relation.

Carrier frequency is the frequency at which the RF energy is generated. The higher the carrier frequency, the shorter the wavelength and thus the smaller the antenna required. The frequency of the radar signal is produced in the transmitter by the magnetron or klystron. These tubes can produce high-frequency, high-power RF signals.

The unique characteristics of the pulse-modulated signals create difficulty in amplifying returned signals. The RF amplifier cannot simply attach the amplified signal to the carrier wave. Instead, the frequency of the incoming echoes are mixed with that of a locally oscillated signal. This mixing is referred to as heterodyning the signal. The resulting frequency, known as the intermediate frequency, is now low enough to be amplified through a simplified system and then converted to video pulses.

The pulse repetition rate is the number of pulses transmitted per second. After a signal is transmitted, time must be allowed for the echo to return and be received. If this time was not allowed, the transmitted signal would block the returning signals. The PRR establishes how long the radar listens for the returned echoes. The maximum range of a radar depends upon the unit's peak power in relation to its pulse repetition rate. Transmitted RF energy can be increased by lowering the pulse repetition rate to provide additional time between transmitted pulses. The signal, however, must have a high enough PRR so that enough pulses hit the target and return to allow detection of that target. Maximum range of the system can be determined by dividing the constant 80,915 by the PRR.

As the antenna rotates, the radar beam strikes a target for only a short time. During that time, enough signals must be transmitted in order to produce sufficient echoes to allow annunciation (the accumulated display of many amplified echoes) to be presented on the radar screen. For an average system with an antenna rotation of 15 rpm, a unit having a PRR of 800 pulses will produce 22 pulses for each degree of antenna rotation. PRRs are between 500 and 4,000 pulses per second in most radar sets.

The pulse length, measured in microseconds, is the transmission time of a single pulse of RF energy. The pulse length determines the minimum range at which a target can be detected. If a target is very close to the radar, the echo will return so quickly that it can't be received, as the TR tube is still engaged. The target will not be seen on the radarscope at a critical close range, a serious situation in restricted visibility.

Generally, short pulse lengths of about 0.1 microsecond are used for close ranges. Most radar units are designed for operation with both short and long pulse rates. On some units, this is automatically connected to the range selector. Usually when an operator selects a range scale below 6 miles, the unit will switch to the shorter pulse length. On some older sets, it is left to the operator to select a long or short pulse length based upon the same criteria. With the shorter pulse length, maximum detection range is compromised but better range resolution is obtained. There is also better definition of the target on the radarscope with the shorter pulse length.

In considering power relation, the useful power of the transmitter contained in the radiated pulse is referred to as the peak power of the system. Power output from the radar antenna is measured in kilowatts.

INTERFERENCE

Radars are simply radio transmitting, receiving, and displaying systems. As with any radio device, static or noise can be a major inconvenience. When interference adversely affects a device aboard ship installed to increase safety, a very serious and potentially dangerous situation can be created. The skilled operator should know how to recognize certain interferences and possess knowledge of how to minimize them if possible. Sometimes the term noise is used to describe interference.

Sea return was mentioned in the sea surface effect section. Sea return, or sea clutter, is unwanted echoes from the ocean waves displayed close to the center of the sweep of a radar. The danger of sea return is the possible nondetection of a contact close to the ship, or loss of contacts that are being tracked. Sea return really can't be eliminated unless the radar is shut down, but it can be minimized by either reducing the RF gain or lowering the range scale in use. Radar units are equipped with sea clutter control switches called sensitivity time control (STC). The STC reduces the CRT sensitivity near the center of the sweep. Care must be taken to use this control judiciously, and to switch it off when not needed.

Rain clutter is unwanted return being displayed from echoes bouncing off precipitation. The existence of this clutter can be useful in determining if heavy rain is approaching, but it is dangerous in that it may mask out contacts. Again, reducing RF gain can help. Radars are equipped with a variety of controls and methods to attempt to minimize rain clutter. The basic means is by a fast time constant (FTC) switch, which reduces receiver sensitivity and reduces amplified signals transmitted to the CRT, often called rain clutter or antirain. Other methods include polarization and rain rate switches, which sometimes work as multipliers of FTC. Manufacturer operations manuals should be consulted as to the best methods to use these additional clutter controls. Any antirain clutter switches should be used carefully since they affect the entire screen, and they should be turned off when no precipitation is present.

Indirect or false echoes are interference incurred by the ship's superstructure appendages, such as masts, kingposts, or stacks. These obstructions interfere with the propagation of RF energy as discussed under "Propagation of RF Energy" on page 212, and are referred to as blind or shadow areas. Indirect echoes are always displayed in known shadow areas of the ship. They are created by RF energy directed toward the obstruction then being deflected out to a solid object, then returning by the same path. These echoes should always be at the same range as a contact already being displayed on the screen. They are basically unimportant, and usually will disappear relatively soon when the angles of incidence are changed by the combined motion of the own ship (radar observer's term referring to the radar operator's ship, as opposed to the target or contact ship) and the target ship. Temporary removal of indirect echoes can be accomplished by a minor course change, or sometimes by a reduction of RF gain.

Multiple echoes are interference that occurs when the own ship is passing close to large, steeply walled obstructions or high freeboard ships at beam ends. The RF energy reflects off the target and is returned to the own ship, but some of it bounces back off the own ship toward the target ship for another reflection. Each time RF energy is returned to the own ship, some of it makes it to the antenna and is displayed. The displayed image is successive contacts, an equal distance apart, on the same bearing. This occurrence is usually temporary and is easy to recognize as not being very serious. If the operator wishes to reduce the effect, reduction of RF gain should do the trick.

Second-trace echoes, sometimes called ghost targets, are echoes which have traveled out beyond the range scale in use and have returned after a subsequent pulse emission. This concept was discussed in "Propagation of RF Energy." Changing the pulse repetition rate using the range scale can help the operator recognize this type of interference.

In "Characteristics of Radar Propagation" (see page 209), side lobes were mentioned as a characteristic of RF propagation. It was also noted that slotted wave guides have effectively eliminated unwanted side lobes. If there are some side lobes to the own ship propagation, however, close-in contacts can produce side lobe effects. Side lobe effects are unwanted echoes on either side of a known contact, creating an arc. There are usually two or three echoes on each side of the target, getting progressively weaker as they move away from the target. These are temporary in nature and can be eliminated by reducing RF gain.

Electronic interference occurs when an own ship radar is operating near another ship with the same or nearly the same carrier frequency. The display will show segmented spirals emitting from the sweep center. These are temporary and there is little the operator can do about them.

Overhead cable effect is another nuisance interference, but one which should be known about because of the circumstances in which it occurs. When navigating in rivers or narrow waterways, overhead power cables or high tension wires can occasionally reflect RF energy. They do not appear as a line across the screen, but usually as one large target at the lowest point of the cabling. Naturally, it could be very unnerving when, navigating down a river, one suddenly detects a contact immediately ahead. NIMA's *Sailing Directions* and U.S. Coast Guard's *Coast Pilots* will often warn mariners of this effect, and pilots will sometimes make the circumstance known.

There are a number of interferences that really are equipment malfunctions. The mariner must be able to recognize them and conclude that maintenance is required on the radar. When one of the following occurs the operator should note in the radar logbook which interference took place. This will assist the service technician in finding the radar's problem.

Spoking occurs when there is a modulator problem, indicated by many radial lines showing up on the radar screen. Sectoring occurs as a result of problems with the automatic frequency control and the radar display's large, pie-slice sectors. Serrated range rings occur as a result of problems in the sweep. PPI distortion is a result of static electricity soon after power up on older CRT displays. Hourglass effect is an expansion or constriction near the center of the screen because of time base or modulator problems, and usually occurs in narrow rivers or canals.

FACTORS AFFECTING MAXIMUM RANGE DETECTION

The following factors should be considered regarding maximum range detection in radar systems. The higher the frequency the greater the attenuation, regardless of weather. Lower frequencies are more effective for long-range detection. For this reason, the 10-cm S band radar is often considered the long-range collision avoidance radar. The higher the peak power output, the longer the range. This relationship is not proportional, as doubling the power increases the range by only 25 percent. The longer the pulse length, the greater the range of the system. The lower the PRR, the longer the detection range will be since the pulses are longer, allowing returning echoes to be detected from greater distances. The more concentrated the beam, the greater the detection range of the unit.

Larger, more solid objects are more easily detected. Targets that are high above the surface can also be picked up at greater distances. More sensitive receivers pick up targets at greater ranges. They are, however, more sensitive to jamming and interference from atmospherics or other radars on the same frequency. The slower the antenna turns, the greater the detection range.

FACTORS AFFECTING MINIMUM RANGE DETECTION

The following factors affect the ability of the radar unit to pick up targets at close range. Since minimum range is equal to one-half the pulse length, the shorter the length the closer the targets that are picked up. Therefore, the higher the PRR, the shorter the pulses, and the shorter the detection range. Proper operation of the duplexer, or the TR/ATR assembly, is critical to minimum detection range. Signals returned by ocean waves can cause sea return or clutter at the center of the scope and can mask targets. Side lobe effects create additional clutter at the center of the scope that also masks targets. Targets close in under the vertical beam angle, particularly at beam ends, can escape detection.

FACTORS AFFECTING RANGE ACCURACY

Range accuracy depends upon the exact time interval between the instant a pulse is transmitted and the instant an echo is received. Factors that affect range accuracy include fixed error, which occurs when the sweep starts before the RF energy leaves the antenna. This is a modulator time problem that may affect accurate ranging of the device. Voltage drops or fluctuations of the line voltage can cause variations in the range rings or variable range marker. Frequency drift causes variations in the frequency of the transmitter's oscillator and may affect ranging. Target alignment by the operator can yield more accurate ranges when the leading edge of a target is placed against a fixed range ring. The variable range marker (VRM) is not as accurate for determining range as fixed rings. The higher the range scale setting, the greater the error in the VRM or the fixed ring alignment. The further the target is out on the PPI from the center, the greater the range inaccuracy.

FACTORS AFFECTING RANGE RESOLUTION

Range resolution is the capability of the radar to distinguish between two targets on the same bearing that are close together. This is dependent upon several principal factors, which include pulse length, receiver gain, CRT spot size, and range scale being used. For the best results, the user should employ the lowest possible range scale that includes short pulses and minimum receiver gain.

FACTORS AFFECTING BEARING ACCURACY

Bearing accuracy is dependent upon several factors. The narrower the horizontal beam width, the more accurate the bearing measurement. The center of the target is easier to discern and measure on the PPI scope. Effective beam width can be reduced by lowering the gain. Bearings of small targets are more accurate than bearings of large targets. Slow or stationary target bearings are more accurate than fast-moving target bearings. Stabilized displays are more accurate than nonstabilized displays. If the origin of the sweep is not at the center of the scope, the accuracy of the bearings is off. Bearings are affected by the improper use of the mechanical bearing cursor due to parallax error. Using an electronic bearing line is more accurate. If the heading flasher and the ship's head are not aligned, bearing errors can result. Check the alignment accuracy by checking that the heading line crosses targets dead ahead.

FACTORS AFFECTING BEARING RESOLUTION

Bearing resolution is the ability of a radar unit to separate contacts that are at the same range but close together. Certain factors can affect bearing resolution. Horizontal beam width from the antenna can distort numerous targets so they appear as one. The narrower the beam, the better the ability to discern more than one target at close bearing at the same range. Bearings should also be read at the center of the contact. Slotted wave-guide antennas generally produce narrow horizontal beam widths and thus produce better bearing resolution. The farther away the target, the poorer the bearing resolution simply because of the angular distance relationship to linear distance. The smaller the screen, the poorer the resolution.

MISCELLANEOUS DETECTION FACTORS

Two miscellaneous factors finally must be considered in the effectiveness of the radar to detect targets: weather and target aspect. Weather generally reduces the effective range and creates unwanted echoes. The observer should note that sea return is greatest from the direction that the wind and sea travel. To reduce the effect of sea clutter, you can lower the gain or use the STC or anticlutter sea/sea clutter control. The other condition is precipitation including fog, rain, snow, or hail. The FTC or differentiator or anticlutter rain/rain clutter control will shorten the echoes that are reproduced as video signals. It will also reduce receiver sensitivity. Adjustment of gain or use of the STC or FTC will compromise maximum detection range.

Aspect is how the other vessel is viewed by the radar. High vessels with a lot of freeboard viewed from the side will be seen earlier and better than low targets viewed end-on.

TYPES OF RADAR DISPLAYS

As stated earlier, modern marine radar units are pulse-modulated. Radar users must be aware of different types of pulse-modulated radars. There are two types of radar units found aboard ships today. The difference is referred to in terms of display.

The first kind of display is relative-motion display. In this display the own ship is shown as a fixed point around which the objects surrounding it are moving. In the relative-motion display, when the own ship is making way, all detected objects including land appear to be in motion. Hence, everything else is relative to the own ship. Obviously, landmasses cannot move, but they will be displayed as moving at the exact reciprocal course and speed of the own ship. Only a ship moving at the exact same course and speed of the own ship will appear stationary.

The other type is true-motion display. Here the own ship is put in real motion, actually moving across the indicator screen consistently with the course and speed of the ship. All fixed objects, such as land, will remain stationary. Any object that is moving will appear to be actually moving. This type of display is obviously more difficult to accomplish, as the unit must have references to course, speed, or some fixed object.

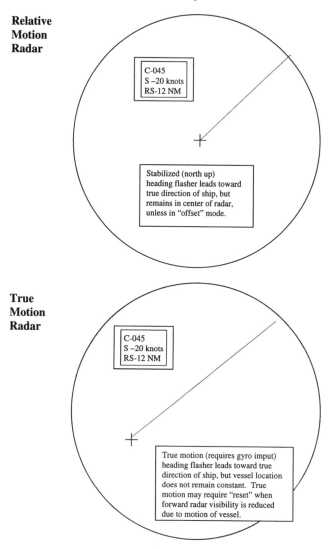

Relative Motion Radar

C-045
S –20 knots
RS-12 NM

Stabilized (north up) heading flasher leads toward true direction of ship, but remains in center of radar, unless in "offset" mode.

True Motion Radar

C-045
S –20 knots
RS-12 NM

True motion (requires gyro imput) heading flasher leads toward true direction of ship, but vessel location does not remain constant. True motion may require "reset" when forward radar visibility is reduced due to motion of vessel.

Fig. 9-14. Relative motion/true motion displays.
Drawing by Thomas Bushy.

It is fair to say that the relative-motion radar is less difficult to make and to maintain. Yet is equally fair to say that the true-motion display is easier to use. Ease of use may be a relative term, however, since mariners have long proved relative-motion as a useful and preferred display. Modern true-motion units are far superior today than were their predecessors. The reality is that both have unique benefits to the mariner. When operating in confined waters where precision navigation and ship control is imperative, most users will agree the true-motion wins hands down. On the other hand, a relative-motion radar is easier to use and observe while under way in open waters because of its simplicity.

The two radar displays also have available options. Stabilization refers to the direction the radar unit is pointing, or the direction toward which the heading flasher is aligned. Although the ship is following a course track, it also is following the bow. The two choices, course or bow, are available to operators when using a relative-motion display. When a radar display is stabilized it has directional sensors or course input. A radar without course input must logically be unstabilized.

Early radars were unstabilized displays, even before the units were known to have stabilization. The focus of the radar was on the bow, and the heading flasher was aligned to it. This was the easiest method to install, and it required no confusing external information imputs to the radar. Unstabilized displays are also known as heading-up displays, or simply head-up. This method of display will always be available on relative-motion radars since the unit is acting independently of all other sources, notwithstanding electricity. This type of display can introduce errors to radar observation that could be dangerous and that could make radar plotting techniques difficult. Because the unit is stabilized to the bow, any change in direction will cause contacts displayed to drift in the opposite direction. If an observer is using the unit for rapid radar plotting on the plotting head, when the vessel changes course, new plotting information must be reinitiated. If accurate bearings to determine position or risk of collision are desired, meticulous note of accurate ship's course must be taken.

Stabilized relative-motion radars, sometimes called north-up displays, have compass information imput to the unit, called compass sensors. The electric gyrocompass and the newer flux gate compasses can send directional information to the radar unit, which can then use this as the heading flasher alignment. Older mariners may remember the first stage of this innovation in the late 1950s and early 1960s when gyrorepeaters were installed as an azimuth ring outside of the relative bearing ring of the indicators. Actually, the radar remained unstabilized, yet the mariner could cross-check the heading without leaving the radar. This practice was relatively short-lived, when in the early 1970s the compass data was fed directly into the heading flasher alignment.

Stabilized radar display units were a significant benefit to mariners. Now the operator could expect the contacts to remain relatively constant in displayed position as the ship changed course. No longer was the radar observer constantly looking for a compass, because the heading flasher was the compass. Unfortunately, there was a problem. Radar indicators had always been installed on the bridge of ships facing forward, and the operator stood astern of them. This was a tradition held over from the unstabilized displays. Once compass information caused the heading flasher to move off top dead center, or dead ahead of the operator, confusion arose. Now the operator steering a course of 180 degrees was standing in such a location that the own ship was coming aft. The image displayed by the stabilized radar might be totally different than the view out the windows. Practice makes all tasks easy, and the difficulty was soon overcome.

Technology has recently changed, and another choice is now given the operator that may finally alleviate any confusion, while giving him or her all the benefits of stabilized orientation. Stabilized course-up is now available. In this display orientation, the operator selects the stabilized function, offering the benefits of north-up, but also with the heading flasher placed at the top of the screen, regardless of the direction of travel. As the ship yaws through its course, the small deviations do not affect target display. If the ship makes a small course change, the operator can reset the course-up and bring the heading flasher to the top, while all the targets are moved along with it. Larger course changes usually cause an automatic reset to actuate.

Stabilization has a slightly different meaning in true-motion radars. Since the radar is designed to display the own ship course as true, it requires manual input or gyrocompass input. But ocean or tidal currents create set and drift, which in turn modify the course and speed made good. Early true-motion radars were equipped with set and drift compensating control knobs, where the navigator had to manually input corrections. It is this circumstance which caused early resistance to true-motion radars and continued resistance when operating in the open sea. The early units also allowed for sea-stabilized or ground-stabilized displays. Debate continues as to the accuracy of either selection, but technology and preference has probably quelled most disagreement. Modern ARPA units which have true-motion capability are fitted with autodrift functions. These functions allow the operator to select a known fixed object and lock on. The unit then computes and compensates for any variation of course or speed inputs. This will be discussed further in chapter 10.

PLOTTING

Radar is mentioned in the Rules of the Road as a means of determining safe speed and risk of collision. There remains no doubt that mariners have learned to effectively utilize radar, and this has prompted international standards of safety to demand proper use. Virtually every licensed officer aboard merchant ships must have completed a specific course in radar operations. In the United States mariners have the title "radar observer" clearly added to their licenses. Such endorsement is valid for 5 years, at which time the officer must attend a 1-day refresher course. Most maritime training institutions throughout the world have gained approval to conduct this training and are using radar simulation in the process.

Probably one of the most difficult things to understand about radar is how to derive valid information from it and use that information effectively in determining risk of collision. The skill is essential to proper watchkeeping.

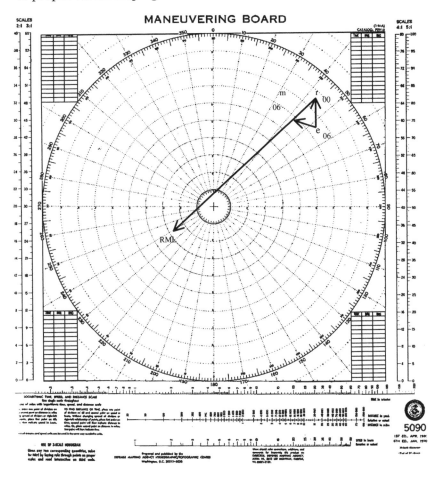

Fig. 9-15(a). Basic rapid radar triangle. Drawing by Thomas Bushy.

Vector method plotting is considered the manual means of determining collision information. This is what is meant when the rules mention "radar plotting." There are a number of different methods within the area of manual plotting. The method most frequently used throughout the world today is the rapid radar plotting method. The operator uses a grease pencil and a speed stick on a reflective surface installed on PPI-type radar indicators. This method of plotting is a requirement of the U.S. Coast Guard and is found in many other nation's regulations. The method is very useful and time-efficient on the scope, and the same method may be accomplished on radar plotting sheets after extracting the data from the radar. This

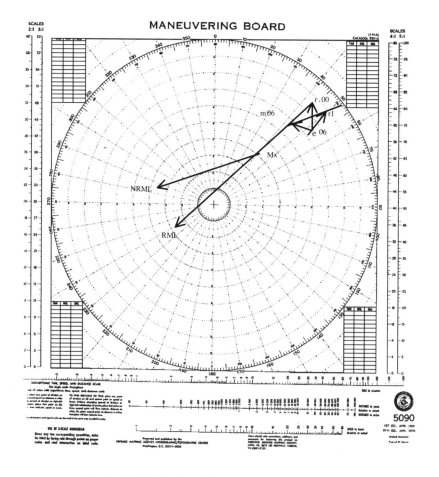

Fig. 9-15(b). Basic collision avoidance triangle.
Drawing by Thomas Bushy.

may be the only alternative a radar observer has for determining exact radar information if computer-aided systems fail.

Rule 7 of the Rules of the Road allows "equivalent systematic observation" to be conducted in determining risk of collision, in lieu of radar plotting. Modern technology has been added to radar to aid the mariner in using it. Rule 7 refers to these computer-aided radar plotting devices called ARPA, briefly introduced earlier in this chapter. Detailed discussion of these systems can be found in chapter 10.

Rapid Radar Plotting

Rapid radar plotting is a term used to describe a method of vector analysis intended to give the radar observer information about the movement of contacts on his or her display. In this discussion the reader will notice the use of terms which are synonyms. The term "own ship" will be used to describe the operator's vessel only. The terms "target," "contact," and "pip" are synonyms referring to the other ship in a collision analysis.

Three pieces of information must be known about a vessel's navigation in order for the radar observer to be able to effectively plot radar contacts: the vessel course made good, speed made good, and radar range scale in use. "Course and speed made good" is used as opposed to "true course" because current effects on the own ship should be approximately the same as for target ships. Range scale in use is important because it is used as a distance base for the vector analysis.

Course information is usually provided to the radar by a mechanical gyrocompass or an electronic flux gate compass. Each of these external sensors inputs data to the radar when in stabilized mode. Under most circumstances mariners prefer to plot targets using the stabilized function, as it negates time wasting cross-check of own ship heading. It is important to understand that rapid radar plotting can be done in unstabilized mode provided care is taken when observing bearings. When performing rapid radar plotting, speed is not input directly into the radar, but must be inserted into the vectors analysis on the screen. Range scale in use is displayed clearly when viewing the scope, as required for any radar meeting international performance standards.

The concept of using the range scale as a basis for time intervals is necessary because radar plotting requires very precise use of fractions of the hour. When an observer intends to plot targets, he or she must select an interval of observation. An interval of observation is the time period between observations of contacts. This time interval must be both large enough to generate large vectors, but not so long as to waste valuable time, particularly for fast-moving targets. Most mariners will select an interval of observation in minutes by dividing the range scale in use by two. If the range scale is 12 miles, then the time between observations of a contact will be 6 minutes. This is the normal observation period because the scale and time creates large vectors, and the mental arithmetic is rather easy. It should be understood that the radar observer must be capable of gathering accurate information in a timely fashion. Any delays in lengthy computations could lead the vessel into danger.

The range scale and the interval of observation share a relationship that lends itself to simple use of the speed stick. A speed stick is a transparent straightedge that has been calibrated with vessel speed. Most training institutions provide students with speed sticks that have a scale printed on them. This scale is based upon the distance between range rings on standard 16-inch displays, or the diameter of a radar screen. Mariners should always check to make sure the scale printed on the screen in fact matches the intended scale on the radar. To check the stick, draw a radial line on the screen, mark off the intersection of at least two consecutive range rings, then compare. If there is a variation, obviously the speed stick graduations must be modified, as changing the location of range rings is difficult and confusing.

Once sure the speed stick has a useful scale, use an indelible marker to depict the distance the own ship will move in 6 minutes, or $\frac{1}{10}$ hour. This distance will be used when doing standard 6-minute plots of contacts. When using a range scale other than 12 miles, the own ship vector length will remain the same, as the operator changes the interval of observation rather than the vector length.

As an example of this important concept, imagine your vessel is operating at 20 knots. Its motion over 6 minutes will be $\frac{1}{10}$ of the 20 knots, or 2 miles. If using the 12-mile range scale with six range rings, each ring would be 2 miles apart. Own ship vectors would also be 2 miles long since the interval of observation is 6 minutes. When the operator chooses to plot contacts on a 24-mile range, the interval of observation is now 12 minutes. The vessel would travel 4 miles in that period, and that also is the distance between range rings on a 24-mile scale. The rule is useful on all range scales where six rings are given. Rarely would observers plot on 48- or 60-mile ranges, so the rule works with ranges from 24 to 1.5 miles. At the 1.5 mile range the interval of observation would be a mere 45 seconds. Although unlikely, if a target was suddenly displayed at 1.25 miles in fog, performing a 45-second plot for more information might be better than taking the wrong action. Remember that the *Rules of the Road* specifically warn against using scanty radar information to determine risk of collision.

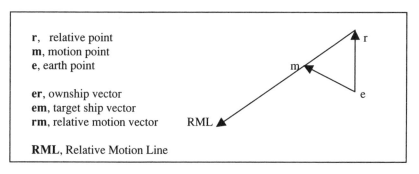

r, relative point
m, motion point
e, earth point

er, ownship vector
em, target ship vector
rm, relative motion vector   RML

RML, Relative Motion Line

Fig. 9-16. Radar plotting symbols. Drawing by Thomas Bushy.

Once the radar observer is confident of the course, speed, and observation time, plotting targets to effectively monitor collision is possible. Upon detecting a target, the observer should mark the pip with an X. The use of X is recommended over dots since dots may be obliterated when drawing in vectors later. The first marking is labeled "r" and given a time, usually real time in minutes. The "r" point is so labeled since it begins the relative motion analysis, and is so called the relative point. The observer now must insert the own ship vector, labeled "er." The creation of the "e," or the earth point, is integral to proper plotting. Once the "e" is put into the plot, it will remain stationary in all future analysis. This is why it is called the earth point. To draw in the own ship "er" vector, the observer draws a line parallel with the heading flasher, starting at "r" and the reciprocating course for the distance appropriate to the interval of observation. Carefully mark "e," the distance own ship will travel based upon the interval of observation. Once placed, the "er" vector should accurately represent own ship motion for the interval of observation. Always make a quick check by reading the "er" vector, where the direction of "e" to "r" is actually own ship course. Mariners often go the wrong way, particularly when plotting contacts abaft the beam.

After the interval of observation elapses, the present position of the contact is carefully marked with an X and labeled "m." The "m" stands for the motion point, as it represents the relative motion of the contact over a determined time interval. This is the last point of observation of the base triangle. By connecting "r" to "m," the speed and direction of relative motion (SRM, DRM) are seen, and by connecting "e" to "m," the course and speed of the target ship is seen.

The collision analysis usually begins by extending the relative motion line (RML) beyond own ship's beam. This line will represent the relative motion expected of the contact provided all things remain the same. In other words, the validity of this prediction for the future is wholly dependent upon the own ship and target ship continuing on the same courses and speeds as were maintained during observation. It is for this reason that most mariners will take another observation, usually at 12 minutes, to have confidence that the situation is as was predicted at 6 minutes. Any variation of the contact from the RML is evidence that something is not as was predicted and that the information gathered was insufficient to make firm decisions.

To most mariners the RML tells the whole story. It is the line that represents what is going to happen. If the line comes directly to the center of the sweep (own ship location), then risk of collision exists and some form of action will be required. If the line passes astern at a significant distance, there probably is no risk. If the RML passes ahead, there exists a bow crossing range (BCR), and if it is far enough away no real danger is present. Some mariners will actually only draw in the RML and make decisions from it. Although this sounds foolhardy to the novice, it really is not. If the mariner can ascertain that risk of collision does not exist, and can continue to monitor the situation until finally past and clear by using the RML, then proper watchkeeping is being maintained. Usually further analysis is desired only if risk of collision is present and detailed information about the other contact is needed to plan an evasive maneuver or to assist in providing information useful in communications.

The RML can provide more than risk of collision information. The closest point of approach (CPA) is derived from the RML. As the name describes, the CPA is a point on the RML depicting the exact location where the target vessel will be nearest the own ship. This point is found by finding the shortest perpendicular to the RML connecting the sweep's center. CPA is expressed in range and bearing, and can be given a predicted time by advancing the SRM. Mariners must be guided at this point by the practices of safe watchkeeping established by their vessel master. The master will have prepared detailed information about watchkeeping, in particular regarding identification of what is a risk of collision and what is not. It is fair to say most captains will consider CPAs of less than 2 miles to represent risk when operating in open sea, but may lessen this distance when conditions of better readiness to take action by the own ship exist.

To determine more information about the target ship the observer must go back to the original triangle and focus on the "em" vector. The direction from "e" toward "m" is the vessel's course, and the length of the vector represents speed. It is commonly accepted practice to determine target ship speed by comparing the length of the "em" against the own ship vector. If, for example, it is 50 percent longer, then the contact is going half again own ship speed. Once the target's course and speed are known, evasive maneuvers may be planned as required or communications can be made more easily.

The question of evasive maneuvers to avoid a risk of collision is a matter of study in the Rules of the Road. Under the Rules, some vessels must give way to others. In order to give way, a vessel has only course and/or speed to choose from. Most captains will select course change on their vessels, as the Rules encourage, provided certain checks are made. Speed changes take a little longer for oceangoing vessels and therefore are avoided if possible.

To plan an evasive maneuver the observer must know when and where the action point will be. This distance from own ship is contained in the master's standing orders. At that point on the RML an X is placed and labeled "Mx" for maneuvering point. The time of this action point should also be noted by advancing the known SRM. From the "Mx" a line is drawn tangent to the range at which the captain desires to pass the contact. This line is called the new relative motion line (NRML). The line is transferred back to the original triangle so that it remains parallel with the drawn NRML. It is added to the original triangle at the "m" point. Students should note that bringing the NRML to a motion point makes sense because it is the "er" line that must be modified if own ship intends to take action, not the "em" vector. Once placed, the NRML represents the desired relative motion own ship wants the contact to follow. If the NRML cuts through the existing "er" vector, a speed change can be determined quickly, at the point of intersection called "r^1." If a course change is desired but not speed change, the observer must arch the existing "er" vector length from "e," until the arc intersects the NRML. The intersection is also called "r^1." By connecting "e" to "r^1," the mariner can ascertain the new course to steer.

Execution of the predicted action should be carefully monitored by observing the relative motion of the contact on the NRML. If for any reason, after the own ship has taken determined action, the target vessel does not follow the NRML, the mariner should be alerted that the contact also took action, and further action may be required under the Rules of the Road.

The original triangle can be extremely useful to the watch officer if a target vessel proposes taking action via radio communications. Simply draw in a new "em^1" vector and determine the NRML. Transfer the NRML to the action point to ascertain if the action will satisfy the own ship's needs. This process is also used when determining whether the predicted action of the own ship will have detrimental effects on another contact that otherwise would pass safely. Simply draw the new "er[1]" into the original triangle of the target in question. Connect the new r[1] with the existing "m" and transfer to the maneuvering point.

Use of rapid radar plotting is essential to safe watchkeeping practices. Although modern ARPA equipment suggests that manual plotting is no longer needed, nothing could be further from the truth. Should the microprocessor fail, radar information can still be displayed. Although accurate scope plotting isn't easy on a rasterscan display, ranges and bearings of targets can be transferred to maneuvering boards for determination of risk of collision. As a matter of fact, the prudent mariner will practice radar plotting frequently, even in clear visibility, so as to be assured the skills are not lost. This is very important for U.S. mariners who must recertify their radar plotting skills every five years.

RADAR NAVIGATION

The radar has become an integral part of navigation in recent years. Where mariners once were forced to accomplish mathematical computations to determine distance off, or to use various forms of navigation to gather position information while making landfalls, today most doubts about position have been eliminated due to radar.

The radar unit has an inherent strength in being able to display distance off an object. It also may, with proper use, give reasonably accurate bearings. That is to say, if the mariner can positively identify an object present on the navigational chart with radar, then a simple range and bearing can affix position with pretty good accuracy.

The trouble for most new users of radar for navigation is the identification problem. Learning to navigate for most is a challenge, to take a bird's eye perspective given on the chart and transfer this information to the plane view from the earth's surface. With radar this problem has come around full circle. Now the radar observer attempting to navigate must take the bird's eye perspective of radar to the chart. The trouble is, they rarely look exactly the same. All the issues discussed in this chapter concerning strengths and weaknesses of radar can cause tremendous confusion. The more rapid attenuation of 3-cm RF energy, the composition and shape of targets, and the limitations of radar horizon are examples of a few problems still faced by navigators using radar.

The one key to effective radar use for navigation is the same as with virtually every other form of navigation. If you have a reasonable idea of where your vessel is, then it can be confirmed or denied rather quickly. To accomplish this the mariner must maintain as accurate a dead-reckoning track as possible. With a good DR position the perception of what the radar might display is made easier. If the shoreline nearby is rocky in most places yet has low sand beaches at other points, then the radar observer will visualize a broken coastline before consulting the radar. City skyscrapers may be useful targets well beyond the anticipated range of the radar. Yet radar will be the last choice of navigators if approaching a low, swampy coastline.

Basically, radar navigators should rely upon ranges first. When more than one range is taken, the range information is scribed onto the chart by swinging an arc with compasses from the known terrestrial object displayed on the radar. When two of these ranges intersect a fix is made. Of course more than two ranges are desired, and the established rules of angular distances between lines of position

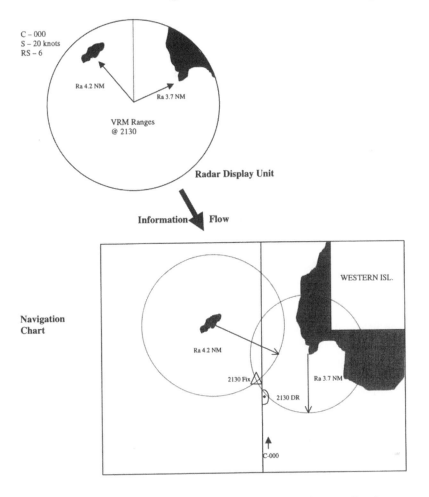

Fig. 9-17. Navigation by radar. Drawing by Thomas Bushy.

(LOP) should be followed. When taking distance measurements that are relatively large the use of bearing can be rather handy in reducing the amount of range arcs to be plotted. Use the bearing as an approximate LOP to the object, then step off the range on that line. Remember that the bearing will have error, which can become rather exaggerated at large ranges. Use more than one range if at all possible.

Radar units are handy tools for navigation in close to shore or within the confines of harbors. The navigator used to have to rush from bridge wing gyrorepeaters to the chart table to get a fix in congested waters. This long-distance run was shortened by using radar. New techniques of placing grease pencil lines on the plotting surface can assist the watch officer in positively monitoring track position at a glance. Called parallel index lines, they are referenced to known terrestrial objects.

For example, if own ship wished to parallel index when entering a harbor where a prominent lighthouse on a small island is known to be an excellent radar target, the navigator would plan on using this as a turn point. An index line can be drawn on the scope parallel with the approach heading flasher. As the ship approaches the harbor, the ship can be guided in by bringing the lighthouse onto the index line. As the ship progresses in, the lighthouse apparently moves down the line. Another index line can be drawn on the scope from the turn point, representing the ship's second course required for safe entrance. Once the target moves to that point the ship is turned so that the lighthouse begins to follow the second line. Many methods have been presented, involving using multicolored lines, different symbolization, or multiple terrestrial points. The concept remains the same. Take an object that can be clearly identified and track out a reciprocal line for each leg of the transit. The navigator will always be assured at a moment's notice of where the vessel is. Obviously this method does not relieve the navigator of plotting the own ship's position frequently, but it can allow for more time to concentrate on serious traffic situations. The ARPA has added many new dimensions to radar navigation, particularly regarding index lines, navigation lines, and map programs. More details are given in the following chapter.

Taking a range and bearing of a target at close range will invariably give the navigator a good fix. Taking three ranges will afford a better fix. Dropping an index line down will make close-in navigation easier. It cannot be emphasized too many times, however, that the prudent navigator will not rely solely upon any single aid to navigation. He or she will look upon radar navigation as just one more means to be positive about where his or her vessel is located.

RADAR MAINTENANCE

Unless an individual has a valid radiotelegraph or general radiotelegraph license with a radar endorsement, routine maintenance of radar is restricted to simple activities. This includes keeping the unit dry and clean and free from dust, dirt, or ashes, which can foul controls. An unused paintbrush is very effective along with a soft, lint-free rag.

Units that have reflection plotters need to be cleaned regularly because of residue left from using grease pencils. Any standard

---

1. Ensure the vessel is on internal ship's power, not shore power, before operating or servicing radar.
2. Check the scanner to be sure it is clear and no personnel are aloft. Keep all flags or dayshapes clear of radar scanners.
3. Set all controls to zero, including gain, contrast, and brilliance.
4. Power up on standby and await warm-up period. Most units will automatically not allow transmission until all components are ready.
5. Switch radar to transmit, check scanner to see if it is turning free and clear.
6. Set range to 6 or 12 miles (midrange). Increase gain, contrast, and brilliance up about three-quarters and adjust each for a bright picture. Use focus or tuning controls to sharpen known displayed information. Tuning knobs should not be adjusted once under way unless assurances exist that they should.
7. Adjust illumination controls for desired brilliance of both screen and user panel.
8. Use sea or rain clutter as necessary for heavy weather or precipitation. Do not use these controls to protect the center of the screen from damage by keeping the center clutter low. Remember, use of sea clutter or rain clutter may compromise the unit's maximum range detection. In close waters, it is sufficient to lower the gain. Keep in mind that a new radar CRT is cheaper than a collision.
9. Change ranges frequently, adjusting gain accordingly to search for targets. During periods of no targets at sea, utilize performance monitors or echo box functions as installed to be assured of proper functioning. If none, occasionally lower range scale and gain to lowest settings and note vessel wake.
10. Never rely solely upon radar as a single means of determining position or risk of collision. Use visual bearings to confirm risk of collision if possible, and alternative position fixing techniques.

Fig. 9-18. Radar startup procedure

household cleaner that cuts grease or similar film will be effective. The plotter should be removed on occasion and the underside of the plotter and top of the screen face should be cleaned. Most screen faces are made of plastic today and a small amount of liquid cleaner and a nonabrasive, lint-free rag should be used to wipe the screen. The face of the control unit can also be opened on some units, and with power secured, the face of the CRT and underside of the screen should also be cleaned.

Illumination lamps and plotter lamps should be replaced as soon as they burn out and spares should always be kept aboard. Spare fuses should also be kept aboard, but if the unit blows fuses regularly a technician should be called. Of primary importance is keeping the filters clean at cooling intakes. These intakes should be checked weekly.

All maintenance performed on the radar, whether routine or by a technician, should be logged in a radar maintenance manual. This must be made available to the Coast Guard or the FCC on demand.

Other general areas that should be checked include the wave guide, to ensure connections are tight and supports secure. The scanner should be checked to ensure its mounting is secure and all connections are tight. Some scanner motors require routine maintenance including checking lubricating oil and replacing drive belts. These inspections should be made monthly and logged. Refer to your operator's manual for other routine procedures.

A common problem, simple to correct, but serious in its implications, is indicator scanner misalignment. When the scanner is not aligned with the indicator's heading flasher, a technician should be

---

1. Wipe clean plotting surface, stow plotting tools.
2. Turn all controls to minimum.
3. Switch to standby if you plan use within 24 hours.
4. Switch off radar if use is not planned in the next 24 hours, or if switching over to shore power.
5. Open supply breakers if the plant is being secured for an extensive period of time. Use this time to thoroughly clean the screen and panels, perform routine maintenance, cover the unit, and log all accomplishments.
6. Heating the space in cold weather is recommended. Use a dehumidifier in a damp environment. Unit should be started and checked monthly during extensive lay-ups if possible. If the unit is secured for any time frame above 30 days, have manufacturer's service representatives available during start-up.

Fig. 9-19. Radar securing procedure

called to adjust the operating mechanism in the scanner motor unit. One final note: log all problems with your radar unit and have them corrected as soon as possible. Remember, you may be ashore when the radar repair person is aboard. Irregular presentation, spoking, flare-ups, or other similar problems can seriously affect the unit and will probably lead to complete breakdown. Have these problems checked and corrected as soon as possible. Remember, your radar system is your second set of eyes, so take care of it.

BASIC SYSTEM OPERATION

Every radar varies in its operational functions based upon the manufacturer and the level of technology installed. Baseline starting operational procedures are included in figures 9-18 and 9-19. These are not intended to replace any specific requirements of manufacturers.

CHAPTER 10

AUTOMATIC RADAR PLOTTING AIDS

INTRODUCTION

ARPA is an acronym for automatic radar plotting aid. ARPA is an electronic device interfaced with a radar display unit that can continuously interpret the motions of contacts on the radar display as an aid to the navigation of the vessel. Originally referred to as collision avoidance systems or computer radars, ARPA systems presently meet stringent international specifications and governmental regulations, which call for plotting reliability to be as effective as manual plotting techniques.

Most nations require ARPA systems on their registered unlimited tonnage ships that are generally over 10,000 gross tons. The United States has specific requirements for ARPA installation and performance under 33 CFR 164. International requirements are also specified under IMO Resolution A.218(vii). The IMO recommendations further stipulate that masters and watchstanders on these ships possess certification to effectively operate an ARPA unit. At present there are many training facilities in the world. In the United States such training is approved by the U.S. Coast Guard.

ARPAs improve the standard of collision avoidance at sea by automatically providing information to radar observers and thereby reducing their workload. ARPA, therefore, allows the mariner viable information on multiple targets, where a manual plot may only allow data on one target. In addition, they are designed to provide continuous accurate and rapid situation evaluation. ARPA performance must be equal to that which can be obtained from a standard radar unit. It must be capable of target acquisition by manual or automatic means, but if an automatic system is employed, the unit must have the capability of manual acquisition and cancellation of targets. In the automatic acquisition mode the unit must be capable of suppressing acquisition of targets in certain areas.

ARPA units should be able to automatically track, process, simultaneously display, and continuously update information on a minimum number of targets. If the system is equipped with automatic tracking, the number of targets must be at least twenty, but only ten if manual. The unit should also be able to continue to track and acquire a target which is clearly distinguishable for five out of ten consecutive scans.

There must also be a history capability providing at least four equally spaced past positions of targets over a period of at least 8 minutes. ARPA units may be stand-alone systems or may be attached to a radar unit. Stand-alone units were popular in the early years of ARPA, but most second-generation ARPA manufacturers have elected to use the attached approach. It must be understood that the failure of the ARPA unit must not affect the performance of the radar unit.

ARPA units must be available on specific range scales for both short and long detection of vessel movements. The system must be capable of operating with a relative-motion display, with north up, and either head-up or course-up stabilization. They may also provide a true-motion display (which is used as a sales option).

Course and speed information generated by an ARPA for acquired targets must be displayed in a vector or graphic form, which clearly shows the operator a target's predicted motion. Information presented in vector form should show both true and relative vectors, and in most cases will not only give vector information, but information in graphic form showing target course and speed. Vector information should also include the time scale for operator interpretation.

ARPA information is computer-generated on the display screen, and it is a requirement that this information cannot obscure other information or degrade the process of detection targets. All ARPA data must be under the control of the radar observer, who must have the capability to cancel any unwanted data displayed.

The display is a critical function of the ARPA unit. The presentation is such that it must be clearly visible to more than one observer at a time, in the conditions of light experienced on the bridge of a ship, during day or night conditions. These "day bright" screens require very little shading that might impair the radar observer's ability to maintain a proper lookout.

Fig. 10-1. Typical ARPA units. Courtesy of Litton/Sperry Marine Systems, Raytheon Marine Company, and Furuno Marine Systems.

In practical application, the ARPA unit must be able to obtain quickly the range and bearing of any object that appears on the display. Once a target is acquired into the system the unit should present in a period of not more than 1 minute an indication of the target's motion. It must also provide the target's predicted movement in no more than 3 minutes. This information must appear quickly after the operator changes range scales.

ARPA units are equipped with some basic operational warnings that must include targets entering selected danger zones or ranges, or predicted to close within a minimum time and range chosen by the observer. In addition there should be a warning if a target in track is lost. These warnings must be visible and/or audible. Manufacturers will usually make audible alarm options user-friendly to minimize bridge distractions in congested waterways.

The radar observer must be able to access six pieces of critical information about a target in track in alphanumeric form. This information must include present range to the target, present bearing, predicted target range at closest point of approach (CPA), predicted time to CPA (TCPA), calculated true course, and speed of target.

Trial maneuver functions are required on ARPA units, including a clear indication that this function is being operated. Requirements further stipulate minimum system accuracy under various environmental conditions such as weather, vessel motion, and trim.

Finally, the ARPA system must be fully integrated into other types of bridge equipment, such as radionavigation receivers, speed logs, and compasses. Of course this integration must be designed in such a manor that malfunctions of any integrated units must not degrade the performance of the ARPA. In the case of malfunctions, the unit must provide a suitable warning to the operator.

The mariner must recognize that even though manufacturers may have provided units that vary in construction and operations, their performance is based upon these specific requirements. Every ARPA unit in use today should have these similarities, which should make operation of different units easier. Consult manufacturers' operation manual for precise key options of these functions.

THEORY OF OPERATION

An ARPA primarily relies upon a radar and a microprocessor computer. The radar unit must have digital bitmapping of the display, either rasterscan or cathode ray tube, so as to allow a processor to mathematically approach problems involving relative motion. The data gathered by the ARPA is then processed into an anticollision loop, or a logical progression of analysis, which aids a mariner in determining the best actions to avoid collision. The anticollision loop is an interactive process involving both man and equipment. ARPA turns bits of data into information useful to the watchstander, but lacks complete interpretation of the information. This is because the unit is incapable of interpreting the prevailing circumstances and conditions under the applicable collision regulations. Forward-thinking readers may envision a level of computer technology in the future capable of full interpretation, but until nearly every vessel afloat is equipped with an interactive ARPA system, no substitute is possible for an experienced mariner in the decision loop.

ARPA units are programmed to be able to extract and store viable contact information, analyze data and display results, and provide the operator a means of interpreting information to plan evasive actions if needed. ARPA units can be invaluable because of their inherent ability to circumvent the boredom of manual plotting, because they are capable of plotting multiple targets simultaneously, because they can be programmed to be meticulous in avoiding errors of analysis, and because they are blind enough to display information without bias.

An ARPA unit begins with a radar unit. Most are of the raster display type. (Rasters are sometimes called rasterscan or television-type screens.) Course information is provided to the unit via a mechanical gyrocompass or a flux gate electronic compass. Speed information may be input from one or more different speed logs, but manual input of speed is always possible. These three devices, each integral to the ARPA, are referred to as sensors. Failure of ARPAs based upon sensor error or failure is only possible due to failure of radar. If the course or speed sensors fail, the ARPA must be capable of providing tracking capability. The ARPA will still be able to track contacts and display information about them, but many functions may be lost.

The essence of the ARPA is the tracker. The tracker works by dividing the radar screen into relatively small cells. The size of the cells can be made extremely small for the most advanced radars, but will consist of a large number of radial wedges and numerous concentric circles. These cells usually measure less than one-half degree in angular measure and no more than 0.025 nautical miles in range.

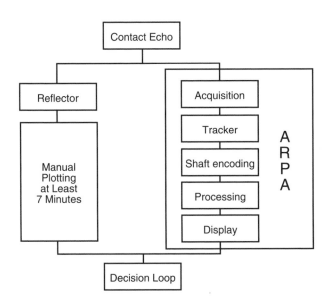

Manual Plotting as Opposed to ARPA Plotting

Fig. 10-2. ARPA decision loop

This division of the screen is called shaft encoding, which incorporates the angular position of the radar antenna in relation to the bow.

When the tracker is activated it will record target locations as they move through these cells. The tracker records a series of radar pips, looking for a successive repetition sufficient to register a hit. A hit means the ARPA has not stopped the tracking of the contact due to poor return or inconsistent display. Very persistent contacts will register hits more quickly, and weak contacts, such as sea return, will not. This is both a strength and a weakness in that elimination of returns that are of no danger is preferred, but elimination of small vessels is not desirable.

When a registered hit is tracked, its position is then encoded simply by a digital zero or one. Once approximately six hits are encoded, the microprocessor of the ARPA begins to function to its fullest potential. As hits are encoded, and the contact moves on the radar screen, a different code is recorded for the subsequent contact hit. Encoders can provide bearing accuracy of tracked contacts down to a thousandth of a circle, thereby allowing for very accurate coding of contact position.

The encoded signal is placed in an X- and Y-coordinate system, where plus indicates north and east, and minus equals south and west. From the track of a series of hits the ARPA then determines a

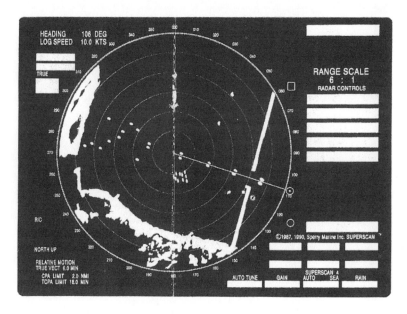

Fig. 10-3. ARPA screen. Courtesy of Litton/Sperry Marine Systems.

probability of where the next hit will be. This process predicts the location the target should be for the next hit. If it encodes a hit in the predicted location, a greater confidence level exists that the next hit can be more accurately predicted. Once the unit is satisfied that specific lines are being followed by a tracked contact, information is displayed to the operator.

Another function the ARPA utilizes is called window size or gate. Windows are the small area in which the tracker will look for a target upon demand. Window size begins relatively large, but once a hit occurs it narrows down to a smaller focus. If a strong contact is detected, the window will shrink and a more rapid analysis of the data can take place. But if a weak contact is windowed and is temporarily lost, the window opens for a larger view. This is not a reaction that helps track smaller weak targets, but one that accepts the reality that a contact has relative motion and may have moved out of the smaller window.

The ARPA processor continues predicting the location of the hit for a period of time even if the contact has not been detected. This is called rate aiding. This term describes the mathematical prediction of where a contact is most likely to be displayed in the future beyond a sweep or two. Since the tracked contacts are encoded for prediction purposes, rate aiding helps maintain a contact's relative motion, even if a poor return was experienced and no hit was encoded at the predicted location.

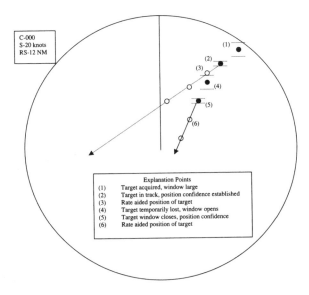

Fig. 10-4. Rate aiding. Drawing by Thomas Bushy.

Rate aiding and window size work together as the unit tracks a known contact. By rate aiding, the ARPA is allowed to keep the window size smaller, with confidence that it will track the next hit. This allows the processor to display more accurate information. This function has weaknesses in that the contact could change course or speed, or the own ship might do the same. For this reason the window size will be manipulated based upon tracked information.

As an example of rate aiding, suppose a contact being tracked on an own ship's port side turns to the right to avoid the own ship. When the unit looks for the hit at a particular point by rate aiding, it is no longer there. By opening the window size very quickly, the contact can be reacquired into the linear equation.

A similar function to rate aiding is the ability of the processor to purposely stop tracking a contact. When the operator tries to place a target in track too close to a tracked contact, or if two tracked contacts pass close together, the unit will default to coasting. This takes rate aiding a step further, in that the processor will look for the contact's hit in a position further down the relative motion line, based upon the time since it last tracked a hit, using the contact's last known relative course and speed. Modern ARPA units will warn the mariner when the ARPA has temporarily lost the contact, or if coasting was utilized.

OPERATION

The operator of an ARPA can activate tracker function in two ways. Manual acquisition is when a contact is specifically highlighted by the operator within an acquisition window by use of a joy stick or track ball. Automatic acquisition is when the tracker is sensitized to a window, or looks for hits either over the whole display or in particular areas. Manual acquisition allows the experienced operator to select which targets he or she considers necessary to track, but it requires continuous surveillance of the screen and time to acquire or delete targets. Automatic acquisition relieves the operator of constant monitoring, but may clutter the screen with unwanted information. ARPA units must be capable of tracking ten targets when using manual acquisition and twenty targets when operating in automatic acquisition.

Automatic acquisition incorporates the use of guard zones and exclusion zones. Guard zones are similar to range rings, which when called up default to established inner and outer guardian zones. Guard zones can be moved further away from a vessel for open ocean tracking, or in closer for coastal navigation. Targets that pass through the outer guard zone are automatically plotted. Targets that are not

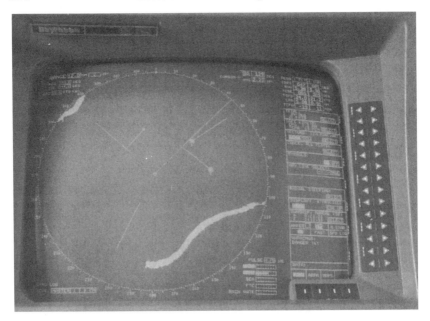

Fig. 10-5. ARPA guardian zones.
Photograph by Forlivesi Photography.

displayed until inside the outer guard zone are intended to be
automatically acquired at the inner guard zone. Note that the guard
zone rings have depth, which allows for automatic acquisition. If a
small contact were to be detected inside the inner guard zone, the
ARPA unit would not plot the target automatically. Exclusion zones
are offered to the operator as a means of limiting the automatic acquire function in areas where plotting of targets is not desired, such
as when passing a fishing fleet or a large anchorage. An operator
may utilize the exclusion capability when navigating near a coastline, or where indirect echoes frequently occur.

After tracking the target for approximately six sweeps, the processor is usually capable of displaying relatively accurate collision
information. The ARPA must be able to render relative motion information within 1 minute of steady tracking at a level of accuracy of 95
percent, and target motion information within 2 minutes thereafter
at the same level of accuracy.

A description of the means of displaying this information to the
operator continues in the following section. The processor collision
information is compared to the operator-selected minimum range
and time to potential collision. The operator must use this informa-

tion intelligently to close the anticollision loop. The first issue the operator must recognize is the value of the information. The accuracy of the ARPA is based solely upon the sensors. Usually there isn't a problem with the radar information since the ARPA will not display information from nonpersistent targets. But the course and speed inputs play a vital role in the value of the displayed information.

The microprocessor will display specific details concerning potential collision points or areas. Such information will be used by the mariner to plan actions. The mariner must seriously consider how much to rely on the ARPA. Most people have heard the term "Garbage in, garbage out" when talking about computers. *The ARPA is a computer.* Sensor information must be valid if the operator plans on getting useful knowledge out. The first rule to be followed when operating the unit is to always be critical of the information given, and careful that over-reliance is not allowed. Constant doubt, however, would lead to neglect of a valuable device. So use the ARPA, but be certain that the sensor inputs are accurate.

Course input is usually relatively good. The means by which the gyro information is inputed is accurate and reliable, and it is clearly displayed. When a course changes, either intentionally or unintentionally, the watchkeeper watching a radar can catch it quickly. If a course change occurs, the operator must dismiss ARPA displayed information for at least one minute before having confidence in

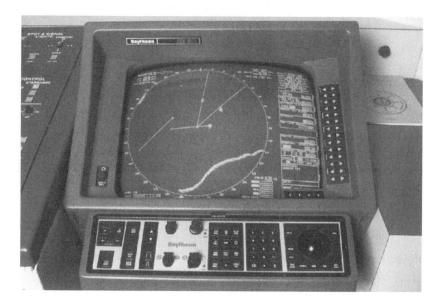

Fig. 10-6. ARPA data display. Photograph by Forlivesi Photography.

collision information. Since the tracker probably was forced to open the window wider to find the target, it must now begin recomputing next position before confidence is restored. Remember, if compass imput fails, the ARPA must and will still function in the unstabilized head-up mode. This equates to manual course selection. If head-up is required, remember that the tracker must continually compensate for the vessel's yaw, and ARPA information should be given a conservative margin for error.

Chapter 7 detailed varieties of speed logs. This information about the theory of speed logs is important to ARPA operation. The ARPA wants to know how fast the vessel is going in relation to the other targets it is tracking. As the tide raises all vessels, so too do the currents affect all vessels. Vessels about which collision information is desired are usually subjected to the same currents, or set and drift. Therefore selection of ground-stabilized speed logs should be discouraged by ARPA users. The best selection for speed logs are double-axis, water-stabilized Doppler or electromagnetic logs. These will give the best accuracy of speed through the water. The worst type of log to use for anticollision assessment is single-axis, ground-stabilized Doppler. It should be noted that the radar can provide ground lock, or auto drift, true course, and speed information. Under all circumstances these are excellent for radar navigation, but not for anticollision assessment.

If the vessel is equipped with a speed log that has proven unreliable, the best action for the ARPA operator is to manually input dead-reckoning speed. Under most circumstances this will render collision information to be considered slightly inaccurate. If the dead-reckoning speed is correct however, the displayed vectors can be considered accurate.

Remember the anticollision computer relies heavily on speed inputs. If you have any reason to doubt the accurate speed through the water of your ship, do not use collision information for precision passes with other vessels. The operator should consult the manufacturer's accuracy disclosure statement in the ARPA technical manual. Accuracy of collision points or predicted areas of danger are usually dependent on the target contact's computed true speed and time to closest point of approach. Accuracy of closest point of approach is reliant upon the target's relative position from the own ship and speed measurements. The prudent watchstander will therefore be meticulous in inputting speed into the ARPA, and rely less on collision information for targets at greater range.

To assist the operator in making better decisions concerning collision avoidance, ARPA units are equipped with a function called trial maneuver. The trial maneuver modifies the own ship course

and speed within the processor. When the operator selects trial maneuver the electronic bearing line (EBL) becomes the "new course" of
the own ship, and speed differences are programmed in via a thumb
wheel or keypad. As the EBL is manipulated, all displayed target information changes to meet the own ship trial course and/or speed. A
visual warning is displayed in the shape of a "T" on the screen. Operators should take care when making decisions about contacts
when the trial maneuver is functioning, and should never leave the
unit in trial when unattended.

ARPA units are now being programmed to give the operator
more useful functions associated with radar navigation. Index lines
and navigation lines are available. Index lines are used by mariners
who wish to practice parallel indexing. These lines are placed into
the display unit and are fixed to the own ship and will move with it.
Parallel indexing allows the operator to program the radar screen to
provide time-saving reference lines useful in navigation. Units frequently have procedures that call for the lines to be programmed in
specific display modes, such as true motion.

Navigation lines, or nav lines, are lines oriented to earth. A ship
can then navigate on these lines, or between a succession of nav
lines. This function requires the unit to have course and speed input,
or it may have a function referred to as ground lock or auto drift. This

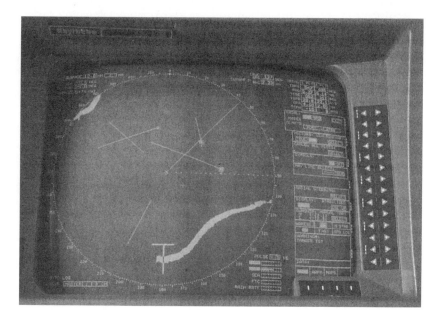

Fig. 10-7. Trial maneuver. Photograph by Forlivesi Photography.

function allows the operator to acquire a contact that is known to be stationary, such as a lighthouse, beacon, or small island. Since nav lines are frequently used in true-motion displays, they may require programming in that mode. Never rely strongly on collision assessment information when working an ARPA in ground lock.

Numerous terms have been assigned to the ARPA. "Target loss," usually displayed as a target lost to the operator, indicates that no registered hits have taken place on a contact upon demand. This is the expected result when an operator demands information on a contact at greater ranges, or weak contacts close in, as is the case with sea return. "Coasting" helps to prevent the unit from opening the window too quickly and allowing another, close contact to jump into the window. "Target swap" occurs when the unit begins tracking a contact different from the one originally tracked. This can occur when a close, untracked contact passes close to a tracked contact, or when two tracked targets pass close together. ARPA units that have very accurate tracking systems are less prone to this problem. Mariners are warned to be aware in advance of possible target swap, as displayed information may suddenly no longer be valid.

DISPLAYED INFORMATION

ARPA units must be able to display information concerning targets at a minimum of one long range and one short range. The long range is either 12 or 16 miles, and the short range is either 3 or 4 miles. Most units, however, are capable of displaying data from relatively close ranges, of about 1.5 miles up to 24 miles. Units allow operator input called safe limits, usually minimum CPA and time to CPA. Operators should definitely be aware of larger safe limits when switching down to shorter range scales.

Up to this point in the analysis of ARPA, no mention has been made of the details of information. It goes without saying that a unit must give the operator information on target range, bearing, course, speed at CPA, and TCPA. Vessels' vectors must be shown on the screen. Some units will display bow crossing range (BCR), if any, and time to BCR (TBCR). The ARPA unit must be able to continue displaying information when the observer switches range scales, provided selected range scales are within the tracking capability. Display methods fluctuate among different manufacturers, and the trained ARPA operator will study the operation manual to ascertain these differences.

ARPA units display information in two ways. This earliest method, and one that continues to exist today, is for the unit to display an electronic vector. The vector will begin at the target or from a symbol created on the display screen representing the target's actual relative position. The vector will usually be the same color as used to display all target relative positions, electronic bearing lines, and range rings. As advancements in radar technology and color radars become more common, mariners can expect to see different colors for different types of displayed information.

The vector may be selected to show either a relative vector or a true vector of the target's motion. The length of the vector indicates the contact's speed over a time period selected by the operator. By interpreting the relative vector the operator can glean information useful in satisfying risk-of-collision questions, and from the true vectors the operator can gather information about the target's approximate course, speed, and potential actions. These so-called potential actions are determined solely by the experienced operator and are based upon the area being navigated.

To further aid in the anticollision loop decision process, ARPA units provide the operator with potential collision points (PCPs) and predicted areas of danger (PADs). PCPs are basic information based on a similar system as rate aiding. Usually displayed as a dot or small circle, more than one point could exist for a single own ship.

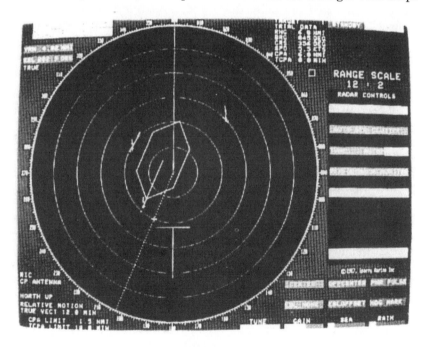

Fig. 10-8. Predicted area of danger (PAD).
Courtesy of Litton/Sperry Marine Systems.

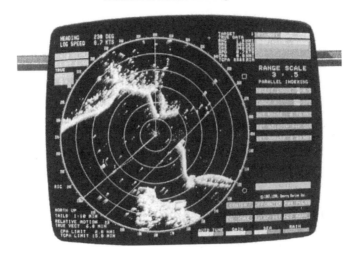

Fig. 10-9. Target trails. Courtesy of Litton/Sperry Marine Systems.

When two ships encounter one another at sea, the faster ship will have but one collision point displayed, as it could always outrun a slower ship or purposely attempt to collide with it. But the slower ship has two collision points, one where collision would occur if it were to change course to intercept or collide with the other ship, and another point based upon the other ship attempting to intercept the slower ship.

PADs incorporate a bit more information. They display not only a point, but also either a circle or a hexagon. This display includes the danger area selected by the operator plus system inaccuracy probabilities and the size of the contact being tracked. Specific criteria incorporated in these determinations are detailed in the fine print of operating manuals.

The second method ARPA uses to display information is through digital readouts. These information windows digitally detail the other ship's range, bearing, course, speed, CPA, TCPA, and other information such as BCR or TBCR.

Target information may also be displayed based on historical tracking. In other words, points can be placed on the screen to represent where the contact was in the past based upon operator selected time intervals. Target trails show the true course and speed of the target ship over time by small dots on the screen. Many operators use target trails to keep informed on the target's course and speed, and simultaneously use the relative vectors to keep abreast of collision information.

DISPLAY WARNINGS

Probably the most important and frequent alarm an ARPA unit gives the operator is when a contact in track is approaching closer than established parameters the operator selects using the safe limit function. As an example, an operator may select a minimum CPA of 2 miles, and a minimum time to CPA of 12 minutes. If the relative motion line of a contact in track violates either of these parameters, an audible and visual alarm is indicated by the unit. This allows an operator not to have to stand by waiting for displayed information, so he or she can listen or watch for a warning alarm. These alarms, like others on the unit, may be suppressed for certain targets, but will rapidly default to full function. Some older units allow for the silencing of the audible alarm, but this choice is discouraged.

ARPA units must have self-diagnostic equipment monitoring and alarms. When a self-test function is randomly run on the processor and failure is detected, the unit will give an audible and visual alarm to alert the operator that the unit is not functioning properly. Reference to a particular unit's operating manual will then guide the operator in a series of further tests or part-exchange processes designed to fix the fault.

ARPA units provide operational warnings that aid the operator in using the equipment. When guard rings are activated and when automatic acquire function is operating, the unit will display the guard rings clearly on the screen. Should the unit detect a contact within an acquisition window, the unit will give an audible auto acquire alarm and a visual warning that a contact has been acquired.

If a manually tracked target is lost in the rate-aided window, an audible and visual alarm called "target lost" indicates to the observer that the target has been lost. In many cases it is possible for the operator to suppress the audible alarm for target lost, but never the visual alarm.

The unit will also alert the operator if "trial maneuver" is activated. Remember a trial maneuver is when the ship's heading and speed are adjusted within the processor only to make collision avoidance decisions. When trial maneuver is activated, a large "T" will appear on the lower half of the screen and will remain there until the operator stops trial maneuver function.

ADDITIONAL FUNCTIONS OF ARPA

The "Displayed Information" section above detailed what an ARPA must be capable of displaying for the mariner. In a few cases, the section mentioned information that the radar observer frequently wants, so it is often added to displayed information. The interesting thing about ARPA units is that they are merely computers. That statement may sound unusual since computers are very technical devices. However, currently there is scarcely a trained mariner who hasn't worked with a personal computer or with some form of computer system aboard ship. The reality is that computers permeate our lives and promote design innovation.

ARPA units are capable of providing the mariner with more information than many may desire. (The expression "information overload" comes to mind.) The people who design and build radar and ARPA units are engineers. Most are not seamen. In the beginning the computer programming engineers gave the mariner what the mariner wanted. But their ambition to provide the mariner with as much information as he or she needs has been overwhelming. It is a challenge for the mariner to sort out optional functions from needed functions on modern equipment.

Machines will continue to advance and improve. The manufacturer must be sure to provide a user-friendly means of gathering needed information and to create a more user-friendly choice of options.

Exclusion boundaries, target trails, and navigation line functions mentioned earlier are options. But these functions have become almost expected of computer radars. There are many more options that should be mentioned since they are becoming more and more common.

Probably the most interesting advancement in ARPA usage is the mapping function. This is a direct result of the increased memory capability of computers. The operator may carefully build a map of a particular harbor, river, or bay that is frequently navigated. This map can then be saved in memory for use another day. The maps must function in ground-locked stabilized mode to be effective. Manufacturers today can produce maps and distribute them to ships on demand.

Displayed information has taken tremendous steps forward with the advancement of rasterscan screens. Time and date readouts can be found. Detailed information about gyrocompass selection, speed log selection, and interswitched radars is common. The radar pulse lengths for certain range scales, as well as increases and decreases, are shown graphically and alphanumerically. Digital readouts of EBL direction and offset distances are common. Graphic displays of the gain and FTC and STC intensities are available.

The same technology that makes gyro and log sensor inputs easier is now being used to input latitude and longitude from radionavigation aids onto the screen. The ability of this information to interact with EBL and VRM allows the operator to position a target for easier identification in search and rescue or routine communications. This data transmission system can also be found when a personal computer is connected to be used as a voyage record or management system.

CHAPTER 11

INTEGRATED BRIDGE SYSTEMS

GENERAL

Over the course of time, technology aboard ships has become extremely reliable. Where once the mariner looked toward new electronic devices with skepticism, he or she now finds the units ready and able to assist in even the most severe conditions. Integrated electronic systems have been reliably used in most segments of the transportation industry. Airliners, railroad locomotives, and vehicles are finding their operations more dependent upon computerized electronic systems.

Manufacturers faced a number of challenges in applying technology to the harsh marine environment. High levels of moisture, vibration, long periods of improper maintenance, and resistant operators all contributed to a difficult transition.

Integration is not a new concept. For years the interfacing of some basic electronic devices has been successfully accomplished aboard ships. Gyrocompass inputs to steering systems and radars are among the most familiar. The concept of the integrated bridge, however, transcends these accomplishments. We now have technology available where interfacing is easily accomplished. This technology allows microprocessors to assist in situational awareness and decision making for the watch officer. This concept can be applied not only to direct control of a vessel's movement and navigation, but to virtually every shipboard system controlled by computer. Ultimately, full control of all shipboard systems can be incorporated into one computer terminal. This permits one trained individual to control the ship's navigation and engine room operations, as well as handle cargo condition monitoring, vessel stability, communications, fire and safety monitoring, voyage planning, preventative maintenance programs, and future cargo loading arrangements. This information can then be transmitted to shoreside managers for detailed cargo planning, optimization of vessel movements, and voyage analysis.

In this modern world where "just in time" concepts are critical in intermodal logistics, these systems can help vessel owners and operators maximize vessel and system efficiency. The marine world may be heading for the day when the safe navigation of ships at sea could conceivably be controlled from a computer terminal in, for instance, Fort Wayne, Indiana.

CONCEPTS OF INTEGRATION

Integrated bridge systems (IBS) are designed to allow a vessel operator to plan, execute, monitor, and record the performance of a vessel in normal operations. The system utilizes a specialized local-area network, known as ethernet, which allows each piece of integrated equipment to exchange specific information. This information is provided to the controlling mechanism of the vessel under the watchful eye of the vessel operator. In most cases, all information within the

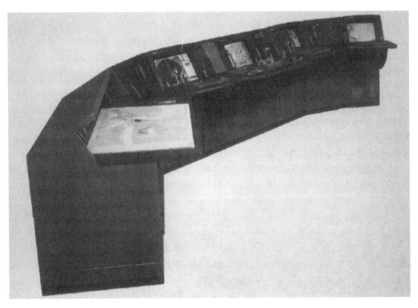

Fig. 11-1. Raytheon Marine Company's "Bridge Control" integrated bridge system (IBS). Courtesy Raytheon Marine Company.

network is provided to a master control station on the bridge where the watch officer can access and utilize this critical data continuously. This includes navigational information, collision avoidance data, steering and propulsion control, emergency systems, communications, and environmental data.

To put it simply, a trained bridge watch officer is able to lay out the ship's voyage using a personal computer (PC) equipped with an electronic chart display and voyage information database. This planning information is electronically transmitted to a central control system. In addition to general control functions, the system utilizes an electronic chart with positional information and vessel status provided by inputs from the radionavigation equipment, gyrocompass, speed log, and steering system.

Once the ship departs port, the vessel's control is maintained by this central control station, located on the bridge. As the vessel travels along its intended track, environmental conditions of weather, sea state, and vessel motions can be factored into navigation by the computer. In addition, radar information provided through an ARPA unit is projected onto the electronic chart, providing a more comprehensive display of the vessel's navigational condition. Every action of the vessel is recorded. This data, including positional information, updated estimated time of arrival, fuel economy, cargo status, and other critical information, is transmitted back to shore over modems using a radio system such as SATCOM.

BASIC COMPONENTS

The key component of the IBS is the local area network, which links a central control station, a navigation station, a voyage planning and recording system, collision avoidance ARPA units, navigation sensors, the steering stand, the communications console, and machinery and emergency systems monitors. All units are tied into the central control station. This station includes a conning display, steering controls, an automatic pilot, a navigation display, a radar display, communications, and the main engine and thruster controls. Shipboard personnel can also be provided information on vessel motion, hull stresses, trim conditions, and other data necessary in making key operational decisions. The central control station will often have remote consoles located on bridge wings or other critical locations used for navigation. There is also a steering stand with a traditional helm, with autopilot and steering system controls linked to the central control station.

Information for voyage planning is generated on a separate computer that provides all track data to the control and navigation sta-

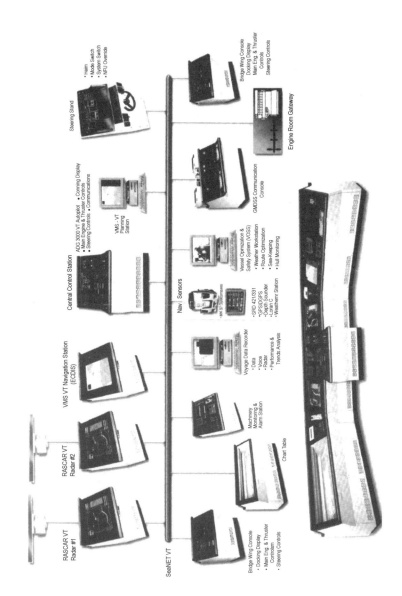

Fig. 11-2. Sperry Vision 2100 integrated bridge system. Courtesy of Sperry Marine Systems.

tions. The navigation station will generally have an electronic chart system displayed with the vessel track, and other navigation information provided by navigation sensors. These sensors include at least one gyrocompass, speed log, GPS/DGPS, loran C, a depth sounder, and a weather station. Also included in this integrated network are the 3- and 10-centimeter ARPA units. Target information can be displayed at the navigation station.

Linked to the navigational and ship control components is a voyage data recorder. This additional computer keeps a record of system and vessel data, electronic logbook voice recordings from the bridge, radar display records, and vessel performance and trends. In addition to the ship control systems there are separate monitors for machinery, shipboard emergency surveillance systems, communications, and alarms.

The entire system is interfaced with a communications network system that includes GMDSS and a direct ship-to-shore communications link. This communications system provides a connection to shoreside managers for monitoring vessel location and performance. In addition to vessel location and performance, shoreside managers can monitor cargo information, slip, fuel consumption, engine performance, available horsepower, generator power availability, parts inventories, and a host of other types of information.

VOYAGE MANAGEMENT SYSTEMS

The international maritime community has determined that the single most important element of a safe ocean passage is comprehensive voyage planning. The details of good voyage plans have for years been included within the job description of the master and the navigation officer. Together they would devise a plan using charts and assorted publications to lay out their course lines, taking into account those factors that might interfere with safe navigation. Their plans were translated into a simple pencil line on the chart. This system, however, has proven to be insufficient in today's world of reduced manning and efficient vessel movement demands from the home office.

These methods began changing when modern radionavigation equipment became available to the navigator. The practice of programming waypoints, or points where courses are changed in a voyage, into a piece of radionavigation equipment has become commonplace. Now the voyage is not just a pencil line, but a systematic list of planned positions, running times, course, and required speeds. As PCs were introduced, navigators started placing this information into spreadsheet formats or similar types of databases. This has

Voyage plan:		SS American Sailor			Voyage # 333 3–12 March 1998		
Waypoint	Latitude	Longitude	Course	Distance– NM	Speed	ETA	Remarks
1							
2							
3							
4							
5							
6							
7							
8							

Fig. 11-3. Voyage plan spreadsheet

become an operational tool and is added to the documented paper-work for a voyage.

Simple techniques incorporate spreadsheets with recorded and anticipated information, which are listed as a reference. Information showing waypoints, courses, anticipated speed, measured distances, predicted estimated times of arrival (ETA), and other key data can be laid out by the navigator. This information is used to lay out the courses on paper charts. The voyage plan has become a companion to the charts and publications used in navigation. With the introduction of computers, it is now commonplace to find this information in electronic form in the chart room. Figure 11-3 is a simple example of a spreadsheet-format voyage plan.

Recording data is as important as predicting it. A careful record of fixes and experience with different systems allows the operator a frame of reference on which to rely. This information becomes useful to the navigator in routine conditions, and much more valuable in extreme circumstances. Critical to the plan's execution is the recording of key data such as electronic fixes, terrestrial fixes, and other pertinent information. In most cases, this information is carefully entered into the watchkeeper's navigation notebook or the vessel's navigation log.

In a voyage management system, the data is compiled and entered into a spreadsheet computer program or similar database. The system automatically translates this information into courses, distances, and waypoints which are displayed on the electronic chart. The navigation sensors provide input that shows the vessel's position in relation to the intended track. This eliminates the requirements of using paper charts and position fixing, which may tend to distract the watchstander from more essential tasks such as collision avoidance. Provisions are incorporated to allow the navigator to introduce terrestrial observation information onto the electronic chart. Once the vessel is under way, the same system automatically records all information regarding the vessel's movements into a real-time database.

Once the voyage plan is electronically recorded, surveillance of the vessel's track is monitored by not only the watch officer but also by the computer. If the vessel's actual performance deviates from the plan, the voyage management system incorporates alarm mechanisms intended to alert the watch officer.

ELECTRONIC CHART SYSTEMS

The International Maritime Organization and the International Hydrographic Organization (IHO) have classified emerging electronic chart technology into two basic groups. The first classification is known as the electronic chart display and information systems (ECDIS), and the other is non-ECDIS electronic chart systems (ECS).

ECDIS equipment and chart data are designed to meet strict specifications laid out by the IMO and IHO. Generally, data for ECDIS systems has to be equivalent to the latest edition of material originated by a government-authorized hydrographic office and must conform to IHO standards. ECDIS data should be capable of accepting official updates to correct changes in the chart's database. This database, known as the electronic navigational chart (ENC), is in a specified electronic format and must be provided by official government sources.

The ECS classification comprises all other types of electronic charts that do not comply with the IMO and IHO ECDIS specifications. These systems are not regarded by the IMO as acceptable equivalents to paper charts.

Electronic charts are also designed on a computer-generated database. Like ECDIS charts, they can be electronically updated as actual hydrographic conditions change. The databases can be provided from any source and generally use government hydrographic information. These databases vary according to the equipment's manufacturer.

In the United States, the Radio Technical Commission for Maritime Services (RTCMS) is developing a minimum standard for non-ECDIS systems that can be used within the United States. This will provide a standard that is lacking for the international group of electronic chart systems.

The greatest advantage of electronic charts is that they provide the user with the ability to create electronic route planning in the form of vectors and other superimposed electronic functions. In addition, they allow the user to easily update the charts with electronic corrections. The hardware associated with these systems allows the operator to zoom in or out on a specific location. The equipment interfaces with radionavigation receivers to permit the operator to monitor through superimposed electronic fixes. The equipment can also be linked to radar systems, which can provide identification of landmasses and incorporate collision avoidance information. These units can be placed at the vessel's control station, allowing the watch officer to avoid frequent trips to the chart room.

Certainly the ECDIS standards are at a level at which most manufacturers of IBS equipment will utilize them. There are a large number of manufacturers of electronic chart equipment who provide their own custom data for their particular device. The RTCMS is working with these manufacturers in the United States to develop a minimum standard that they can use as a guideline in developing chart databases. This type of ECS equipment will most likely be confined to noncommercial applications.

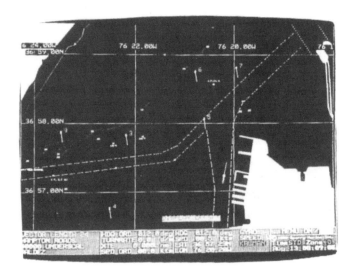

Fig. 11-4. ECDIS chart. Courtesy of Litton/Sperry Marine Systems.

VESSEL SYSTEM MANAGEMENT

Most modern ships are equipped with controls for propulsion and thruster systems. In many cases these vessels have the capability of monitoring propulsion performance at remote locations outside the engine room. The technology exists to have full propulsion control and monitoring accomplished on the ship's bridge.

This innovation may well advance the concept of dual training of navigational officers, who are referred to in the United Kingdom as polyvalent officers. The Japanese have experimented with this concept with some success. The governing administrations of the maritime states must decide whether the technology will eventually allow for single-man operation of a ship under way.

Not only are tremendous advances taking place by incorporating engine room operations and cargo management into bridge operations, but maritime application of high-technology "fly by wire," used in the aeronautical world, is now in place. Engines, steering, and thrusters are now being directed automatically in a way only a computer could accomplish. Ship's officers now, with the simple motion of a steering stick much like the control handle of an small airplane, can expect all propulsion and steering forces to act together in a predetermined and efficient manner. This allows for a properly fitted

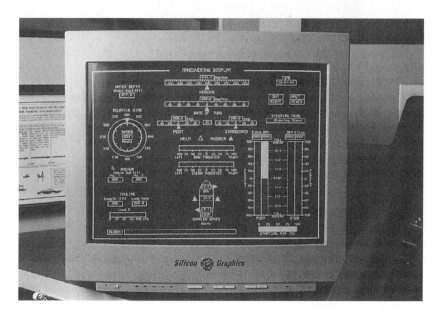

Fig. 11-5. Propulsion monitoring station.
Photograph by Forlivesi Photography.

ship to dock without the aid of tugs or anchors with a level of safely previously unseen.

Navigation inputs from radionavigation receivers are also utilized in station-keeping operations using dynamic positioning systems. Vessels requiring precise positioning, such as cableships or research vessels, can predetermine their track or station on an electronic chart and by using GPS or other similar systems, and can automatically keep the vessel within the parameters defined by the accuracy of the radionavigation system being employed.

PRACTICAL APPLICATION

As the ship's officer faces the strict needs of safe navigation, as well as the demands of maximum economic performance, the proper application and use of modern technology is essential. Ships today are not operated with the levels of freedom once enjoyed. They have

Fig. 11-6. Vessel control system.
Photograph courtesy of Forlivesi Photography.

tighter schedules to maintain. Ocean passages, port time, downtime for maintenance are all carefully calculated. Companies are facing fierce competition, and customer service is a critical part of their corporate philosophy. Errors in navigation can seriously affect a vessel's arrival time. As a result, port costs can increase dramatically, fuel consumption can rise above projections, and deliveries can be impacted. All of this affects the company's bottom line. There is little flexibility left as the master runs his or her ship.

As reliance upon these modern systems grows, so too must the diligence of the ship's officer to use them properly. The systems themselves, for all their capabilities, are only as good as the performance of the numerous components that are incorporated within them. While they can calculate and track a vessel's performance faster and more accurately, human error can compromise even the most technologically advanced systems. Only after proper training in the equipment's use, careful application of the information it offers, and vigilant surveillance can the officer expect the most out of the equipment.

Technology is no substitute for human instinct, perseverance, and fundamental navigational skill, as evidenced by the numerous casualties when ship's officers relied too heavily upon technology, and not enough on their experience and skill. For example, a simple problem in the form of a bad antenna connection compromised the integrity of a GPS receiver integrated into an IBS system and led to a grounding. Misunderstanding complex ARPA information has led to collisions. Ultimately this can lead to loss of life and property.

Since the days of the radar-assisted collision between the *Andrea Doria* and *Stockholm,* dependence upon electronic systems has grown immensely. Human nature can allow the ship's officer to become complacent. In many cases, the complexity of these new systems is such that, without extensive training and practice, they can be grossly misused. These systems bring a new measure of efficiency and safety to vessel operations. They offer capabilities never before available in the maritime world. As the individual whose license and career is on the line, the modern ship's officer must remember that no matter how dynamic the system is, or how dependable the software or equipment might be, there is just no substitute for looking out the window.

GPS INFORMATION SYSTEMS

GLOBAL POSITIONING SYSTEM BULLETIN BOARD

The bulletin board service (BBS) telephone number is (703) 313-5910 and handles modem speeds of 300–14,400 bps. Communications parameters are 8 data bits, no parity, 1 stop bit (8NI), asynchronous communications, full-duplex. The BBS SprintNet number is 311035011328. (This can be abbreviated to 501-1328 if accessing SprintNet via telephone to one of SprintNet's modems.) Users must set up their own accounts to access SprintNet. Internet access is indirect, via the FedWorld BBS at Internet address "fedworld.gov." From FedWorld, take gateway 54 to the Navigation Information Service BBS.

WATCHSTANDER

Watchstander is available 24 hours a day by phone (703) 313-5900 and fax (703) 313-5920. The navigation information (NIS) 24-hour voice recording, (703) 313-5097, provides access to a 90-second message giving current system status. Forecast outages, historical outages, and other changes in the GPS are included as time permits. The service is operated by the U.S. Coast Guard.

NAVINFONET

To register, contact the DMA Hydrographic/Topographic Center at Navigation Division, ST D 44, National Imaging and Mapping Agency, 4600 Sangamore Road, Bethesda, Maryland 20816-5003.

INTERNET

U.S. Coast Guard Navigation Center, Alexandria, Virginia; (301) 313-5900; http://www.navcen.uscg.mil

GENERAL

To comment on any of the GPS services or ask questions about GPS status, contact the Navigation Information Service at Commanding Officer, U.S. Coast Guard, 7323 Telegraph Road, Alexandria, Virginia 22315-3998; NIS phone: (703) 313-5900; NAVCEN fax: (703) 313-5920.

CIVILIAN GPS SERVICE INTERFACE COMMITTEE (CGSIC)

Points of contact are the following: U.S. Department of Transportation (DRT-20), Research and Special Programs Administration, 400 7th Street S.W., Room 9420, Washington, D.C. 20590-0001; phone: (202) 366-4355; fax: (202) 366-3272 *or* Commanding Officer, U.S. Coast Guard NAVCEN, 7323 Telegraph Road, Alexandria, Virginia 22315-3998; phone: (703) 313-5900; fax: (703) 313-5920.

The program manager for all U.S. Coast Guard civilian GPS activities is Commandant (G-NRN), U.S. Coast Guard; phone: (202) 267-0298; fax: (202) 267-4427.

NOTICE TO MARINER UPDATES

The information listed above should be checked and updated from *Notices to Mariners* and the information systems.

THE NATIONAL IMAGERY AND MAPPING AGENCY

NAVIGATION INFORMATION NETWORK (NAVINFONET)

The Navigation Information Network (NAVINFONET) is a special service to mariners that provides ready access to extensive files of maritime safety information. The primary function of NAVINFONET is to bring the user closer to the data needed while at the same time providing selective query options to minimize the connect time and associated costs involved with interactive data exchange over commercial communications circuits. NAVINFONET is the query system for the Consolidated Navigation Systems (CNS). The Navigation Division of the National Imagery and Mapping Agency (NIMA) controls CNS/NAVINFONET. Its mission is to promote safety of life at sea through up-to-date, accurate, and inexpensive nautical charts and publications.

NAVINFONET has multiple uses and benefits. It can be queried from anywhere in the world using voice grade telephone circuits and modern communications equipment on a 24-hour basis. There is no cost for this service, but the user must bear the cost of the communications connect time to the common carrier plus the purchase cost of the equipment being used. A variety of computer programs are available to extract data from NAVINFONET. Broadcast warnings are generally available by 1000 EST on the next regular workday (Monday through Friday, excluding federal holidays) following transmission. Chart corrections, catalog corrections, and NIMA and U.S.

Coast Guard (USCG) lights and radio navigational aids are updated by 1500 EST each Friday. All users of the NIMA's navigation publications and charts, National Ocean Service (NOS) charts, and USCG *Light Lists* can benefit from the increase in data accessibility and the decrease in notification time.

Currently, NAVINFONET is accessible over voice grade telephones (including INMARSAT voice circuits) as follows:

Baud Rate-Phone Number		Compatible Modulation Standards	Phone Lines Available
1200	301-227-5295	VADIC 3400, BELL 212A, BELL 103/113	5
2400	301-227-4360	CCITT V.32, V.22bis, BELL 212A, BELL 103	5
9600	301-227-4424	CCITT V.32, V.22bis, BELL 212A, BELL 103	14

All modems should be connecting with NAVINFONET. A conversational series of prompts will lead the user step by step to the needed data. Preformatting requests can be very helpful to users unless they are just experimenting with the system. It is emphasized that, although there is no charge for the use of NAVINFONET or its data, the connect cost is paid by the user. NIMA issues individual user identification codes (IDs) that permit access to the NAVINFONET system. To receive a user ID or for further information concerning NAVINFONET, contact the NAVINFONET staff at:

Navigation Division
ST D 44
National Imagery & Mapping Agency
4600 Sangamore Road
Bethesda, MD 20816-5003
Telephone: 301-227-3296 or DSN 287-3296
Web Site: http://www.nima.mil

Reprinted from *Radio Navigational Aids,* Publication 117, United States Government, National Imagery & Mapping Agency

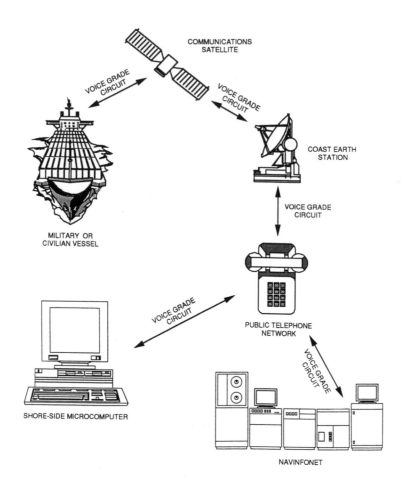

NAVINFONET flow diagram

GLOSSARY

Absolute accuracy. The accuracy of a position compared to the actual geographic coordinates of the earth, as measured by loran C.

Absorbed. Soaked up by the atmosphere (as with waves) so as to dissipate.

AC. See Alternating current.

Additional secondary phase factor (ASPF). A factor based on the variation introduced when signals travel over or near landmasses, since loran C navigational patterns are based upon signal propagation over water, not over land. Therefore, a correction must be utilized by the navigator seeking a high degree of accuracy.

ADF. See Automatic direction finder.

Admiralty List of Radio Signals. A publication by the Hydrographer of the Royal Navy of the United Kingdom that contains information on the range, frequency, characteristics, and position of radio beacon transmitters.

Aerial. See Antenna.

AF. See Audio frequency.

Alert data. The generic term for COSPAS-SARSAT 406-MHz and 121.5-MHz data received from distress beacons.

Alternating current (AC). Current that oscillates in one direction and then reverses its polarity periodically.

AM. See Amplitude modulation.

Ambiguity. A situation in which a loop antenna picks up a signal when either edge of the loop is aligned with the transmitter, causing a potential 180-degree error in the user's radio bearing.

Amperage. The measure of the amount of current moving through a conductor.

Amplifier circuit. A component that increases the oscillator's output within a transmitter.

Amplitude. The height of a wave along the y-axis from its baseline.

Amplitude modulation (AM). AM is a common form of voice transmission system where intelligence is conveyed through the modulation, or alteration, of a signal's amplitude.

Antenna. A conductor common to both transmitters and receivers that converts high-frequency electrical current into radio waves or vice versa.

Antenna gain. The ratio of output voltage or signal strength to input voltage or signal strength.

Antenna system. An assembly consisting of the antenna as commonly understood, the feedline to the transmitter and receiver, and any coupling devices for transferring power from the transmitter to the feedline.

Antenna tuner. A device that matches the antenna to the transmitted frequency by varying the capacitance and resistance that the signal will encounter as it moves to the antenna.

Anticollision loop. A logical progression of analysis that aids a mariner in determining the best actions to avoid collision.

Anti-transmit-receive (ATR) tube. A component used to block the passage of echoes to the radar transmitter.

Approved ARPA. Automatic radar plotting aid with design capabilities and functions that conform to the specifications of the International Maritime Organization (IMO).

ARPA. See Automatic radar plotting aid.

Aspect. The angle at which radar energy hits a radar contact.

ASPF. See Additional secondary phase factor.

Atmospheric noise. Interference usually caused by the buildup of static electrical charges in the atmosphere. This commonly is caused by thunderstorms associated with a passage of a cold front.

ATR tube. See Anti-transmit-receive tube.

Attenuation. The decrease of signal strength due to the medium through which it passes.

Audio amplifier. The final-stage amplifier within a receiver for communications equipment. It generates input to a speaker, finally converting electrical energy into acoustic energy, or sound.

Audio frequency (AF). The range of frequencies detected by normal human hearing (15 to 15,000 hertz).

Aural null indicator. A type of receiver that depends on the ability of the user to listen for and, sometimes with visual assistance, locate the null of a transmitted signal to determine direction.

Auto acquire alarm. An audible and visual warning that a contact has been acquired on an ARPA unit.

Auto drift. A function that allows the operator to acquire a contact that is known to be stationary, such as a lighthouse, beacon, or small island.

Automated mutual assistance vessel rescue (AMVER). An international search and rescue system operated by the United States Coast Guard. Through international cooperation, ships and other vessels on the high seas report their positions and route of travel so that in case of emergency, they may be called upon to render aid to another vessel in distress.

Automatic acquisition. A function by which an ARPA tracker is sensitized to window, or look for, hits either over the whole display or in particular areas.

Automatic direction finder (ADF). A receiver that searches for the direction of a carrier wave and then locks onto the broadcasted signal.

Automatic radar plotting aid (ARPA). Computer-assisted radar data processing systems that generate predictive vectors and other vessel movement information for the purposes of rapid collision avoidance decision making.

Automatic repeat request (ARQ). A mode used with narrow band direct printing (NBDP) that allows the receiving system to detect errors and make corrections. In the ARQ mode, an acknowledgment signal or repeat request is provided by the receiving station for each block of data that is transmitted.

Automatic steering system. A system that utilizes input from the master gyrocompass or other direction finding system through the repeater system to automatically keep the vessel on the course set.

Ballistic gyro. A gyrocompass that utilizes a ballistic (a free-flowing heavy liquid such as mercury or silicone) within the element to apply precessive forces to the gyro.

Band filter. A filter that passes all frequencies between a high and low cutoff frequency.

Bands. Categories having specific names and frequencies within the electromagnetic spectrum.

Bar antenna. An antenna sometimes used by direction finders, utilizing a piece of soft iron with a section of wire wrapped tightly around it. The wrapped wire around a soft iron core eliminates the need for external antennas because of the bar antenna's efficient pickup and induction of weak RF currents.

Baseline. In a hyperbolic navigation pattern, the line connecting two established points at a specific distance from each other at which transmitting stations are placed.

BCR. See Bow crossing range.

Beams. The extra elements on an antenna that make them more directive by changing the shape of the emission pattern of the radio waves for transmitting antennas and enhance reception for receiving antennas.

Bearing repeater. Gyrorepeaters usually located on the wings of the bridge to aid the mariner in taking true-direction visual bearings or for compass comparisons.

Bearing resolution. The radar's ability to distinguish between two ships, or other targets, on the same bearing, at nearly the same range. If the two ships, or targets, are at equal range from a radar unit and are separated by a relatively small angle, then the narrower the beam, the more capable the unit is of discerning between the two. This principle is primarily dependent upon the horizontal beam width.

Beat frequency oscillator (BFO). A device that provides a locally generated signal that can be mixed with a continuous-wave signal when received, allowing the user to hear the carrier wave.

Bellini-Tossi antenna. See Crossed-loop antenna.

BFO. See Beat frequency oscillator.

Binnacle housing. A protective container for all the components of the master gyrocompass.

Blackout. See Night effect.

Blink. A loran C receiver alarm that is triggered by the performance pulse of the master station indicating a systemwide transmitter malfunction.

Bottom return mode. Depth sounder readings that indicate speed over ground.

Bottom track. See Bottom return mode.

Bow crossing range (BCR). Distance ahead of own ship course where it intersects a target's relative motion line.

Bridge-to-bridge. Marine radiotelephone communication, VHF-FM.

C/A code. See Coarse acquisition code.

Carrier frequency. The frequency of the unmodulated signal produced by a radio transmitter.

Carrier wave. The transmitted base signal of all forms of transmitting systems.

Centerline. The line perpendicular to and through the midpoint of the baseline in a hyperbolic pattern.

Centilane. A percentage of a lane, determined by a Decca receiver through a phase comparison measurement.

CGS. See Civil GPS service.

Chain. A group of specific stations that interact with each other in hyperbolic systems such as loran C or Decca.

Chain of soundings. A method of navigation using water depth to determine a vessel's track with reasonable accuracy. The depth readings and the distance between them are then compared to the charted contours near the vessel's dead-reckoning position. Where they match the contours is the vessel's most probable track and approximate position.

Chip log. The earliest type of speed log employed, which was trailed astern of a vessel to measure the distance traveled through the water over a specific period of time.

Civilian GPS service (CGS). A service consisting of the GPS Information Center (GPSIC) and the Precise Positioning Service Program Office, which provides information to and is the point of contact for civilian users of the GPS system.

Closest point of approach (CPA). The minimum distance a target's relative motion line will pass around the own ship.

Coarse acquisition (C/A) code. Segment of the transmission of a GPS satellite that, along with the precision (P) code, is used to identify a specific satellite and its signal. The code, unique for each satellite, allows a receiver to determine the difference between signals, which are all broadcast on the same frequencies.

Coastal confluence system. A category within hyperbolic radionavigation systems designed to provide highly accurate position-fixing information in potentially hazardous navigation areas. Its accuracy decreases the greater the distance from shore.

Coastal refraction. A signal alteration caused by the passage of radio signals over or near a landmass, particularly where topographic features are prominent.

Coast earth station (CES). A land-based earth station in the INMARSAT satellite communications system that connects the space segment to ground-based telecommunication networks.

Coasting. Method used in an ARPA unit to prevent switching of close targets by the processor. If two tracked targets pass very close to each other, the ARPA processor looks for the contacts hit in a position farther down the relative motion line, based upon the time since it last tracked a hit using the contact's last known relative course and speed.

Coaxial cable (Coax). A cable consisting of a center conductor placed in the center of a nonconducting tube. Then a second conductor, called the shield, is placed around the nonconductive tube which in turn is surrounded by thick insulation. This construction causes the fields to remain entirely inside the tube, which prevents RF energy from appearing outside the cable or other fields from mixing with the signal in the line. The shield is grounded to protect the internal fields of the cable and to dissipate any external RF energy.

Collision avoidance system. A computer-assisted radar plotting aid that allows rapid decision making to avoid collisions between vessels.

Composition. The basic electrical properties of the radar contact's surface. Steel offers an excellent composition, whereas wood or fiberglass offers very little reflective composition.

Compulsory ship. A ship that is required to comply with global marine distress and safety system regulations.

Computer radar. A synonym for automatic radar plotting aid.

COMSAT. Comsat General Corporation, the United States partner in the INMARSAT system.

Conductor. A medium that allows current to flow within it.

Confederation of Independent States' (CIS) Intergovernmental Radionavigation Program. The program that now operates GLONASS, the Russian satellite positioning system.

Consol. A navigation system that was designed to provide long-range navigation from shore stations and was considered a radio directional system. It has been shut down virtually all over the world.

Continental United States (CONUS). U.S. coastal navigation zone that is covered by the more powerful coastal radio beacons extending out to 50 nautical miles.

Continuous wave (CW). The most basic form of RF energy, dispersed into the atmosphere at a specific frequency.

Controlling element. The portion of the gyrocompass that contains the ballistic or pendulous weight. Application of this weight creates the precessive forces toward a particular direction.

Control segment. A component of satellite navigation systems that utilizes earth-based tracking stations to monitor the satellite's orbit and provide corrective information to the system.

CONUS. *See* Continental United States.

Conversion angle table. Data used to establish the appropriate correction to apply prior to plotting radio bearings from a station more than 50 miles away.

Coordinated universal time (UTC-universal time, coordinated). The coordinated time kept by a uniformly operating clock, corrected for seasonal variations in the earth's rotation.

Correction cam. A device used to correct a radio direction finder for quadrantal error. Once RDF correction factors are calculated, the device is custom cut to correct the unit.

Correction factors. Factors applied to the user's radio bearings to compensate for quadrantal error.

COSPAS-SARSAT. The joint cooperative satellite search and rescue system operated on 406.025 MHz and 121.5 MHz. The system uses low earth orbit satellites and provides specific coverage area. It was established by participating members in the United States, Russia, Canada, and France. COSPAS is an acronym for the Russian Cosmicheskaya Sistyema Poiska Avariynich Sudov, meaning Space System for the Search of Vessels in Distress. SARSAT is an acronym for search and rescue satellite.

Course alarm. An alarm that activates when the vessel varies beyond a set parameter for the intended course.

CPA. See Closest point of approach.

Crackling. A sound that may arise from faulty parts in a receiver, poor contacts, or improper grounding and that allows static electricity to build up in the electrical components.

Crossed-loop antenna. An antenna that focuses radiated energy into a relatively narrow beam. It also picks up signals at varying levels at different points on the antenna. These levels are analyzed by the receiver to determine transmitter direction.

Cross-track error (XTE). The loran C term for a vessel's ability to navigate on a straight rhumb line from point A to point B by compensating for external forces.

CRT (Cathode ray tube). A component of the radar used to form the video display. The CRT screen is coated with a film of phosphorescent material that reacts when excited by the narrow beam formed as the cathode draws electrons from a filament. The beam also passes by a series of coils that focus and deflect the beam to create images on the screen.

CW. See Continuous wave.

Cycle. One complete oscillation or one complete wave, beginning when the wave passes zero in one direction until it passes zero in the same direction.

Cycle alarm. A loran C receiver alarm that appears when initializing the receiver or when the signal is lost. It indicates that the receiver is not reading the transmission pattern correctly because it has not picked up the performance pulse.

DC. See Direct current.

Deactivation control. If the steering system is installed as a secondary system to a hydraulic system, a control on the telemotor steering stand to cause the system to automatically shut down the electric steering if the telemotor is engaged.

Decca. A phase comparison hyperbolic system first developed by the British. It is considered to be a relatively accurate, short- to medium-range radionavigation system designed for use in coastal confluence areas. Decca operates in the low-frequency band, 70 to 130 kHz.

Decca lane. The distance or interval between each successive zero phase point for the Decca system.

Decometer. The Decca digital readout that simultaneously indicates the phase comparisons between the master and each of the slave stations.

Deep scattering layer. See Thermocline.

Depth sounder. A hydrosonic system specifically designed to generate sonic pulses that are directed toward the ocean floor. The system then measures the amount of time it takes for the echo to be received and, based on an average velocity of sound through water, calculates depth.

Detector. Through the use of a tuning control, frequencies of desired radio signals are located and passed on to this second stage of a receiver.

DGPS. See Differential global positioning system.

Differential global positioning system (DGPS). A system designed to provide the same information as the regular global positioning system, except that an additional correction, or differential signal, was added to improve accuracy. This correction signal is broadcast over a specific frequency that covers particular geographic areas.

Differential Global Positioning System (DGPS) Navigation Service. A U.S. Coast Guard service designed to provide coverage at the specified levels for all harbors and harbor approach areas and other critical waterways for which the Coast Guard provides aids to navigation.

Diffraction. The bending of waves around a solid object and filling in behind it. This can be seen when radio waves pass around an object or can be picked up over the horizon.

Diffuse reflection. When waves reflect back at various angles caused by contours and the variability of the reflective surface.

Digital readout. ARPA information windows that digitally detail another ship's range, bearing, course, speed, closest point of

approach, time to closest point of approach, or other information such as bow crossing range or time to bow crossing range.

Digital selective calling (DSC). A system used for the transmission
of critical information such as distress calls, navigational
alerts, automatic position reporting, routine communications,
communication relays, and reception acknowledgments between ships and coastal radio stations.

Direct current (DC). The continuous flow of electrons in the same
direction.

Directional loop antenna. See Crossed-loop antenna.

Direction of relative motion (DRM). Compass direction toward
which a relative motion line on a radar plot leads.

Direct waves. Radar waves travelling outward in a straight manner.

Display type. The way the radar image presents changes in the
vessel's surroundings.

Doppler effect. The frequency shift of an approaching signal due to
the signal's velocity/distance relationship.

DRM. See Direction of relative motion.

Ducting. An extreme condition of reflection when a wave is re-
bounded off the surface of two separate layers of different
densities, such as an atmospheric layer and the earth's surface, and can travel great distances within these two layers.
This is also known as trapping.

EBL. See Electronic bearing line.

ECDIS. See Electronic chart display and information system.

Echo. A reflection of a radar wave or hydrosonic signal.

Echo sounder. See Depth sounder.

ECS. See Electronic chart system.

Effective power gain. The signal leaving a transmitting antenna
that is powerful enough to induce a current in a receiving antenna. It is expressed as the ratio of power required to produce a certain signal strength at a receiving comparison
antenna to the power needed to have as strong a signal with
another specific antenna.

EGC. See Enhanced group call.

EHF. See Extremely high frequency.

Electric current. The rate of flow of electrons through a conductor.

Electricity. A physical phenomenon, it is the existence of moving
electrons by means of a conducting element such as air, water, or solid material.

Electric stylus. A pen used in conjunction with an electronically
driven clock mechanism in newer course recorders.

Electromagnetic radiation. Radio signals or the radiated radio signal energy that travels in open space.

Electromagnetic spectrum (EMS). The classification structure of all radio frequencies based on frequency value.

Electromagnetic speed log. A system that utilizes a flow probe or rodmeter that extends out beyond the ship's hull. The probe contains a coil through which an electric current is passed, producing a magnetic field around the probe. As water moves past the probe, the magnetic field becomes altered, producing a variation in the signal voltage. The measurement of this variation can be utilized to indicate the vessel's speed through the water.

Electromechanical. Both electronic and mechanical.

Electronic bearing line (EBL). Electronic device on a radar unit that allows the operator to determine approximate bearing to a target or navigational aid.

Electronic chart display and information system (ECDIS). Data equivalent to the latest edition of material originated by a government-authorized hydrographic office and in conformance with International Hydrographic Organization standards. ECDIS data should be capable of accepting official updates to correct changes in the chart's database.

Electronic chart system (ECS). A system that comprises all types of electronic charts that do not comply with the International Maritime Organization and International Hydrographic Organization ECDIS specifications. These systems are not regarded by IMO as acceptable equivalents to paper charts.

Electronic interference. A situation in which an own ship radar is operating near another ship with the same, or nearly the same, carrier frequency. The display will show segmented spirals emitting from the sweep center. These are temporary and there is little the operator can do about them.

Electronic navigational chart (ENC). A database with a specified electronic format that meets International Maritime Organization and International Hydrographic Organization ECDIS specifications and must be provided by official government sources.

Electronics. Motion of electrons in which the conduction is controlled within the component, such as a vacuum tube or a semiconductor.

Electrostrictive. A type of transducer used in depth sounders to convert electrical signals to sound vibrations by passing a current through two plates that sandwich a nonconductive material. The electrically induced magnetic field causes the plates to vibrate, creating the sound vibrations.

Emergency generator. An alternate source of power on larger vessels used in case of a loss of power from the main engineering system.

EMS. See Electromagnetic spectrum.

ENC. See Electronic navigational chart.

Enhanced group call (EGC). Used by a GMDSS coordination center to contact vessels, it allows broadcast messages to be made to selected groups of stations located anywhere within a satellite's coverage area. Information regarding vessels in need of assistance can be put out to vessels in a specified geographical area that may be able to render aid.

Equipment monitoring and alarms. Audible and visual alarms, generated by a radionavigation system processor following a self-test and detection of a failure, that alert the operator that the unit is not functioning properly.

Ethernet. A specialized local area network that allows each piece of integrated equipment to exchange specific information.

Exclusion zone. An option that offers the ARPA operator a means to limit the automatic acquire function in areas where no unwanted plotting is desired.

Extremely high frequency (EHF). The range within the electromagnetic spectrum (beginning at 3 GHz) that includes the heat and infrared ranges, invisible light, ultraviolet light, X rays, gamma rays, and cosmic rays.

Fading. The variation in the strength of signals received by a transmitter.

False echo. Interference on radar caused by the ship's superstructure appendages, such as masts, kingposts, or stacks.

Fast time constant (FTC). A switch on a radar that reduces receiver sensitivity and reduces amplified signals transmitted to the CRT to reduce rain clutter.

Fathometer. See Depth sounder.

FCC. See Federal Communications Commission.

Federal Communications Commission (FCC). The government agency charged with control of all forms of communications within the United States, it classifies radio wave emissions according to their characteristics.

Feed horn. An antenna component at the end of the wave guide that radiates energy in a highly directional pattern from the focal point of the directional reflector of a parabolic radar antenna.

FFU. See Full follow-up control system.

Fidelity. The degree of clarity and completeness with which a receiver can reproduce the original characteristics of a received signal.

Field strength. The strength of a signal measured as the distance between peaks of a wave.

Filter. A component in a power supply that cleans the electrical power that flows through it.

Fixed crossed-loop antenna. Used on newer RDF/ADF receivers, an antenna that is placed higher for better reception and that does not require adjustment, as did those placed on top of the receiver.

Fixed errors. Those errors in the Decca system that are relatively constant and are caused by the path that the ground waves travel, particularly over or near land. This type of travel introduces diversions in the signal path because of the terrain and can cause the speed of the signal to vary from its point of transmission until the time it is received.

Flow probe. A component of an electromagnetic speed log. The probe contains a coil through which an electric current is passed, producing a magnetic field around the probe. As water moves past the probe, the magnetic field becomes altered, producing a variation in the signal voltage.

FM. See Frequency modulation.

Forward error correction (FEC). A method of reducing errors and poorly received characters utilized with narrow band direct printing.

Frequency. The number of cycles a wave completes in a specific period of time.

Frequency control. The ability of a tuner (which can be variable, crystal-controlled, or synthesized) within a receiver to receive one or more frequencies.

Frequency modulation (FM). System where intelligence is conveyed through modulation, or alteration, of the frequency of a signal. FM is commonly used in voice transmission and in radionavigation systems due to signal clarity.

Frequency range. The spectrum of frequencies within an upper and lower limit of a receiver that determines what specific signals can be tuned and reproduced. A unit may cover a broad group of frequencies, such as on a multiband communications receiver, or a single frequency, as in a radionavigation receiver like loran C.

FTC. See Fast time constant.

Full follow-up control system (FFU). A joy stick or control lever that allows direct control of the rudder without use of the wheel. This unit is designed as the primary steering station or as a remote station that can be placed anywhere on the vessel. This system will automatically return the rudder to amidships when the control lever is released.

Gain control. See Volume.

Gate. *See* Window.

GDOP. *See* Geometric dilution of precision.

Geometric dilution of precision (GDOP). Based on the geometric relationship of the GPS satellites to the receiver, a measurement of the spacing or spread of the satellites, with the best situation being one satellite nearly overhead and the others equally spaced around the horizon.

GeoSAR (geographic search and rescue). A commercially operated radar system utilized on aircraft and designed for terrestrial mapping which can also be used for land or sea surface search and rescue.

Giga-. Metric prefix for one billion.

Global coverage system. A category within hyperbolic radionavigation systems that was designed to provide position-fixing information in all areas with the same average accuracy throughout the system. There was only one global hyperbolic system and it has been terminated.

Global marine distress and safety system (GMDSS). An automated vessel-to-shore emergency and distress alerting system utilizing satellite and earth station links.

Global navigation satellite system (GLONASS). The Russian equivalent of the U.S.-operated global positioning system. Designed to function in a similar manner, the system may ultimately use more satellites, resulting in greater accuracy than the Western system.

Global positioning system (GPS). A satellite-based radionavigation system designed to provide continuous worldwide coverage of navigation, position, and timing information to marine-, air-, and land-based users.

GLONASS. *See* Global navigation satellite system.

GMDSS. *See* Global marine distress and safety system.

GMDSS radio maintainer's license. The accepted certification for a GMDSS radio maintainer (separate from the GMDSS radio operator's license). The maintainer is responsible for preventive and corrective maintenance to equipment to ensure it is available in case of emergency.

GMDSS radio operator's license. The accepted certification for a GMDSS radio operator. This license is approved in the United States by the FCC, which did not permit existing licenses to cover GMDSS requirements. This license is issued separately, by authorized agents, and is not an endorsement attached to existing FCC or U.S. Coast Guard licenses.

Goniometer. A device in the RDF receiver that separates the incoming signals by their varying strengths to determine signal direction.

GPS. See Global positioning system.

GPS constellation. The layout and spacing of the satellites used by the global positioning system.

GPSIC. See GPS Information Center.

GPS Information Center (GPSIC). A U.S. Coast Guard center providing information to and that is the point of contact for civil users of the GPS system. Unplanned system outages resulting from system malfunctions or unscheduled maintenance are announced by the GPSIC system as they become known.

Gradient. The difference between each hyperbolic line within a hyperbolic pattern on a chart, represented as a specific distance in nautical miles.

GRI. See Group repetition interval.

Ground lock. See Auto drift.

Ground segment. Portion of the COSPAS-SARSAT system composed of local user terminals and mission control centers.

Ground waves. Waves that travel parallel to the earth's surface due to the refractory tendency of RF energy in the atmosphere.

Group repetition interval (GRI). Used in the loran system, the amount of time it takes for a chain to broadcast all of its signals in sequence from the beginning of the first pulse of the master to the beginning of the first pulse of the master station transmission in the next cycle. Group repetition intervals are established between 40,000 and 99,000 microseconds.

Guard zone. Electronic boundaries set by an operator on an ARPA to provide automatic acquisition and tracking. Targets that pass through the outer guard zone are automatically plotted, those which are not displayed until inside the outer guard zones are intended to be auto acquired at the inner guard zone.

Guardian Zone. See Guard zone.

Gyro. Anything that spins rapidly enough to render stability of motion.

Gyrocompass. An electromechanical compass that uses the properties of gyroscopic inertia, precession, gravity, and the rotation of the earth to line up with the geographical meridians of the earth and assist the mariner in discerning true north.

Gyropilot. See Automatic steering system.

Gyrorepeater. An element within the repeater system for the master gyrocompass, designed to give indication of ship's heading.

Gyroscopic inertia. Gyroscopic inertia or rigidity in space is the property that causes a gyro or spinning element to remain stable and in the same plane of rotation.

Half-power points. Predetermined points along the radar beam
where power has decreased by 50 percent.

Half-wave antenna. The most fundamental antenna type, where
the total length of the antenna is equal to half of the wavelength of the transmitted frequency.

Half-wave dipole antenna. A common variation of the whip antenna that, when mounted over earth, is bidirectional and radiates equally well in both horizontal directions
perpendicular to it. In order for a half-wave dipole to take on
unidirectional characteristics, it needs additional elements. It
has excellent directive capabilities and is very efficient when
placed at least a half wavelength above the ground.

Heading-up. An unstabilized display available on relative motion
radars. The vessel's heading is straight up at 0.

Heat. A factor caused by resistance within an electrical component.

Height. The distance above the sea surface that a target must have
to expose itself to radar waves. Also, the distance above the
sea surface of a radar antenna that determines the radar
horizon.

Hertz. One cycle per second.

HF. See High frequency.

High frequency (HF). The range in the electromagnetic spectrum (3
to 30 MHz) where shortwave broadcast and single-sideband
ship-to-shore communications occur. Many nations broadcast
radio time signals, or time ticks, in this range, as well as
shortwave programming.

High-pass filter. A type of filter that allows all frequencies above a
certain specified frequency to pass through into an electrical
system.

Hit. A circumstance where an ARPA has not stopped the tracking
of a contact due to poor return or inconsistent display.

Home. To tune a signal and allow the bearing to be used as the vessel's course.

Hop. The bouncing back of a sky wave from the ionosphere.

Horizontal beam width. The angular distance, parallel to the
earth's surface, of a radar beam. It is relatively narrow, measuring between 0.65 and 2 degrees.

Horizontal whip antenna. The most commonly used antenna by radiotelegraph aboard ship. Horizontal receiving antennas work
best with horizontal transmitting antennas. *See* Whip antenna.

Hourglass effect. An expansion or constriction near the center of
the radar screen because of time base problems. It can be detected in narrow rivers or canals.

Hum. A common type of equipment noise caused by antenna lines picking up the magnetic fields of power lines when they are located too close to each other.

Hydrosonic. Systems designed to generate sound waves that are directed through the water medium and reflected off the sea bed to provide required information, such as water depth or speed over ground.

Hyperbola. The locus of all points in a flat plane that have a constant difference of distance from two fixed points.

Hyperbolic radionavigation system. An electronic navigation system created by establishing a specific hyperbolic radio pattern over a geographical area. This pattern is established through a series of mathematical calculations that define the exact coordinates of each point. To utilize this as a navigation system, transmitting antennas are placed at separate points and broadcast signals in a specific sequence on a specific time base. The system receiver can measure the difference in time or the variance in the phase of the two received signals. This information is used to determine where the vessel is within the hyperbolic pattern.

IBS. *See* Integrated bridge system.

IHO. International Hydrographic Organization.

IMO. International Maritime Organization.

Impedance (Z). The vector sum of the resistance, inductive reactance, and the capacitive reactance in a circuit.

Impeller log. A device that uses a small propeller to drive a geared mechanism, which produces a measurable electrical impulse or mechanical force that is converted to a speed measurement.

Index line. Used for parallel indexing, this line, when placed into the display unit, is fixed to the own ship and will move with the own ship. This allows the operator to program the radar screen to provide time-saving reference lines that are useful in navigation.

Indicating depth sounder. An instrument that provides some form of visual presentation of depth using one of a variety of methods of presenting information. These include a rotating neon light, a digital readout, or a CRT (cathode ray tube) presentation.

Indicator. A cathode ray tube in a radar system that reproduces radar echoes as video signals. It uses a polar diagram with the transmitting ship's position located at the center. Images of target echoes are displayed in either their true or relative bearings at their distances from the indicator center. Also called plan position indicator.

Indicator unit. A component of a depth sounder that contains an oscillator that creates the electric signal at the desired frequency and provides depth indication in a digital or graphic form.

Indirect echo. See False echo.

Indirect waves. Radar waves that are reflected off the surface of the water, causing a pattern of waves to reflect upward and mix with the direct waves in the outward path of travel.

Ink stylus. A pen used in conjunction with a wind-up clock mechanism in older-style course recorders.

Inner guard (guardian) zone. Used by ARPA, a zone that establishes the inner limit of the guard zone and has a depth that provides for automatic acquisition. When a target passes through this zone it is automatically plotted.

Integrated bridge system (IBS). A system designed to allow a vessel operator to plan, execute, monitor, and record the performance of a vessel in normal operations.

Interference. Unwanted and confusing signals or patterns produced by a transmitter of the same frequency, or more rarely, by the effects of nearby electrical equipment or machinery, or by atmospheric phenomena.

Intermediate frequency. A frequency produced when the local oscillator within an amplifier mixes its signal with the carrier.

International Association of Lighthouse Authorities (IALA). International organization charged with the responsibility of setting standards for safe navigation in coastal waters and heavy traffic navigation areas.

International Telecommunications Union (ITU). An international organization that through cooperation sets the standards for use and performance of radio equipment utilized in the maritime industry.

International Maritime Satellite System (INMARSAT). The international satellite system used for maritime communications supported by member nations throughout the world.

Inverter. A special supply system used to convert DC to AC.

Ionosphere. A layer of the earth's atmosphere beginning at around 30 miles above the surface of the earth and extending out to about 250 miles.

Iron mike. See Automatic steering system.

Jamming. Signal interference caused by the reception of extraneous RF energy being specifically targeted by a transmitter. Used as an intentional military tactic.

Janus configuration. A speed measurement system with two transducers, one set facing forward and a second facing aft. This allows the system to calculate frequency shift in two directions, thus ensuring a more accurate speed measurement.

Kalman filtering computer. GPS receivers that include this program are able to determine the quality of signals received and weigh them against each other to provide a more accurate fix.

Kilo-. Metric prefix for one thousand.

Land effect. See Coastal refraction.

Lane slip. A major error encountered with Decca that results when the receiver fails to keep a continuous count of the lanes through which it passes. This error or incorrect lane identification primarily is caused by an interruption or disturbance in transmissions, incorrect initializing or referencing of the receiver, or interference.

Lattice tables. Numeric tables for loran C that assist the mariner in developing lines of position based upon dead-reckoning positions.

LEO. See Low earth orbit.

LEOSAR. Low-earth-orbit search and rescue satellite system.

LF. See Low frequency.

Light lists. Information published by the U.S. Coast Guard on the range, frequency, characteristics, and position of radio beacon transmitters.

List of lights. Information published by the National Imagery and Mapping Agency on the range, frequency, characteristics, and position of radio beacon transmitters.

Loaded/light condition adjustment. A gyropilot control that sets the vessel's condition. The vessel reacts differently depending upon its condition, which is most noticeable in vessels such as tankers. Loaded vessels react more slowly and require larger rudder movements. Vessels in a ballast condition react faster and require less rudder.

Local user terminal (LUT). A terminal that processes the signals relayed via COSPAS-SARSAT satellites to determine the originating radio beacon's location.

Loran (long-range navigation system). A terrestrial radionavigation system that establishes a hyperbolic surface pattern for the purposes of determining lines of positions to create a fix.

Lost signal. A loran C receiver alarm that indicates that the received transmissions are unusable or unheard above background noise.

Low earth orbit (LEO). Doppler-based satellite systems, each utilized in different Russian communities. These include the military Parus or Tsikada-M system, which utilizes six satellites, and the Tsikada system, designed for civilian use and consisting of four satellites.

Low frequency. The range in the electromagnetic spectrum (30 to 300 kHz) where the loran system and low-frequency radiotelegraph are used.

Low-pass filter. A type of filter that allows all frequencies below a certain specified frequency to pass through into an electrical system.

LUT. See Local user terminal.

Magnetostrictive. A type of transducer for use in depth sounders that uses a form of electromagnetics to create vibrations in a diaphragm, thus producing an ultrasonic signal.

Manual acquisition. When an ARPA contact is specifically highlighted by the operator with an acquisition window by use of a joy stick or track ball.

Mapping function. A computer ability whereby the operator may carefully build a map of a particular harbor, river, or bay that is frequently navigated. This map can then be saved in memory.

Marine radio beacons. Shore-based radio stations that transmit coded signals intended to be received by ships for positioning purposes.

Maritime safety information. Navigational/weather warnings and communications associated with search-and-rescue activities. MSI is broadcast over NAVTEX, SafetyNET, and high frequency narrow band direct printing (HF/NBDP).

Master station. In the loran system and Decca system, the principal station that controls system transmissions and begins transmission sequences.

"Mayday." Prefix for communication relating to a vessel in distress and requiring immediate assistance.

MCC. See Mission control center.

MCW. See Modulated continuous wave.

Medium frequency (MF). The range within the electromagnetic spectrum (300 kHz to 3 MHz), where the marine radio beacon system is found. The old radiotelegraph international calling and distress frequency (500 kHz) was located here, as is the familiar AM broadcast band.

Mega-. Metric prefix for one million.

MF. See Medium frequency.

Microphone. A piece of equipment that converts acoustic energy into electrical energy for radiotelephony systems.

Microphonic noise. Noise caused by moving elements within a unit. It results from connections becoming loose from vibrations

aboard the vessel, or sometimes because components within
the radar were improperly assembled or soldered.

Microsecond. One millionth of a second.

Millington's Method. The mathematical method of determining
ASPF corrections for loran C as presented on chart lattices or
in correction tables.

Minimum shift keying (MSK). A method of modulation of the
medium-frequency radio beacon signals that enables data formatting to be done in the reference station, and puts real-
time differential corrections in the RTCM SC104 format and
sends them through a broadcast transmitter.

Mission control center (MCC). Personnel and equipment whose functions include the validation and exchange of alert data and system (technical) information, both within the COSPAS-SARSAT
system and with the search and rescue (SAR) networks. Specifically, they collect distress alert data from local user terminals and other mission control centers, and geographically sort
and redistribute them to appropriate SAR authorities.

Modulated continuous wave (MCW). A transmission system that
superimposes audio information on the carrier wave prior to
transmission. This altered signal is then broadcast and received by any simple receiver. Most modern radiotelegraph
systems use this transmission system for Morse code radio
transmissions.

Modulation. The effect that occurs when a signal is altered by the
addition of a superimposed wave over a carrier wave before
the signal is broadcast.

Modulator. A component that superimposes intelligence on the carrier wave emitted from a communication device.

Morse code. System of dots and dashes that provides communication using continuous-wave or modulated continuous-wave
transmitting systems.

Motor generator. A piece of equipment that converts mechanical
energy into electrical energy.

MSK. See Minimum shift keying.

MTR. Modulator, transmitter, and receiver.

Multiple echoes. Interference that occurs on radar when the own
ship is passing close to large, steeply walled obstructions or
high freeboard ships at beam ends. The RF energy reflects off
the target and is returned to the own ship, but some of the RF
energy also bounces off the own ship's side and is returned to
the target ship for another reflection.

Narrow band direct printing (NBDP). Medium frequency and high
frequency radiotelegraphy system transmitting data in

alpha-numeric characters for the transmission and reception of general communications, distress communications follow up, and maritime safety information (MSI).

National Oceanic and Atmospheric Administration (NOAA). U.S. Government Department responsible for ocean survey, research, weather tracking, and publication of U.S. territory nautical charts.

NAVAREA. Specific navigational area on the globe defined by general navigational parameters and numbered for reference when used for the broadcast of safety information.

Navigation Information Service (NIS). A service established by the U.S. Coast Guard to meet the needs of the civil GPS user. The information provided includes planned, current, and recent satellite outages and constellation changes, user instructions and tutorials, other GPS-related information, system status and information about other Coast Guard-provided radionavigation systems, and general information about federal radionavigation policy and systems.

Navigation line. A line oriented to earth on which, or between a succession of which, a ship can navigate. Since they are frequently used in true motion displays on ARPAs, they may require programming in that mode.

NAVINFONET. Computer link system operated by the U.S. Government for the purpose of providing current navigational and safety information to the maritime user community.

Navstar system. See Global positioning system.

NFU. See Non-follow-up control system.

Night effect. The problematic effect that occurs when bearings are taken within half an hour before sunset to about half an hour before sunrise, caused by introduction of sky waves as well as radio errors that occur during twilight.

NIS. See Navigation Information Service.

Noise. Unintentional signal interference.

Noise limiter. A device within a receiver that blocks out unnecessary background noise or all signals above or below a certain level.

Non-follow-up control system (NFU). A joy stick or control lever that allows direct control of the rudder without use of the wheel. This unit is designed as the primary steering station or as a remote station that can be placed anywhere on the vessel. It allows the operator to move the rudder into any position and leave it where placed.

NOTAM. See Notice to Airmen.

Notch filter. A filter used by loran C receivers to eliminate unnecessary background noise on the broadcast frequency.

Notice Advisory to Users (NAU). General information regarding safety and system performance broadcast to the maritime community.

Notice to Airmen (NOTAM). Information provided by the Federal Aviation Administration to the civilian user concerning unplanned system outages resulting from system malfunctions or unscheduled maintenance.

Null point. The point at which the signal almost disappears using a radio direction finder.

Ohm. The unit measure of resistance within electrical components.

Omega. A hyperbolic radionavigation system. Its coverage grew to extend beyond the coastal zone areas to include the open ocean, making it the first global coverage system. The system operated in the very low frequency band in the internationally agreed-upon frequencies between 10.2 kHz and 13.6 kHz.

Omnidirectional. In all directions.

Open scale repeater. A form of gyrorepeater that shows a larger but only partial section of the azimuth ring.

Oscillation. A cycle in alternating current.

Oscillator. A component that converts direct electrical current into the RF signal of the carrier frequency.

Outer guard (guardian) zone. A zone that establishes the outer limit of the guard zone and has a depth that provides for automatic acquisition. When a target passes through this zone it is automatically plotted on the ARPA.

Overhead cable effect. An effect observed when navigating in rivers or narrow waterways, where overhead power cables or high-tension wires can occasionally reflect RF energy. They do not appear as a line across the screen, but usually as one large target at the lowest point of the cabling.

PAD. See Predicted area of danger.

"Pan Pan." Prefix for communications related to the safety of a vessel or a threatened person.

Parabolic reflector antenna. An antenna whose emitter/receiver element is usually a feed horn. It uses a curved section behind the element to focus transmitted or received signals. Generally, marine types are reflector antennas with signals emitted back into a curved dish, where they are focused and then sent outward. In reception, the opposite occurs. These antennas are very directive and cannot pick up or distribute signals in all directions at the same time. They have better output range and detection ability from a single direction.

Parallel index lines. Grease-pencil lines, referenced to known terrestrial objects, on the plotting surface of a radar, used to

assist the watch officer in positively monitoring track position
at a glance.

Parasitic element. An element of an antenna that receives power by
either induction or radiation from the driven element. It then
reradiates it in the proper phase relationship to achieve directivity or gain over a simple half-wave dipole in free space.

Pattern corrections. Corrections that compensate for fixed errors
found in Decca. Pattern corrections are available in various
publications.

P code. See Precision code.

PCP. See Potential collision point.

Peak. The highest and lowest point on the crest and trough of a
wave, respectively.

Pendulous gyro. A type of gyrocompass that uses a solid weight
suspended from the gyro frame to apply precessive forces in a
particular direction to the gyro.

Performance controls. Controls, possessed by most automatic steering units, that include a rudder adjustment, weather adjustment, speed adjustment, and loaded/light condition
adjustment.

Performance pulse. Broadcast by a loran master station as a ninth
pulse, it allows the receiver to determine which of the transmissions is coming from the master, thereby giving it an indication of where the cycle of transmissions begins.

Persistence. The glow remaining on the radar screen when an electron beam is shut off, caused by the electron beam reacting
with the phosphorescent material on the screen. It decreases
in strength when the electron beam is not present.

PF. See Primary phase factor.

Phantom element. The frames and mechanisms within a gyrocompass that shadow the movement of the sensitive element
without interfering with it. This element also contains the
compass card off which is read the ship's heading.

Phase comparison. The variance in the phase of two received signals measured by the receiver of a hyperbolic radionavigation
system.

Plan position indicator (PPI). See Indicator.

Plan position indicator (PPI) distortion. An effect that occurs as a
result of static electricity soon after power-up on older radar
CRT displays.

PN. See Pseudo-noise generator.

Polarization. The orientation in space of the electric axis of a radar
wave. This axis is at right angles to the magnetic axis and
may be either horizontal, vertical, or circular. Also, a switch

on a radar that will act as a multiplier to the fast time constant to reduce rain clutter; *see* Fast time constant.

Polarization error. See Night effect.

Polyvalent officer. An officer with dual training in both ship's propulsion and bridge procedures.

Potential collision point (PCP). A dot or small circle on the radar
screen that shows the position of a potential collision with the
own ship along a target's course.

Power control. A switch used to turn a navigation or communications system on and off.

Power failure alarm. An alarm that sounds from a system if the
power supply is cut off from the main unit or secondary unit
on such systems as the gyro, steering, or radar systems.

Power supply. A component within an ARPA that receives electricity from the ship's generators and distributes filtered voltages
as required for the production of RF energy and for the components of the operational controls. It performs the key function of providing regulated and constant operating current
throughout the entire unit, providing protection from variations of current often found in a vessel's electrical system.
Power supplies are common in all types of marine radionavigation and communication systems.

PPI. See Indicator.

PPS. See Precise positioning service.

Precession. The external force applied to a gyro to change its plane
of rotation. Precession causes the body to move in a direction
nearly perpendicular to the application of the applied force.

Precise positioning service (PPS). A form of GPS restricted to use
by U.S. Armed Forces, U.S. federal agencies, and selected allied armed forces and governments for security purposes.

Precision (P) code. Segment of the transmission of a GPS satellite
that, along with the coarse acquisition (C/A) code, is used to
identify a specific satellite and its signal. The code, unique for
each satellite, allows a receiver to determine the difference
between signals, which are all broadcast on the same frequencies.

Predicted area of danger (PAD). Displayed as either a circle or a
hexagon on a radar screen, it includes the danger area selected by the operator, plus system inaccuracy probabilities
and the size of the contact being tracked.

PRF. See Pulse repetition rate.

Primary phase factor (PF). A factor based on an average variation
of signal propagation for loran C in the geographic area due to
atmospheric conditions.

PRN. See Pseudo-random noise.

PRR. See Pulse repetition rate.

Pseudo-noise generator (PN). A device used by each global positioning system satellite to produce a specific code corresponding
to each satellite for identification.

Pseudo-random code. Phase comparison by the global positioning
system of these codes is used to determine the precise time.
Both the satellite and the receiver generate the same code at
exactly the same time. The receiver synchronizes itself to the
satellite time frame by comparing the two codes and correcting for the discrepancy.

Pseudo-random noise (PRN). Sequence-modulated radio signals
used by the global positioning system containing a coarse acquisition code (C/A code) and precision code (P code). There is
a navigation message superimposed on the codes which contains satellite ephemeris data, atmospheric propagation information, and satellite clock bias.

Pseudo-range. Developed as the receiver begins to determine range
from each of the satellites and begins to adjust itself to determine the most precise position. This process contains some error, primarily of timing. The microprocessor in the global
positioning system receiver continues to adjust the pseudo-
ranges until the signals from at least three satellites intersect
as closely as possible.

Pulse length. The length in microseconds of a particular burst of
radar energy.

Pulse modulation. A type of transmission system that functions
through the modulation of the amplitude and frequency of the
signal attached to the carrier wave, which are in turn molded
into short bursts of RF energy. These systems are very effective in the application of RF energy to radionavigation systems and radar.

Pulse repetition rate (PRR). Also called pulse repetition frequency
(PRF), the number of pulses per second emitted from a radar.

Quadrantal error. Deviation introduced by the vessel itself. This
error is caused by the ship's metal, masts and stays, deck
cargo such as containers, and electrical/magnetic character.

Quarter-power points. Predetermined points along the radar beam
where the power has decreased by 25 percent.

RACON. Radar beacon. A radar transponder device designed to
produce a distinctive image on the screens of ships' radar
sets, thus enabling the mariner to determine position with
greater certainty than would be possible using a normal radar
display alone.

Radar. Radio detecting and ranging.

Radar horizon. The distance to which radar waves reach, taking into account antenna height and refraction.

Radar wave. Radio waves that are comprised of electromagnetic energy with power output expressed in watts. They are considered electromagnetic because they have both electrical and magnetic fields.

Radio beacon segment. A segment of the COSPAS-SARSAT system. It includes emergency beacons designed to transmit distress signals on 121.5 or 406 MHz. Most 406-MHz beacons also include a 121.5-MHz homing transmitter. These beacons transmit signals that are detected by COSPAS-SARSAT polar-orbiting satellites.

Radio direction finder (RDF). Radio receivers installed aboard vessels and at shore stations that have direction-sensitive antennas for the purpose of determining the direction of a transmitter.

Radio ducts. "Pockets" formed by specific prevailing atmospheric conditions that allow radio waves to become trapped between two layers of differing densities.

Radio frequency (RF) energy. The energy with which electrons, emitted from an antenna, travel through the atmosphere and are received by another antenna.

Radio navigational aids. Any system designed to assist in navigation based upon the propagation of radio waves, to determine lines of position.

Radio signals. Electrical current transformed into radiant energy.

Radio Technical Commission for Maritime Services (RTCM) SC104. A system used by DGPS that employs differential or pseudo-range corrections broadcast over the existing network of marine radio beacons.

Radiotelegraphy. Another name for continuous-wave or modulated continuous-wave transmissions through the use of Morse code.

Radiotelephony. A form of voice transmission system.

Rain clutter. Unwanted return being displayed from echoes bouncing off precipitation.

Rain rate. A switch on some radars that works as a multiplier to the FTC to reduce rain clutter. *See* Fast time constant.

RAMARK. A older system which broadcast continually, and only provided bearing information.

Range resolution. Dependent upon pulse length, the ability of a radar to distinguish between two targets that are close together and on the same bearing.

Range rings. Rings designating a set distance from the center of a radarscope.

Rapid radar plotting method. A method of vector analysis intended to give the radar observer information about the movement of contacts on his or her display.

Rasterscan. An ARPA unit of the raster display type with a television-type screen.

Rate aiding. The mathematical prediction of where a contact is most likely to be displayed in the future beyond a sweep or two on the ARPA screen.

Rate of turn indicator. A component of the steering system that allows the operator to determine the vessel's rate of turn when the rudder is applied. It is very useful when maneuvering and allows the person controlling the maneuver to see the effect of various rudder angles.

RCC. See Rescue coordination center.

RDF. See Radio direction finder.

Receiver. A piece of equipment that reconverts the incoming radio waves into RF current within a radar or radio.

Receiver segment. A component of satellite navigation systems consisting of government-provided or commercially available units to receive and display the navigation information.

Recording depth sounder. An instrument that produces a graphic record of depth against a time base.

Recording graph. An element of a depth sounder that displays the depth data collected by the instrument.

Reflection. The bouncing of waves off an object or a medium of a different density than the one through which they were initially traveling, such as a dense atmospheric layer or a topographic feature.

Reflectometer. The instrument used to measure the standing wave ratio for an antenna in the transmission of radio waves.

Refraction. The bending of a wave as it passes through a medium. It can be seen by the tendency of radio waves to follow the curvature of the earth.

Relative accuracy. The comparison of two loran C operators who are using the same system at the same time.

Relative motion display. A radar display in which an own ship making way is shown as a fixed point and all detected objects, including land, appear to be in motion.

Relative motion line (RML). A line on the radar scope that represents the relative motion expected of the contact with respect to one's vessel, provided all things remain the same.

Relative vector. The length of this vector on the ARPA will depict the contact's speed over a time period also selected by the operator. By interpreting this information the operator can glean information useful in satisfying risk-of-collision questions.

Repeatable accuracy. The ability of a loran C receiver to determine a similar position in comparison to the same position measured at a previous time.

Repeater system. A separate transmission amplifier and distribution control system that receives signals from the master gyrotransmitter and distributes this signal to units within the system designed to give indication of ship's heading.

Rescue coordination center. A center that enables GMDSS to link search and rescue authorities ashore with vessel traffic in the immediate vicinity of a vessel in distress or requiring assistance.

Resistance. Opposition to the flow of electrons with respect to the medium in which the energy is transmitted.

RF (radio frequency). The frequency, or cycles per second, of electromagnetic radiation.

RF amplifier. The first-stage amplifier within a receiver.

RF energy. See Radio frequency energy.

RF gain. A signal boost at its primary stage of amplification within a general communications receiver.

Rigidity in space. See Gyroscopic inertia.

RML. See Relative motion line.

Rodmeter. A probe that extends from the hull of a vessel that is used to determine speed through the water in an electromagnetic speed log system.

Rotating antenna system. A radio direction finding antenna that functions like a movable loop unit and is turned by a motor in continual rotation located at its base. The rotating loop picks up the transmitter signals as it passes through the RF field.

RTCMS. Radio Technical Commission for Maritime Services.

Rudder adjustment. An adjustment that sets gyropilot control for the amount of rudder used in returning the vessel to course. It can be used to allow the system to use a smaller or larger amount of rudder depending on prevailing conditions.

SA. See Selective availability.

Safe limit. A parameter set by the ARPA operator that causes an alarm to sound if the parameter is violated by a contact, i.e., if a contact comes within an established minimum closest point of approach.

Saint Elmo's fire. A unique atmospheric phenomenon, the result of an excessive static buildup of electrified particles in still air. It causes rigging and other components of a vessel to glow with a dim green light. It is easily attracted to antennas and

the connected components. Large variations in signal readings or loud static noise on radios is the result.

SATCOM. Satellite communications.

Satellite Control Center (SCC). Ground-based control center that
tracks and predicts orbital positions of communication satellites.

S band radar. Radar that operates on 3,070 MHz with a wavelength of 10.0 cm.

Scanner. See Slotted wave guide antenna.

Scattering. The spreading out of energy waves in many different
directions so that they eventually disappear.

Sea clutter. See Sea return.

Search and Rescue (SAR). System designed to assist vessels in distress through specific procedures for communications, conducting on-water searches, and instituting rescue operations.

Search and Rescue Transponder (SART). Automatic transmitter
designed to react and respond to search and rescue transmitters to indicate the position of a unit in distress.

Sea return. Radar waves that strike the wave action of the ocean's
surface and are returned and displayed at close ranges,
which results in clutter around the center of the indicator
screen.

Secondary phase factor (SF). An accuracy factor for loran C developed by taking into account the effect on a signal of traveling
over water. The SF is accounted for on charts and in the receiver's microprocessor.

Secondary station. See Slave.

Second-trace echoes. Echoes received by radar that have traveled
beyond the range scale in use and return after a subsequent
pulse emission.

Sectoring. An effect that occurs because of problems with the automatic frequency control, resulting in the radar displaying
large, pie-slice sectors.

Selective availability (SA). The intentional downgrading of accuracy for nonmilitary global positioning systems.

Selectivity. The ability of a receiver to limit reception to signals of a
specific frequency and filter out interfering signals near that
specific frequency.

Sense antenna system. A system designed to eliminate ambiguity
in radio direction finding, consisting of a second antenna connected to the receiving circuit. By mixing the current from the
two antennas it can be established whether there is a difference in polarity and thus whether the antenna is facing the
wrong way.

Sensitive element. The central part of the gyrocompass that contains the spinning gyro, called the rotor, an electric motor that drives the rotor, the rotor housing, and the supportive frame.

Sensitivity. The capability of a receiver to amplify weak signals to a useful level so that they can be detected above existing background noise.

Sensitivity time control (STC). A control that reduces the CRT sensitivity near the center of the radar sweep to reduce sea return.

Sensor. A device that allows the input of information into the ARPA unit, such as course or speed, from an outside source like a mechanical gyrocompass or speed log.

Sequencing. A process that involves several different RDF stations broadcasting on the same frequency, one at a time, in a specific order, which allows the user to get more than one bearing for a fix without changing frequencies.

Serrated range rings. An effect that occurs as a result of problems in the sweep on the plan position indicator of a radar.

SF. See Secondary phase factor.

Shadow area. The area behind a solid object where there is reduced signal strength due to diffraction of the waves around that object.

Shaft encoding. Division of the radar screen into small cells.

Shape. With respect to radar contacts, a factor that affects how well a contact reflects back a radar wave. A flat surface is a better reflector than a convex one because the latter tends to diffuse the waves upon reflection.

SHF. See Super-high frequency.

Ship control systems. Systems that utilize not only gyro information, but input from speed logs and radionavigation systems, to maintain the vessel's course and intended track. The units can be used to calculate courses and distances, set a vessel on the calculated track, and maintain that track by analyzing all of the data.

Sideband. The signals attached to the carrier wave used in RF transmission systems.

Side lobes. Undesirable minor lobes of the radiation pattern that are formed due to the shape of the antenna.

Signal loss error. Error associated with the use of a Doppler speed log caused by the attenuation of the vibrations during transit of the signal through the water or upon reflection from the bottom.

Signal-to-noise ratio (SNR). A numeric reading of the ratio between the strength of the received signal and the existing background noise to indicate the signal strength as detected by the loran C receiver.

Single-lobed shaped pattern. A pattern of radiation formed by the directional antenna, which focuses the radiated energy into a relatively narrow beam very similar to the beam of light from a searchlight.

Single movable loop. An antenna employed by earlier RDF systems. It was turned by a hand wheel above the receiver to pick up the strongest signal so it could be easily identified. The antenna was then rotated until perpendicular to the original position. At this point the signal would almost disappear. By carefully moving the antenna back and forth slightly, this null point could be defined within a couple of degrees, thus determining the direction of the transmitter.

Size. A factor with respect to radar contacts that determines the number of radar waves that will be reflected back to the unit. The larger the size the more radar waves will be reflected.

Sizzling. See Crackling.

Skip. To bounce back, as with sky waves.

Skip distance. The range of a signal's reception after it is reflected.

Skip zone. The area of no reception when a receiver is beyond the range of the ground wave but not yet far enough from the transmitting station to pick up sky waves.

Sky waves. Waves that move upward and away from the emitting antenna into the atmosphere. Some pass completely through the atmosphere into space while others are reflected back toward the earth's surface.

Slave. A secondary station transmitter that is synchronized with a master station for loran, allowing a precise time interval between the transmission from each station to be measured. Decca uses a phase comparison between the master and secondary stations to determine position.

Slotted wave-guide antenna. A highly directive radar antenna which consists of a hollow tube with slots in its side allowing short bursts of high energy to radiate out and be subsequently received. A long-angled reflector behind the slotted wave guide shapes and concentrates the signals during transmission and reception. Also known as a scanner.

SNR. See Signal-to-noise ratio.

SOLAS. International Convention for the Safety of Life at Sea (1988).

Space segment. A component of satellite navigation systems that provides transmitted radionavigation information. It includes

all of the deployed satellites, placed in precise orbits via unmanned booster rockets or the space shuttle.

Speaker. A unit that converts electrical energy into acoustical energy so voice transmissions may be heard.

Specific hyperbolic radio pattern. A pattern established for use by
hyperbolic radionavigation systems. A series of mathematical
calculations defines the exact coordinates of each point, leading to a precise pattern.

Specular reflection. The effect when a depth sounder's beam pattern travels downward with the wave front striking the ocean
bottom, and the signals are reflected directly back.

Speed adjustment. A gyropilot control setting for the speed of the
vessel. Many vessels operate at reduced speed for any number
of reasons and when the vessel is slowed, the steering system
must apply more rudder. The system may not need to react as
often. The speed adjustment compensates for these variances.

Speed log. A device used to determine a vessel's velocity while under way.

Spider element. See Transmission system.

Spoking. An effect that occurs when there is a modulator problem
in a radar system, indicated by many radial lines appearing
on the radar screen.

Squelch control. A device within a receiver that blocks out unnecessary background noise or all signals below a certain level.

SRM. Speed of relative motion.

Stability. A receiver's capability to lock onto a desired signal without drifting off frequency.

Stabilization. The direction the radar unit is pointing or the direction to which the heading flasher is aligned.

Stabilized course-up. A radar display orientation that allows the
operator to select the stabilized function where the heading
flasher is placed at the top of the screen, regardless of direction of travel.

Standard repeater. A type of gyrorepeater that exhibits the entire
azimuth ring.

Standing wave ratio (SWR). The most common measurement of radio frequency output for an antenna system. Standing waves
are variations of current and voltage along a transmission
line. These occur when the impedance of the line is different
from that of the antenna at the operation frequency, creating
a mismatch.

Static electricity. An excess of electrons in a nonconductive environment.

STC. See Sensitivity time control.

Steering repeater. A gyrorepeater positioned as part of the ship's steering stand.

Step system. A common type of repeater system for the gyrocompass, this system produces segmented signals driving a repeater motor in three separate "steps."

Subrefraction. Ducting that results in reduced signal distances as signals are bent toward the sky due to a layer of warm moist air lying over a layer of dry air.

Super-high frequency (SHF). In this range (3,000 to 30,000 MHz) the familiar 10-cm wavelength and 3-cm wavelength radars are found (respectively, the S and X band radars).

Superrefraction. Ducting that increases signal distances. It occurs when a temperature inversion layer of dry air sits on top of a layer of warm moist air.

Survival craft transceiver (SCT). Portable transceiver designed to be used on board rescue or survival craft.

Sweep. The motion of the trace as it moves in a clockwise direction around the plan position indicator screen of a radar.

Swept gain circuit. A component that enables a depth sounder to compensate for attenuation of the signal due to varying densities of the water. This essentially increases the amplification of the signal at a rate dependent upon the amount of time the signal takes to return. The farther the signal travels, the more it is absorbed. This absorption can be decreased by lowering the frequency of the signal.

Swinging the ship. The process of determining the correction factors for an RDF by carefully comparing visual bearings of a transmitting antenna with a radio bearing taken at the same time. This determination of correction factors is required to be done annually and checked periodically.

SWR. See Standing wave ratio.

Syncro system. A repeater system for the gyrocompass that uses a different voltage requirement than the step system with a syncro-style operating motor. The movement of this type of repeater is truer to the movement of the master compass.

System data. Information used to keep the COSPAS-SARSAT system operating at peak effectiveness and to provide users with accurate and timely alert data. It consists of satellite ephemeris and time calibration data used to determine beacon locations, the current status of the space and ground segments, and coordination messages required to operate the COSPAS-SARSAT system.

System selector. A function that allows the steering system to be switched between the port and starboard rudder control systems. Each rudder control system is fully redundant to the other and powered from separate sources.

Target loss. When the ARPA indicates that no registered hits have taken place on a contact upon demand. An alarm may sound.

Target swap. When the ARPA unit begins tracking a contact that was not the same as was originally tracked, as can occur when a close, untracked contact passes close to a tracked contact, or when two tracked targets pass close together.

Target trail. An indication of the true course of the target ship over time by a display of small dots on the ARPA screen.

TBCR. See Time to bow crossing range.

TCPA. See Time to closest point of approach.

TD. See Time delay.

Telemetry, tracking and control. Functions performed by a satellite control station in the operation of orbiting satellites.

Texture. With respect to radar contacts, a factor that affects how well a contact will reflect back a radar wave. A smooth surface is a better reflector than a rough one because the latter tends to diffuse the waves upon reflection.

Thermistor. A device installed on most Doppler speed log systems to measure water temperature and adjust for velocity of sound errors.

Thermocline. A layer of equal temperature within the ocean that can give an indication of water depth far less than is the case; a dual trace may appear on a graph.

Time delay (TD). The difference in time of two received signals measured by the receiver of a hyperbolic radionavigation system.

Time to bow crossing range (TBCR). Current time at own ship until vessel reaches the bow crossing range point.

Time to bow closest point of approach (TCPA). Current time at own ship until vessel reaches the closest point of approach.

Trace. A bright line formed by the CRT as it sweeps around the plan position indicator screen of a radar.

Track alarm. An alarm that activates when the vessel is outside of stated parameters for an intended track, if the gyropilot is outfitted with radionavigation inputs.

Tracker. A device that divides the ARPA screen into small cells and records target locations as they move through these cells as a series of radar pips, looking for a successive repetition sufficient to register a hit.

Trail maneuver. A maneuver that modifies the own ship course and speed within the ARPA processor, causing all displayed target information to change to meet the own ship trail course and/or speed.

Transceiver. A component within a marine radio or radar system that contains both transmitting and receiving units installed as one apparent unit.

Transducer. A component of a depth sounder that converts the electrical signal from the indicator unit into ultrasonic vibrations for transmission.

Transducer orientation error. An error associated with the use of a Doppler speed log caused by excessive pitching and rolling of the vessel.

Transformer. A component in a power supply that steps the input voltage up or down as required and may serve as an isolation device between the ship's power and the electrical components.

Transit Navsat. A Doppler-based, two-dimensional satellite system formerly operated by the United States. This system was found to be very accurate, but was slightly inconvenient to use since the radio signals were useful only while a satellite was in an orbit visible from the receiving unit. This off-demand system was therefore often used in conjunction with land-based systems.

Transmission amplifier/distribution control. A unit that allocates a single electrical circuit for each repeater within the repeater system for the gyrocompass, each normally switched and fused. The distribution control system maintains sufficient power to drive all the vessel's repeaters.

Transmission system. A component within a gyrocompass that sends compass signals to the heading indicators throughout the ship's bridge.

Transmit-receive (TR) tube. A component of a radar that rapidly switches from transmitting to receiving functions and vice versa. This prevents damage to the receiver from energy emitted by the transmitter.

Transmitter. A device that generates and amplifies radio frequency signals within a radar or radio. It consists of two main sections, the oscillator circuit and the power amplifier circuit. Each of these segments is in turn divided into multiple components that have specific functions in the production and amplification of a radio signal.

Trapping. See Ducting.

Trial maneuver. Function of an ARPA that allows the operator to predict collision avoidance scenarios based on proposed course or speed changes.

TR tube. See Transmit-receive tube.

True motion display. A radar display in which the own ship is in motion across the radar screen consistent with the course and

speed of the ship. All fixed objects, such as land, remain stationary, and any moving object appears to move.

True vector. A vector whose length on an ARPA depicts the contact's speed over a time period selected by the operator. From
this the operator can gain information with regard to the target's approximate course, speed, and potential actions in the
future.

UERE. See User equivalent range error.

UHF. See ultra-high frequency.

Ultra-high frequency (UHF). The range in the electromagnetic
spectrum (300 to 3,000 MHz) used for a majority of shipboard
walkie-talkie communications and the global positioning L
band system. It includes television channels 14 through 83.

Unstabilized display. See Heading-up.

User equivalent range error (UERE). A random error based on several factors associated with the global positioning system, including the stability of the satellite's clock, predictions of the
satellite's orbit, errors in the 50-Hz transmission, precision of
the correlation process, atmospheric distortion and the applied compensating calculations, and the satellite's signal
quality. It is the result of the functionality of the satellite system and the user's receiver.

User segment. In the GPS system, the operators of receivers that
use the system for navigation and position fixing. The GPS receiver calculates its position and determines exact universal
coordinated time through a series of calculations it performs
when in operation. From this information it can derive the accurate course and speed of the receiver for the user.

Van Allen radiation belt. An extraterrestrial belt of electromagnetic radiation surrounding the earth that can have a dramatic effect on radio signals.

Variable error. Decca error generally caused by sky-wave interference that increases the farther you travel from the transmitters. Sky-wave interference is greatest at night and more
significant in winter than in summer.

Variable frequency oscillator (VFO). A controller attached to the oscillator circuit within a transmitter that is used to determine
the frequency of the signal to be transmitted.

Variable Range Marker (VRM). Electronic device on a radar unit
that allows the operator to determine approximate range to a
target or navigational aid.

Vector. An indication that begins at the target on an ARPA screen,
or from a symbol created on the display screen representing
the target's actual relative position.

Vector method plotting. Considered the manual means of determining collision information from radar.

Velocity of sound error. Error associated with the use of a Doppler speed log caused when there is a change in water temperature or salinity. Most systems are equipped with a thermistor, a device that measures water temperature and adjusts for this type of variation.

Vertical beam width. The angular distance perpendicular to the earth's surface of a radar beam. It is relatively broad, ranging between 15 and 30 degrees.

Vertical whip antenna. An antenna usually used for very high frequency, single sideband, loran C, Decca, Omega, and SATNAV that is efficient for long-distance transmitting and receiving because of the low radiation angle. By standing vertically, the antenna transmits in a more uniform omidirectional pattern. *See* Whip antenna.

Very high frequency. The range in the electromagnetic spectrum (30 to 300 MHz) used by bridge-to-bridge Channel 13 (156.650 MHz) radiotelephone and television channels 2 to 13.

Very low frequency (VLF). The range in the electromagnetic spectrum (10 to 30 kHz) in which distinct radio frequency is found.

Vessel motion error. An error associated with the use of a Doppler speed log that is caused by excessive vibration of the vessel as it moves through the water.

VFO. See Variable frequency oscillator.

VHF. See Very high frequency.

Vital electrical service. The emergency electrical service designed to supply power to emergency circuits on a vessel.

VLF. See Very low frequency.

Voltage. The measure of the force that moves electrons through a conductor.

Volume. A signal boost at the final stage of amplification within a general communications receiver that affects final audio output.

Volume reverberation mode. A mode during which the depth sounder indicates speed through the water.

Water track. See Volume reverberation mode.

Wattage. The measure of the amount of work that electrical current can accomplish.

Wave front. The leading edge of a propagated signal.

Wave guide. The electrical conductor that provides a common path for the transmitted and reflected energy of a radar.

Wavelength. The metric units of distance that the cycle occupies in one second.

Waypoint. A navigation point that has been programmed into the electronic navigation equipment.

Weather adjustment. A gyropilot control designed to slow the response of the rudder by reducing the reaction time of the rudder in heavy seas. Conversely, if the seas are calm, the unit can be set to react faster. The proper use of the weather adjustment will prevent the system from being overworked in heavier seas.

Whip antenna. A single wire either stretched horizontally between two supports, such as ship's masts, or vertically supported by a nonconductive shell such as fiberglass. Used for transmitting and receiving radio waves.

Window. A small area on an ARPA screen in which the tracker looks for a target upon demand. It decreases in size to allow a more rapid analysis of the data within the window of the ARPA, or increases for a larger view when a weak contact is windowed. Also known as gate.

X band radar. Radar that operates on 9,375 MHz with a wavelength of 3.2 cm.

XTE. See Cross-track error.

INDEX

ABOUT THE AUTHORS

Jeffrey W. Monroe, Master Mariner, is director of the Department of Transportation and Waterfront at the Port of Portland, Maine. A former associate professor of marine transportation and electronics at both the State University of New York Maritime College and the Massachusetts Maritime Academy, he also directed SUNY Maritime College's Center for Simulated Marine Operations and Massachusetts Maritime's Center of Maritime Training.

Captain Monroe is a graduate of Maine Maritime Academy and has a master's degree in transportation management from the State University of New York. His sailing experience includes tankers, tugs, research and training vessels; on board ship he has served in all capacities, including master. He holds a professional license as master, steam and motor vessels, unlimited tonnage, upon oceans (radar observer).

Thomas L. Bushy, Master Mariner, is associate dean for commercial maritime training at the Massachusetts Maritime Academy and master of the training ship *Patriot State*. He has served as professor of transportation at the academy and is a senior instructor at the Center of Maritime Training.

Captain Bushy was graduated from Massachusetts Maritime Academy. His professional experience afloat includes all officer positions on tankers, freighters, and research and training vessels; he holds a professional license as master, steam and motor vessels, unlimited tonnage, any oceans (radar observer) (GMDSS operator).

ISBN 978-0-87033-510-5